Likeness and Likelihood in the Presocratics and Plato

The Greek word *eoikos* can be translated in various ways, being used to describe similarity, plausibility or even suitability. This book explores the philosophical exploitation of its multiple meanings by three philosophers, Xenophanes, Parmenides and Plato. It offers new interpretations of the way that each employs the term to describe the status of their philosophy, tracing the development of this philosophical use of *eoikos* from the fallibilism of Xenophanes through the deceptive cosmology of Parmenides to Plato's *Timaeus*. The central premise of the book is that, in reflecting on the way *eoikos* is employed in their accounts, Xenophanes, Parmenides and Plato are manipulating the contexts and connotations of the term as it has been used by their predecessors. By focusing on this continuity in the development of the philosophical use of *eoikos*, the book serves to enhance our understanding of the epistemology and methodology of Xenophanes, Parmenides and Plato's *Timaeus*.

JENNY BRYAN is Lecturer in Classical Philosophy in the Department of Greek and Latin, University College London.

CAMBRIDGE CLASSICAL STUDIES

General editors

LIKENESS AND LIKELIHOOD IN THE PRESOCRATICS AND PLATO

JENNY BRYAN

CAMBRIDGE
UNIVERSITY PRESS

CAMBRIDGE
UNIVERSITY PRESS

University Printing House, Cambridge CB2 8BS, United Kingdom

One Liberty Plaza, 20th Floor, New York, NY 10006, USA

477 Williamstown Road, Port Melbourne, VIC 3207, Australia

314-321, 3rd Floor, Plot 3, Splendor Forum, Jasola District Centre, New Delhi - 110025, India

79 Anson Road, #06-04/06, Singapore 079906

Cambridge University Press is part of the University of Cambridge.

It furthers the University's mission by disseminating knowledge in the pursuit of education, learning and research at the highest international levels of excellence.

www.cambridge.org
Information on this title: www.cambridge.org/9780521762946

First published 2012
First paperback edition 2020

A catalogue record for this publication is available from the British Library

Library of Congress Cataloging in Publication data
Bryan, Jenny, 1979–
Likeness and likelihood in the Presocratics and Plato / Jenny Bryan.
p. cm. – (Cambridge classical studies)
Includes bibliographical references and index.
ISBN 978-0-521-76294-6
1. Xenophanes, ca. 570–ca. 478 B.C. 2. Parmenides. 3. Plato.
4. Resemblance (Philosophy) I. Title. II. Series.
B258.X34B79 2012
182′.3 – dc23 2011031546

ISBN 978-0-521-76294-6 Hardback
ISBN 978-1-108-79346-9 Paperback

CONTENTS

ACKNOWLEDGEMENTS

This book has its origins in a Cambridge doctoral thesis submitted in 2007. My greatest debt, both in writing the thesis and in turning it into a book, is to my doctoral supervisor, David Sedley. He has been an apparently indefatigable source of wisdom, guidance and encouragement. This will surprise no one who knows him. But, more than most, I have felt the benefit of his peculiar ability to combine patience and exhortation.

During my time first as a Ph.D. student at Darwin College and then as a Junior Research Fellow at Homerton College, I have had the enormous good fortune to be part of, and to learn from, a vibrant and welcoming community of ancient philosophers. In particular, I am grateful to Malcolm Schofield, who has examined every thesis I have ever written and to Nick Denyer, who has been a constant source of terrifyingly acute and exceptionally entertaining philosophical insights. I also want to express my gratitude to James Warren, who first introduced me to ancient philosophy and has been encouraging and tolerating me ever since.

Further thanks are owed to Patricia Curd and Kelli Rudolph, both of whom were kind enough to read and comment on drafts of Chapters 1 and 2. I am indebted to the Arts & Humanities Research Council and the Faculty of Classics, Cambridge for supporting my doctoral research and to Homerton College, Cambridge for granting me two years as a Junior Research Fellow. Earlier versions of several parts of this book were presented to audiences at the Classical Association, the American Philological Association, the Scottish Classical Post-Graduate Conference, Darwin College Arts and Social Sciences Seminar and a conference on *Eikos* organized by Victoria Wohl at the University of Toronto in 2010. I am grateful to the audiences at all these meetings for their valuable comments.

I also want to express gratitude to my new communities in the Department of Greek and Latin at University College London and amongst the ancient philosophers of London.

Finally, I want to express some less formal thanks to Emma Buckley and Helen Van Noorden, both of whom have done their best to help me along over the last good few years. And, of course, to my mother, who has been doing that for a good few years more. This book is dedicated to the memory of my brother, John.

ABBREVIATIONS

DK	H. Diels and W. Kranz (1951–2) *Die Fragmente der Vorsokratiker*, vols. 1–3, Berlin.
DG	H. Diels (1929) *Doxographi Graeci*, Berlin.
KRS	G. Kirk, J. Raven and M. Schofield (1983) *The Presocratic Philosophers*, Cambridge.
LSJ	H. G. Liddell, R. Scott and H. S. Jones (1940) *A Greek–English Lexicon*, Oxford.

INTRODUCTION

This book should have been entirely about Presocratic natural philosophy. Casting about for a topic for my doctoral thesis on the Presocratics, I was sent away to read Plato's *Timaeus*. I think the reasoning was that, in this particular dialogue, I could find Platonic responses to Presocratic questions. Thus Plato might identify my topic for me. It will surprise no one who has read Plato's 'prose hymn of the universe' that the *Timaeus* soon inveigled itself into a central role in my project.[1] However, I am aware that it may be unexpected that I should end up choosing the notorious assertion that Timaeus' cosmology is 'likely' (εἰκώς) as a point of connection with the Presocratics. For, whilst the fact that Xenophanes, Parmenides and Plato's *Timaeus* all call (part of) their accounts ἐοικώς/εἰκώς has often been noted, the potential significance of this similarity has been little scrutinized. In general, those who acknowledge it do so in the hope of defining one philosopher's usage in opposition to that of the others. Of course, this approach assumes that the correct reading of at least one has been established. In order to say with any certainty that Plato's εἰκώς does not mean the same thing as Parmenides' ἐοικώς, we need to know, at the very least, what Parmenides means by ἐοικώς. This book offers, in turn, a reinterpretation of the meaning of ἐοικώς/εἰκώς as employed by Xenophanes, Parmenides and Plato's *Timaeus*. My aim is twofold. The first is to analyse the meaning of the term as used by each of these three philosophers. The second is to demonstrate the value of reading each author as alluding to and seeking to correct the thought of his philosophical and, in the case of Xenophanes, poetic predecessors.

For all my claims to originality, of course, I am not the first to suggest a connection between the 'likely story' of the *Timaeus* and

[1] Shorey (1938) 104.

the likelihoods offered by Parmenides' goddess and Xenophanes.[2] More often than not, however, the possibility of such continuity has been rejected or ignored. Some scholars have been uncomfortable with the idea that Xenophanes might have enjoyed any significant philosophical engagement with Homer and Hesiod. Others have sought to resist the suggestion that a thinker as original and impressive as Parmenides might have been influenced by anyone at all, let alone Xenophanes. Whilst few would dispute the influence of Parmenides on Plato, the possibility that the εἰκὼς λόγος of the *Timaeus* might allude in any significant fashion to the ἐοικὼς διάκοσμος of Parmenides (B8.60) or the teachings ἐοικότα τοῖς ἐτύμοισι of Xenophanes (B35) has rarely been considered in any depth.

Each of the texts treated in this book have been discussed and reinterpreted countless times. In surveying the scholarship, I was struck by what I perceived, perhaps unjustly, to be a general reticence to entertain or develop an intertextual reading of their use of ἐοικώς/εἰκώς. One fairly prevalent assumption seems to be that continuity and influence can only be signalled by, or amounts to, similarity. It seems to me to be wrong-headed to assume that, if a word is used in a different sense by various authors, this is sufficient to rule out any relation between their respective usages. Verdenius' discussion of Parmenides B8.60 is illustrative of the somewhat underdetermined thinking that sometimes seems to pervade discussions of a connection between these texts. He rejects the possibility of translating Parmenides' ἐοικώς as 'probable' on the grounds that this would require an addition along the lines of that found in Xenophanes B35 (τοῖς ἐτύμοισι).[3] Now, Verdenius has, earlier in the same work, stated that Xenophanes should *not* be read as ascribing 'probability' to his account: rather he should be understood simply to be describing it as bearing a resemblance to the truth.[4] Yet, in his treatment of Parmenides B8.60, Verdenius assumes that 'probability' is *equivalent to* 'resemblance to truth' so that, since B8.60 does not assert the latter, it cannot be claiming

[2] See, for example, Palmer (1999) 26 and Sassi (2005).

[3] Verdenius (1964) 50–1. See also Owen (1960) 49. Cf. Wilamowitz (1899) 204–5.

[4] Verdenius (1964) 46.

the former either. He goes on to declare that it is 'not likely that ἐοικώς at this period [i.e. Parmenides' *floruit*] already had the technical meaning we find in Plato's term εἰκὼς λόγος'. It transpires that Verdenius understands this technical sense to be 'probable'. Finally, however, he warns that εἰκώς in the *Timaeus* can be translated as '"likely" so long as this is taken literally (seeming like) and not in the modern sense of probable'.[5] So, Verdenius rejects the possibility that Parmenides could be using ἐοικώς with the same sense that it carries in Plato, i.e. 'probable', and then rejects 'probable' as a suitable reading of εἰκώς in the *Timaeus*. My aim with this book is to unravel some of this tangled web of possible implications and allusions.

Without hesitation, I agree that it would be simple-minded to attempt to read all three uses of the term in an identical fashion. There can be no doubt that the meaning of words evolves over time and that Xenophanes, Parmenides and Plato may have used the same vocabulary in different ways. In fact, as I hope to demonstrate with this book, in adducing different senses of the same term, each author is relating his own account to those of his precursors whilst simultaneously seeking to present himself as improving upon those previous accounts.

My first chapter argues that we should read Xenophanes B35 (ταῦτα δεδοξάσθαι μὲν ἐοικότα τοῖς ἐτύμοισι) as setting up a contrast with the Homeric and Hesiodic notion of telling lies like truth (ψεύδεα ἐτύμοισιν ὁμοῖα). Xenophanes deliberately alters the term for resemblance in his formula in order to emphasize that he is claiming a relationship to the truth different from that declared by the poets. Analysis of the Homeric use of ἐοικώς and ὁμοῖος suggests that Xenophanes uses ἐοικώς in B35 to signify a particular kind of similarity between his account and the truth: apparent but potentially specious similarity. He is both recommending (or perhaps simply classifying) his teachings as candidates for the truth and simultaneously warning that they may, in fact, not be true. As such, B35 supports a fallibilist reading of Xenophanes' epistemology: we can hope for the truth but we will never be able to ascertain it with any certainty.

[5] Verdenius (1964) 60n1.

The second chapter treats the promise of Parmenides' goddess to offer a διάκοσμον ἐοικότα πάντα (B8.60). I argue that Parmenides intends the sense of ἐοικώς to be deliberately ambiguous and that interpreters are mistaken in searching for one precise meaning for the term in this context. Parmenides' ἐοικώς should be understood as carrying multiple and connected senses. These multiple meanings combine to describe the subjective plausibility of the erroneous beliefs that mortals tend to fabricate without justification. This subjective plausibility can be usefully contrasted with the πίστις ἀληθής (objective cogency) possessed by successful thought about Being. Our understanding of Parmenides' ἐοικώς needs to take account of the forensic background that informs several of his key terms. Further, I suggest that Parmenides alludes to and alters the formula of Xenophanes B35 in order to challenge the claim that it is possible to achieve any kind of truth at all about Coming-to-be.

My third chapter discusses the notorious issue of the εἰκὼς λόγος of Plato's *Timaeus*. In particular, I seek to challenge the assumption that underlies the majority of interpretations of Timaeus' εἰκώς-claim, namely that it describes some kind of deficiency in his account. I argue that the status of Timaeus' cosmology as εἰκώς derives not from the unstable nature of the cosmos, but from the fact that it is created as a likeness (εἰκών). Just as likeness is primarily a positive relation, so likelihood is, in this context, a positive quality. An account that accurately describes a representation will itself be somehow representative of the original model (whilst remaining an account of the likeness rather than the model). The 'representative' λόγος of the *Timaeus* should be understood as a positive endorsement of cosmology as a means of engaging with the realm of the intelligible as well as of describing the perceptible cosmos created in its image.

The fourth and final chapter argues that the *Timaeus*' use of εἰκώς is also a response to the epistemology of Parmenides and perhaps even Xenophanes. By setting out a positive representational relation between the realm of Coming-to-be and that of Being, Plato is seeking to correct the utter separation of these realms and the denigration of thought about Coming-to-be found in Parmenides' poem. I present the case for reading the proportion of *Timaeus* 29c3

('As Being is to Coming-to-be, so truth is to convincingness') as deliberately echoing and subverting the language of Parmenides. By attributing πίστις to his account of Coming-to-be, Plato is emphasizing that the perceptible world is of both ontological and epistemological value, albeit in some qualified way. I also suggest that Plato is seeking to correct the Xenophanean notion that our mortality prevents us from obtaining knowledge. Insofar as we are mortal, the *Timaeus* seems to agree that there are limits on our cognitive abilities and that we are thus restricted to producing unverifiable μῦθοι about certain areas of inquiry. Our share in the divine, however, allows us to transcend these limits. By studying the way that our cosmos is like the Forms, we ourselves become more like god.

Stephen Hinds introduces his work on allusion in Roman poetry with comments that are just as apposite to a consideration of the development of cosmology:

> Whenever we describe the world, consciously or unconsciously we measure our descriptions against previous descriptions of the world. The words we use have always been used before; we never have a monopoly on their contexts and connotations.[6]

The central premise of this book is that, in reflecting on the ἐοικώς/εἰκώς status of their accounts, Xenophanes, Parmenides and Plato are each manipulating the 'contexts and connotations' of the term as it has been used by their predecessors. By recognizing the continuity in the development of the philosophical sense of ἐοικώς/εἰκώς, we can, I think, greatly enhance our general understanding of the epistemology of Xenophanes, Parmenides and Plato's *Timaeus*.

[6] Hinds (1998) xi.

CHAPTER I

XENOPHANES' FALLIBILISM

Introduction

It is difficult to establish anything with any confidence about the life of the sixth-century poet–philosopher, Xenophanes of Colophon.[1] As will become clear, such uncertainty is rather fitting, for Xenophanes is, I shall argue, the most epistemologically pessimistic of our three protagonists. Fragment B35 provides a tantalizingly truncated snippet of his philosophical poetry:

ταῦτα δεδοξάσθαι μὲν ἐοικότα τοῖς ἐτύμοισι.[2]

Since my primary aim in this chapter is to establish the meaning of these six words, I will, for the time being, let them stand without translation. Despite, or more likely as a result of, its brevity this fragment is 'fraught with ambiguity and uncertainty'.[3] In an effort to flesh it out to a degree more conducive to interpretation, scholars have often treated it in tandem with the more extensive B34:[4]

καὶ τὸ μὲν οὖν σαφὲς οὔτις ἀνὴρ ἴδεν[5] οὐδέ τις ἔσται
εἰδὼς ἀμφὶ θεῶν τε καὶ ἅσσα λέγω περὶ πάντων·
εἰ γὰρ καὶ τὰ μάλιστα τύχοι τετελεσμένον εἰπών,
αὐτὸς ὅμως οὐκ οἶδε· δόκος δ' ἐπὶ πᾶσι τέτυκται.[6]

And there has never been any man who has achieved certainty
Nor will there be anyone who knows about the gods and what I say about everything.
For even if anyone really managed to enunciate how things are
He would still not himself have knowledge. Rather, opinion is allotted to all.[7]

1 See 93–4 for a discussion of the possible dates of Xenophanes' *floruit*.
2 Plutarch *Quaest. Conv.* 746b. 3 Lesher (1992) 171.
4 See, for example, Barnes (1982) 140; KRS 150; Morgan (2000) 50.
5 Following Fränkel (1974) 122ff. in preferring the ἴδεν of Sextus and Diogenes Laertius to the γένετο of Plutarch. See also Ioli (2003) esp. 201–5.
6 Sextus Empiricus *Math.* 7.110.
7 Except where noted, all translations are my own.

Some have suggested that both B34 and B35 are drawn from a preface to Xenophanes' philosophy, others that they are part of his conclusion.[8] If B35 is correctly regarded as prefatory in nature, it would sit well with the tradition for an author to begin his work with a 'truth-claim'.[9] Examples of such claims are the appeals to the Muse for inspiration, which act as a 'guarantee' of accuracy, in the opening lines of the *Iliad* and *Odyssey*.[10] In the *Theogony*, Hesiod's Muses offer a rather more ambiguous introduction with the claim that they have the capacity to inspire the poet with both the truth *and* lies:

> ἴδμεν ψεύδεα πολλὰ λέγειν ἐτύμοισιν ὁμοῖα
> ἴδμεν δ', εὖτ' ἐθέλωμεν, ἀληθέα γηρύσασθαι.[11]
>
> We know how to tell many lies like truth
> And we know, when we want to, how to speak the truth.

Heraclitus, on the other hand, presents a more explicit claim to authority (insofar as anything Heraclitus says can be regarded as explicit), contrasting the accuracy of his account with the incomprehension of those around him:

> τοῦ δὲ λόγου τοῦδ' ἐόντος ἀεὶ ἀξύνετοι γίνονται ἄνθρωποι καὶ πρόσθεν ἢ ἀκοῦσαι καὶ ἀκούσαντες τὸ πρῶτον· γινομένων γὰρ πάντων κατὰ τὸν λόγον τόνδε ἀπείροισιν ἐοίκασι, πειρώμενοι καὶ ἐπέων καὶ ἔργων τοιούτων, ὁκοίων ἐγὼ διηγεῦμαι κατὰ φύσιν διαιρέων ἕκαστον καὶ φράζων ὅκως ἔχει. τοὺς δὲ ἄλλους ἀνθρώπους λανθάνει ὁκόσα ἐγερθέντες ποιοῦσιν, ὅκωσπερ ὁκόσα εὕδοντες ἐπιλανθάνονται.[12]

Of this eternally true account, men are eternally uncomprehending, both before having heard it and once they have heard it. For, although everything comes to be in accordance with this account they are like the untried trying both the words and deeds that I describe, distinguishing each in accordance with nature and saying

[8] Classen (1989) 101 is of the view that both B34 and B35 are drawn from an introduction to the *silloi* (satirical verses). Barnes (1982) 140 asserts that, whilst B34 is from the prologue of 'Xenophanes' *oeuvre*', B35 is from his epilogue. Gigon (1945) 181 and Hermann (2004) 136 have B35 as conclusory.

[9] Runia (1997) 104–5 discusses the role of the truth-claim in Presocratic *proemia* but correctly notes that the evidence is regrettably scanty. Most (1999) 342–3 highlights the importance of truthfulness in Homer and Hesiod.

[10] See also the introduction to the 'Catalogue of Ships' at *Iliad* 2.484–487 in which the poet appeals to the superior knowledge of the Muses in order to guide the correctness of his account.

[11] *Theogony* 27–28. [12] Heraclitus B1 (Sextus Empiricus *Math.* 7.132).

how it is. But other men are as oblivious to the things they do when awake as they are forgetful of the things they do when asleep.

Likewise, the historian Hecataeus of Miletus (*c*.560–480 BC) opens his *Genealogies* by highlighting his own discernment in rejecting those stories he considers 'ridiculous':

τάδε γράφω ὥς μοι δοκεῖ ἀληθέα εἶναι· οἱ γὰρ Ἑλλήνων λόγοι πολλοί τε καὶ γελοῖοι, ὡς ἐμοὶ φαίνονται, εἰσίν.[13]

I write these matters as seems to me to be true. For the stories doing the rounds of Greece are many and, in my opinion, ridiculous.

Such possible parallels give good reason to think that B35, if it is a 'truth-claim', may well have derived from an introduction to (a part of) Xenophanes' philosophy.

The context in which we find B35 preserved, however, demonstrates that it could serve just as well as conclusory. The fragment is quoted by Plutarch's teacher Ammonius in *Quaestiones Convivales* as the conclusion to his discourse on the activities of the Muses:[14]

τούτοις ἐπιφωνήσαντος τοῦ Ἀμμωνίου τὰ τοῦ Ξενοφάνους ὥσπερ εἰώθει
ταῦτα δεδοξάσθαι μὲν ἐοικότα τοῖς ἐτύμοισι
καὶ παρακαλοῦντος ἀποφαίνεσθαι καὶ λέγειν τὸ δοκοῦν ἕκαστον . . .

In his usual manner, Ammonius rounded off his remarks with a bit of Xenophanes:

ταῦτα δεδοξάσθαι μὲν ἐοικότα τοῖς ἐτύμοισι

and encouraged us each to speak up and give our own opinion . . .

Plutarch or, at least, his teacher Ammonius seems to have regarded B35 as suitable to form a conclusion.[15]

In truth, it is impossible to tell whether the fragment was originally prefatory, conclusory or neither. For present purposes, a

[13] Hecateus F1a (Jacoby 1, 7). See 45–6 below.

[14] For a summary of what little is known about Ammonius, see Jones (1961) and Dillon (1977) 189–192.

[15] Thus, Teodorsson (1996) 367 is encouraged by the context of the fragment in Plutarch to suggest that 'the line seems to be a phrase by which Xenophanes concluded an argument, just as Ammonius does here'.

more important issue is whether it is quoted by Plutarch as carrying the force of a recommendation.[16] The question whether B35 was intended by Xenophanes to be read as an endorsement will prove central to this chapter. In particular, the discussion below will focus on what it means for Xenophanes to claim that ταῦτα are ἐοικότα τοῖς ἐτύμοισι. How are we to understand the idea of something being 'like truths' (or 'like the truth')?[17] Some have read this claim as emphatically positive.[18] Others have argued that Xenophanes' primary concern in claiming similarity to the truth is actually to stress the *difference* between ταῦτα and ἔτυμα, i.e. they are *like* the truth but *not actually* true.[19] On this reading, the line is a warning rather than an endorsement. In the treatment offered below, I will propose a reading of B35 as both qualified endorsement and warning. Xenophanes is asserting the similarity of his ταῦτα to the truth whilst simultaneously acknowledging that this similarity is possibly no more than apparent. Fundamental to this interpretation is our understanding of the specific import of the term ἐοικώς. I will argue that this term was quite deliberately chosen by Xenophanes because it expresses a particular kind of contingent and potentially specious resemblance. I will go on to propose that, understood in this light, B35 provides convincing evidence in support of a 'fallibilist' reading of Xenophanes' epistemology, particularly as expressed in the 'master fragment' of B34. According to such an interpretation, Xenophanes thinks that humans are incapable of attaining certain knowledge.[20] I will conclude with some suggestions about the possible source of the

[16] As noted by Lesher (1992) 171. On the choice between the infinitive and imperative forms of the verb, see 21–2 below. Whilst the imperative is more explicitly commendatory, the infinitive can carry a similarly exhortative force.

[17] On ἔτυμος as 'true' rather than 'real', see 25–6.

[18] Such readings tend to understand B35 as expressing a lack of certainty, as opposed to a lack of truth (thus perhaps echoing the message of B34). See KRS 180 and Lesher (1992) 175–6. Guthrie (1962) 396: 'In their [sc. the erroneous beliefs of mankind] place he puts forward what he personally feels is the truth, yet in all modesty and honesty he must confess that as all men are fallible, so may he be.' Fränkel (1974) 128: 'Xenophanes characterizes what he says in B35 not as "illusory opinion" but as "probable".' Hussey (1990) 25–6 argues that the criterion of 'resemblance to truth' is used to categorize opinions as 'more or less useful or reliable'.

[19] See Barnes (1982) 140; Philippoussis (1989) 330; Morgan (2000) 50.

[20] Lesher (1992) 159–60 admits the influence of M. M. Mackenzie in labelling B34 a 'master fragment'.

uncertainty Xenophanes attributes to the truth value of mortal cognition, suggesting that it derives in part from his insistence on the essential disparity between humans and god.

Fundamental to my argument is the suggestion that, in presenting his doctrines as enjoying a specific kind of relationship to the truth, Xenophanes is deliberately alluding to a formula found in both Homer and Hesiod. The motivation behind this allusion stems in part from the desire to correct the attitudes towards truth, certainty and god that he perceives to prevail within the works of these poets. It will therefore prove fruitful to begin by setting out the case for reading Xenophanes as deeply engaged with both the themes and, more significantly, the language of his poetic predecessors.

Xenophanes vs. Homer and Hesiod

Two of the extant fragments of Xenophanes express an explicit interest in Homer and Hesiod.[21] With B10, Xenophanes notes Homer's role as a preeminent authority:

ἐξ ἀρχῆς καθ' Ὅμηρον ἐπεὶ μεμαθήκασι πάντες . . .[22]

Since from the outset everyone has learnt according to Homer . . .

Although the fragment itself is not explicitly derogatory, B11 is often taken to be a criticism of the depiction of the gods presented by Homer and Hesiod:[23]

> πάντα θεοῖσ' ἀνέθηκαν Ὅμηρός θ' Ἡσίοδός τε,
> ὅσσα παρ' ἀνθρώποισιν ὀνείδεα καὶ ψόγος ἐστίν,
> κλέπτειν μοιχεύειν τε καὶ ἀλλήλους ἀπατεύειν.[24]
>
> Homer and Hesiod have attributed all sorts of behaviour to the gods
> Such as is a matter of reproach and condemnation among mortals:
> Stealing, adultery and swindling one another.[25]

[21] Aulus Gellius *NA* 3.11 (B13), although not a verbatim fragment, refers to Xenophanes' interest in the two poets: 'alii Homerum quam Hesiodum maiorem natu fuisse scripserunt, in quibus Philochorus et Xenophanes, alii minorem' ('Some write that Homer was older than Hesiod, including Philochorus and Xenophanes, others that he was younger').

[22] Herodian π. διχρ. 296, 6.

[23] Havelock (1983) 15.

[24] Sextus Empiricus *Math.* 9.193.

[25] It seems likely that B12 (Sextus Empiricus *Math.* 1.289), which echoes the final line of B11, is also aimed at Homer and Hesiod: 'ὡς πλεῖστ(α) ἐφθέγξαντο θεῶν ἀθεμίστια

Equally pertinent is the description of god in B25:

ἀλλ' ἀπάνευθε πόνοιο νόου φρενὶ πάντα κραδαίνει.[26]

But completely without effort he shakes all things with the thought of his mind.

This fragment evokes the description of Zeus at *Iliad* 1.528–530:

> ἦ καὶ κυανέῃσιν ἐπ' ὀφρύσι νεῦσε Κρονίων·
> ἀμβρόσιαι δ' ἄρα χαῖται ἐπερρώσαντο ἄνακτος
> κρατὸς ἀπ' ἀθανάτοιο· μέγαν δ' ἐλέλιξεν Ὄλυμπον.
>
> The Son of Kronos spoke and nodded his dark brow
> And the divine locks quivered on the immortal head of the king;
> And he made great Olympus quake.

By echoing the Homeric portrayal of Zeus as engendering an effect through a physical movement, Xenophanes emphasizes the superiority of the deity of his account, who generates action purely through the power of his thought.[27] The success of Xenophanes' theological message depends on his audience recognizing the allusion. Indeed, it is hard to see how anyone could have failed to do so when one considers Homer's general predominance as a source of authority. We have seen that, in B10, Xenophanes himself comments on the ubiquity of his predecessor's influence. Given Xenophanes' explicitly stated interest in Homer and Hesiod and the fact that he employs the language and metre of the poets, it seems unquestionable that we should read Xenophanes as reacting to and engaged with the themes and language of his predecessors.[28] When reading Xenophanes we should never forget the significance of his engagement with traditional thought and vocabulary:

ἔργα,/κλέπτειν μοιχεύειν τε καὶ ἀλλήλους ἀπατεύειν' ('as they uttered the numerous wicked deeds of the gods, thieving, adultery and swindling one another'). Hershbell (1983) 126 suggests that this repetition may be an example of Xenophanes imitating or parodying the Homeric style.

26 Simplicius *Phys.* 23.19.

27 Lesher (1992) 110. Broadie (1999) 208 suggests that Xenophanes is 'the first to theologise against popular conceptions of the divine'.

28 Thus Xenophanes is engaged in what Havelock (1983) 15 terms 'the insistent polemic that they all [sc. the Presocratics] direct against the language currently in use, which they sometimes identify as that spoken by Homer and Hesiod, and at other times by men generally'. Hershbell (1983) gives an overview of ways in which the poetic tradition may have influenced Xenophanes' thought and composition.

Xenophanes employs familiar phrases, but he uses them in a most unusual manner, in order to stress that he is rejecting old conceptions, replacing them by new ones, never heard of, never spoken of, new and yet related to the old ones which they are to supersede and in contrast to which he wants them to be understood.[29]

B35 as allusion

My contention is that B35 is a prime example of Xenophanes employing familiar phrases in an 'unusual manner' and that, in fact, it can only be properly understood if viewed in this light. Just as it seems impossible that anyone familiar with Homer should read B25 without being put in mind of *Iliad* 1.528–530, so it is unlikely that B35 (ταῦτα δεδοξάσθαι μὲν ἐοικότα τοῖς ἐτύμοισι) could fail to ring the same kind of allusive bell. For both Homer and Hesiod employ a similar (although, as we shall see, significantly different) phrase. In the brief summary of traditional truth-claims given above, we encountered the words of Hesiod's Muses at *Theogony* 27–28:

> ἴδμεν ψεύδεα πολλὰ λέγειν ἐτύμοισιν ὁμοῖα
> ἴδμεν δ', εὖτ' ἐθέλωμεν, ἀληθέα γηρύσασθαι.
>
> We know how to tell many lies like truth
> And we know, when we want to, how to speak the truth.

This formula of 'telling lies like the truth' is also to be found at *Odyssey* 19.203. A disguised Odysseus tells Penelope that he has seen her husband in Crete and it is noted that:

> ἴσκε ψεύδεα πολλὰ λέγων ἐτύμοισιν ὁμοῖα.
>
> He spoke and concocted many lies like truth.

Although the similarity between these passages and B35 has often been noted, opinion remains divided as to whether Xenophanes should be read as deliberately alluding to Homer and Hesiod.[30]

[29] Classen (1989) 94. Classen is discussing Xenophanes' theology in particular, but goes on to give a comprehensive treatment of his interaction with epic poetry throughout the fragments.

[30] In favour of an allusive reading are Guthrie (1962) 396n2; Classen (1989) 101; Morgan (2000) 51. Mogyoródi (2006) 155 suggests that Xenophanes has 'borrowed' the phrase ἐοικότα τοῖς ἐτύμοισι from *Theogony* 27–28 but makes no comment on the change of term for likeness.

Those opposed to an allusive reading tend to base their objections on one of several grounds, each of which is open to the same kind of counter-objection. The first is 'the general improbability that Xenophanes took his cues to philosophical truth from anything Hesiod had to say (except, perhaps, to assume on principle that an opposing point of view would be correct)'.[31] We have seen above that, in the case of his theology, Xenophanes appears to be using Homer as a text to which he can respond in such a way as to emphasize his own message.[32] There is, I contend, no good reason to reject the possibility that he is playing the same kind of allusive game in B35. Why should we not think that Xenophanes is here adducing the poets precisely in order to present an 'opposing point of view'?

The second ground for denying that B35 is a deliberate allusion is that, whilst Homer and Hesiod have 'lies' (ψεύδεα) resembling ἐτύμοισι, Xenophanes is taken to be likening 'truths' to ἔτυμα.[33] It remains to be seen whether the ταῦτα of B35 are rightly understood as 'truths'. For the present it is sufficient to note that, even if there is a difference between the subjects of the Homeric/Hesiodic formula and that of Xenophanes, this is no justification for rejecting the possibility of allusion.[34] For allusion need not and, indeed, often does not operate purely through similarity. It is frequently the case that the significance of an allusion lies in the way that it differs from that to which it alludes. Returning once again to B25, we see that the force of its allusion to Homer lies in the explicit difference between the two versions of divine power. It is not correct to say that Xenophanes cannot there be referring to Homer because he is presenting an unmoving god whilst the *Iliad* features a deity in motion. This disparity is precisely what we are being asked to notice.

[31] Lesher (1992) 172.

[32] As Lesher (1992) 110 notes: 'The allusion [in B25] could hardly have been meant as a concession of a grain of truth in Homer's depiction. On the contrary, by evoking that famous scene, Xenophanes would only have heightened his audience's sense of the contrast between that crudely physical image of divine power and his own idea of an effortlessly telekinetic divine *noos*.'

[33] Lesher (1992) 173. Classen (1989) 101 notes that Homer and Hesiod are qualifying ψεύδεα but, quite rightly, does not regard this as problematic for an allusive reading.

[34] Indeed, Morgan (2000) 51 sees Xenophanes as deliberately contrasting 'his own limited formulations with the claims of the poets'.

This point is equally applicable to the third objection, which is that, whilst Homer and Hesiod have stories ὁμοῖα to ἔτυμα, Xenophanes' ταῦτα are described as ἐοικότα to ἔτυμα. It has been suggested that this difference in terminology of resemblance is enough to undermine an allusive reading of B35.[35] Again, this objection is founded on the erroneous assumption that allusion requires conformity rather than alteration. In fact, as I shall argue, B35 can be properly understood only if it is read as a deliberate reworking and rewording of the poetic formula 'ἐτύμοισι ὁμοῖα'. Xenophanes alludes to his predecessors because he wishes to adduce a species of 'resemblance' to the truth that is explicitly different from that attributed to the words of Odysseus and the Muses.

Before coming to consider exactly what species of resemblance Xenophanes employs in B35, it will be necessary to examine what kind of likeness he is rejecting, i.e. what type of resemblance he takes to be expressed by the term ὁμοῖος. With this aim in mind, I return to Homer and Hesiod.

Theogony 27–28 offers 'one of the most enigmatic statements about poetry to be found in Greek literature'.[36] A variety of interpretations have been mooted for these cryptic verses.[37] Some have suggested that they favourably contrast the truth of Hesiod's poetry with Homeric falsehoods. On this reading, we are being told that, when the Muses inspire Hesiod, they choose to speak the truth (ἴδμεν δ', εὖτ' ἐθέλωμεν, ἀληθέα γηρύσασθαι). Homer, on the other hand, has been led to recount falsehoods, which may have seemed plausible (presumably, both to Homer and to his audience), but were not actually true (ἴδμεν ψεύδεα πολλὰ λέγειν ἐτύμοισιν ὁμοῖα).[38]

Others propose that *Theogony* 27–28 is a reflexive characterization of Hesiod's own poetry, which the Muses warn may contain

35 Rivier (1956) 51n7 notices the similarities and differences between the formulae, but claims that there is no semantic equivalence between the two terms and thus no reason to think that Xenophanes is alluding to Hesiod.

36 Pucci (1977) 8.

37 For a summary of these interpretations see Belfiore (1985) 47–8 and Ledbetter (2003) 42–8.

38 Proponents of this view include Verdenius (1972) 234; Neitzel (1980) 390; Murray (1981) 91; Bowie (1993) 20–3; Morgan (2000) 21.

both truth and lies.[39] Construed in this way, the Muses are taken to be emphasizing the fundamental difference between their privileged position of comprehensive knowledge and the limitations of mortals (including Hesiod) who are unable to distinguish between truth and lies that merely look like truth. According to Glenn Most, these lines represent a claim that 'the understanding of most men is so limited that mortals, in contrast to the divine Muses, cannot tell the difference between truth and lies'.[40]

The relative merits and disadvantages of such rival interpretations of the *Theogony*'s intriguing truth-claim are many and varied. They are also, regrettably, beyond the scope of the present discussion. More pertinent to my argument is that both readings share the same understanding of the phrase ἐτύμοισιν ὁμοῖα. For, on either construal, this expression is understood as describing lies that are *successfully deceptive*, insofar as they are 'indistinguishable from the truth'. On the first reading, it is Homer who is unable to recognize the Muses' lies as such and who thus recounts them as truth. On the second, it is Hesiod and his audience who are incapable of distinguishing between falsehoods and truths. The Muses are not claiming simply that they can produce lies 'similar' to the truth but rather that their lies are in some sense the same as the truth, if only because they appear to be true.[41]

The propriety of reading ἐτύμοισιν ὁμοῖα as 'indistinguishable from the truth' is even clearer at *Odyssey* 19.203:

> ἴσκε ψεύδεα πολλὰ λέγων ἐτύμοισιν ὁμοῖα.
>
> He spoke and concocted many lies like truth.[42]

39 See Stroh (1976) 86–97; Ledbetter (2003) 42–8.

40 Most (1999) 343. Ledbetter (2003) 42–8 argues against those, such as Neitzel, who doubt the possibility that Hesiod might have prefaced his poetry with a suggestion that its veracity could be doubted. She convincingly emphasizes 'the unsettling threat in the Muses' words' and proposes that, rather than a 'truth-claim', the 'proem to the *Theogony* serves as an extended meditation on the nature of poetry and the poet's art'. In these lines, Hesiod is claiming neither that his poetry is true, nor that it is false, but is stressing that there is no criterion available for mortals to distinguish between the truths or lies that the Muses may choose to tell.

41 Thus Pucci (1977) 9–11 suggests 'identical to true things' as a translation for ἐτύμοισιν ὁμοῖα.

42 Some read ἴσκε as 'said' rather than 'made like' on the grounds that the latter translation renders ὁμοῖα redundant. If, however, we understand that ὁμοῖα represents indistinguishability rather than mere similarity, ἴσκε can retain its meaning of 'assimilated'.

The point here is not that Odysseus has manufactured a story that is merely similar to truth, but that he is spinning his wife a line that is *indistinguishable* from truth and which Penelope, as a direct consequence, takes to be true. It is the *verisimilitude* of Odysseus' lies that renders them believable and thus deceptive.[43]

We have seen, then, that both the Homeric and the Hesiodic formulae express the notion of lies that are indistinguishable from truth and which are thus believed by some undiscriminating audience actually to be true. I will argue below that, in altering the term for resemblance in B35, Xenophanes is deliberately distancing himself from this kind of deceptive verisimilitude. He does this, I will contend, in order to emphasize that his poetry possesses a significantly different kind of resemblance to the truth. Of course, any such arguments regarding the broader epistemological significance of this fragment will be predicated on a satisfactory reading of the Greek. With this in mind, it is high time to look again, and in detail, at these six surprisingly troublesome words.

Fragment B35

ταῦτα δεδοξάσθαι μὲν ἐοικότα τοῖς ἐτύμοισι

(a) ταῦτα

Bearing in mind both the potential parallel to Homer and Hesiod and, perhaps more importantly, the context of the fragment as it appears in Plutarch, the best reading of ταῦτα is as referring to Xenophanes' own writings.[44] In Plutarch, Ammonius uses B35, as is claimed to be his habit, as a comment on his foregoing speech about the Muses.[45] In this context, ταῦτα quite clearly refers to

We can understand Odysseus as lying in such a way as to make his fictions seem to be indistinguishable from the truth rather than that he merely speaks lies that are similar to the truth. See Hayman (1882) 326 and West (1966) 163.

43 As noted by Pratt (1995) 91.

44 Lesher (1992) 171–4 convincingly dismisses the possibility that ταῦτα should be read as 'appearances' likened to some more fundamental reality.

45 The possibility, discussed above, that B35 is part of a conclusion would also support reading ταῦτα as referring to Xenophanes' doctrine.

what Ammonius has just said. B35 may represent Xenophanes making the same sort of reflexive comment.[46]

This plausible supposition that the ταῦτα of B35 are Xenophanes' own doctrines provokes a further question regarding the scope of its reference. Does ταῦτα incorporate the totality of Xenophanes' teachings, or only those dealing with particular topics? The general assumption, following Barnes, is that the ταῦτα of B35 coincide with the subject-matter specified in B34: ἀμφὶ θεῶν τε καὶ ἅσσα λέγω περὶ πάντων.[47] Unfortunately, the significance of this reference to 'the gods and what I say about all things' is itself subject to some uncertainty. Is the phrase intended to incorporate everything Xenophanes has to say about anything, or only what he has to say about the gods and natural philosophy?[48] Lesher argues that the scope of ἅσσα λέγω περὶ πάντων cannot be completely general, i.e. 'what I have to say about everything', for several reasons.[49] The first is that such a comprehensive sense renders the specific mention of the gods which precedes it redundant, since 'the gods *are* among the matters discussed by Xenophanes'. Lesher's second objection to a general reading is that in implying that 'men had never known and would never know the certain truth about *anything*, no matter how minor' the line would appear to conflict with the fact that Xenophanes does speak about some topics (such as the writings of Homer and Hesiod) 'as though these were matters of common knowledge among the members of his audience'.[50] In support of this narrow reading, Lesher adduces B27

[46] It is, of course, far from unthinkable that a passage could be misconstrued and quoted in a fashion alien to its original sense. However, it does seem preferable, in the absence of obvious proof to the contrary, to assume that Plutarch was not labouring under a misapprehension.

[47] Barnes (1982) 140. Lesher (1992) 175 cites the fact that '*dedoxasthō* (from *doxadzō*) and *dokos* are cognate expressions' as supporting the suggestion that the ταῦτα of B35 'may be reasonably supposed to be the subject-matters under discussion in fragment 34'.

[48] The former view is represented by the translation of Heitsch (1983): 'die Götter und alles, was ich sage'. For the latter alternative, see Barnes (1982) 139. Finkelberg (1990) 160 has to limit the reference of θεῶν (he takes this to mean only 'the false gods of convention' as opposed to the god Xenophanes himself describes) in order to argue that B34 refers only to the physical realm.

[49] Lesher (1992) 167–8.

[50] See also Mogyoródi (2006) 133. In fact, it is hard to identify any obvious shift in tone between those fragments in which Xenophanes makes assertions about Homer and Hesiod and those in which he talks about the natural world and the gods.

and B29, both of which employ πάντα to refer to the totality of nature:[51]

> B27: ἐκ γαίης γὰρ πάντα καὶ εἰς γῆν πάντα τελευτᾶι.
>
> All things are from earth and all things end up as earth.[52]

> B29: γῆ καὶ ὕδωρ πάντ' ἐσθ' ὅσα γίνοντ' ἠδὲ φύονται.
>
> All things are earth and water which come to be and grow.[53]

Lesher's main concern is to limit the apparent 'scepticism' of B34 to the 'non-evident' realm. On his reading, Xenophanes would be claiming that we cannot have certainty only about those things which are beyond our experience and which we are thus unable to confirm as true. It is, however, possible to argue for a more general application of ἅσσα λέγω περὶ πάντων. Whilst πάντα in B27 and B29 *may* refer to 'nature', there is no reason to think that its occurrence in B18's apparent denial of revelation is specifically limited to natural philosophy:

> οὔτοι ἀπ' ἀρχῆς πάντα θεοὶ θνητοῖσ' ὑπέδειξαν
> ἀλλὰ χρόνῳ ζητοῦντες ἐφευρίσκουσιν ἄμεινον.[54]
>
> The gods have not revealed, from the outset, everything to mortals,
> But, by searching, in time, they discover better.

Equally, although Lesher may feel that Xenophanes talks about some subjects 'as though they were matters of common knowledge among the members of his audience', there is no compelling reason to think that Xenophanes regarded these as common (certain) *knowledge* as opposed to a commonly held *opinion* providing a useful starting point for his inquiries. Lesher's stronger point is his claim that a general application of ἅσσα λέγω περὶ πάντων would not need the supplement of ἀμφὶ θεῶν. However, bearing in mind Xenophanes' obvious preoccupation with matters theological, one might be tempted to take this supplement as emphatic

[51] Note that the more general scope of πάντων would be supported by reading πᾶσι at B34.4 as referring to 'all things' rather than 'everyone'. On this, see Fränkel (1974) 128.

[52] Aëtius 4.5. [53] Simplicius *Phys.* 188.32. [54] Stobaeus *Ecl.* 1.8.2.

rather than exclusive.[55] In summary, the supposition that the ταῦτα of B35 are (some part of) Xenophanes' writings seems fairly well justified. The problems of whether they are coextensive with the subject-matter set out in B34, and whether the scope of that subject-matter is specific or general, are impossible to solve definitively. Whatever tentative answers I am able to offer will depend on my interpretation of B35 as a whole. For the time being, then, it is necessary to set these questions aside and consider the details of the rest of the fragment.

(b) *δεδοξάσθαι*

In LSJ B35 is cited as an example of the passive voice of δοξάζειν as meaning 'to be a matter of opinion'.[56] In fact, a preferable translation of the verb in this context is 'be accepted' or 'be believed'. These renderings more accurately express the sense of completion implied by the perfect tense of the verb. 'To have been believed' is more decisive and complete than 'to have been (made) a matter of opinion' and the latter seems more like a continuous process than a completed action. Translations such as 'be accepted' also do a better job of representing the notions of deliberation and choice identifiable in the etymology of δοκ- words.[57]

Depending on whether and how we read an infinitive or an imperative (on which see below), Xenophanes is telling us either to believe something or that something is believed. Most commentators understand the fragment as encouraging us to accept or believe ταῦτα, a pronoun that I have noted above probably refers to

55 Thus Warren (2007) 50: 'Xenophanes first disclaims any access to the clear and certain truth about all the matters he has addressed in his work and to theological questions in particular.'

56 LSJ 444. DK 1.137 seems to offer something similar with 'Dies soll zwar der bloßen Meinung nach gelten . . . ' See also Gigon (1945) 181: 'Dieses nun soll der Vermutung nach gelten . . . ' Barnes (1982) 140 and McKirahan (1994) 67 have 'let these things be believed', whilst Warren (2007) has 'let these be believed'. Fränkel (1974) 128, Lesher (1992) 39 and Mogyoródi (2006) 145 have 'be accepted'. Heitsch (1983) 79 has 'dieses zwar vermutungsweise gelten zu lassen . . . ', whilst Schäfer (1996) 120 has 'vermutungsweise gelten lassen'. KRS 179 and Popper (1998) 48 seem to stand somewhere in between this latter type of translation and that of LSJ, offering 'let these things be opined' and 'let us conjecture' respectively. Heitsch (1983) 184 notes that this is the first extant occurrence of δοξάζειν.

57 See Lesher (1992) 85 and 175 and Mourelatos (2008) 194–200.

(some part of) Xenophanes' doctrines. On this reading, the phrase ἐοικότα τοῖς ἐτύμοισι is taken to be an explanatory supplement, clarifying *why* we should believe his doctrine, i.e. to believe it *to be true*.[58] An unfortunate consequence of this interpretation is that the explanation why we should believe ταῦτα to be true is given in terms of their relationship to truth (i.e. their being ἐοικότα τοῖς ἐτύμοισι). This is an unwelcome consequence because, in pointing to the relationship between ταῦτα and the truth, Xenophanes must be implying that there is some disparity between the two, at least insofar as they can be compared.[59] It would seem odd for Xenophanes to be recommending that we believe '*x* is (i.e. identical to) *y*, because it is like (i.e. non-identical to) *y*'.

Thankfully, a more satisfactory reading is available. Rather than taking B35 as instructing us to believe Xenophanes' doctrines *because* they are ἐοικότα τοῖς ἐτύμοισι, we can understand it as telling us to accept *that* his teachings are ἐοικότα τοῖς ἐτύμοισι (or that his teachings have been accepted to be ἐοικότα τοῖς ἐτύμοισι).[60] A useful parallel for δοξάζειν functioning in this fashion is Aeschylus' *Choephori* 844:

> πῶς ταῦτ' ἀληθῆ καὶ βλέποντα δοξάσω;[61]
>
> How can I judge this tale to be the living truth?

Here, the verb δοξάζειν describes 'believing *x* to be *y*' rather than 'believing *x* because or as it is *y*'.[62] I suggest that, just as Aegisthus wonders aloud how he can judge or believe ταῦτα to be ἀληθῆ καὶ βλέποντα so, at B35, we are recommended to judge or believe

[58] Lesher (1992) 175 treats ἐοικότα τοῖς ἐτύμοισι as supplementary when he asserts that 'we should expect what accompanies the injunction [that ταῦτα are to be accepted] to square with it and perhaps to bolster the recommendation by explaining why it should be accepted'. He accordingly translates B35: 'Let these be accepted, certainly, as like the realities.' DK 1.137; Fränkel (1974) 128; Barnes (1982) 140; KRS 179; and McKirahan (1994) 67 all seem to follow this reading.

[59] Lesher (1992) avoids this problem by adopting the translation 'realities' for τοῖς ἐτύμοισι. See discussion below 25–6.

[60] Reading δοξάζειν with a double accusative. See LSJ 444.

[61] Note that, just as with B35, the complement contains a participle.

[62] A further, admittedly later, parallel is Plato's *Philebus* 48e8–10: 'πολὺ δὲ πλεῖστοί γε οἶμαι περὶ τὸ τρίτον εἶδος τὸ τῶν ἐν ταῖς ψυχαῖς διημαρτήκασιν, ἀρετῇ δοξάζοντες βελτίους ἑαυτούς, οὐκ ὄντες.' ('But I think that most people err in the third way, with regard to the qualities of the soul, *believing that they are greatest* in virtue when they are not.')

ταῦτα to be ἐοικότα τοῖς ἐτύμοισι (or told that they have been judged or believed to be so).[63]

There is, I think, further evidence against reading B35 as an unqualified exhortation to accept Xenophanes' doctrine. Lesher suggests that this 'comment could well have served as a concluding or summary remark, urging his audience to agree with what he had previously said or to accept as sufficient the account he had provided'.[64] Against Lesher's reading of B35 is the context of its citation in Plutarch:

> τούτοις ἐπιφωνήσαντος τοῦ Ἀμμωνίου τὰ τοῦ Ξενοφάνους ὥσπερ εἰώθει
>
> ταῦτα δεδοξάσθαι μὲν ἐοικότα τοῖς ἐτύμοισι
>
> καὶ παρακαλοῦντος ἀποφαίνεσθαι καὶ λέγειν τὸ δοκοῦν ἕκαστον . . .

> In his usual manner, Ammonius rounded off his remarks with a bit of Xenophanes:
>
> ταῦτα δεδοξάσθαι μὲν ἐοικότα τοῖς ἐτύμοισι
>
> and encouraged us each to speak up and give our own opinion . . .

Note that, immediately after quoting B35, Ammonius urges his audience to give their own views on the matter under discussion. Such encouragement would seem rather futile if it followed on directly from a recommendation that his audience should believe his own account, i.e. accept it as sufficient. For, if his companions were to believe what has just been said, it follows that, in then stating their own opinions, they would merely be *restating* Ammonius' position.

It seems that Plutarch's Ammonius is not citing B35 as a straightforward endorsement of what has just been said. So, how is the fragment being used in this context? Before attempting to answer this question, it is necessary to introduce one further complication. For, in considering the meaning of B35, one must choose between the infinitive δεδοξάσθαι as found in the mss and Wilamowitz's generally accepted emendation to the imperative δεδοξάσθω.[65] For

63 Popper (1998) 48 translates 'let us conjecture *that* these things are like the truth' (my emphasis).

64 Lesher (1992) 174.

65 See DK 1.137, citing the parallel of Theognis 681: 'ταῦτά μοι ἠνίχθω κεκρυμμένα τοῖς ἀγαθοῖσιν' ('let these be my secretive riddles for the noble'). Those who accept this emendation include KRS 179 and Lesher (1992) 38. Heitsch (1983) 104 and Schäfer

those who read B35 as epilogic, the imperative is preferable, at least in part because it echoes the summarizing imperatives employed by Herodotus, as at 1.140:

καὶ ἀμφὶ μὲν τῷ νόμῳ τούτῳ ἐχέτω ὡς καὶ ἀρχὴν ἐνομίσθη, ἄνειμι δὲ ἐπι τὸν πρότερον λόγον.[66]

Let that be that regarding this custom as it was first laid down; I return to my previous account.

In fact, the desire to read B35 as an endorsement seems to be the major motivation for emending to the imperative.[67] However, since the perfect infinitive can just as well be used with the force of the imperative, the emendation seems unjustified on this ground alone. In the absence of any further justification for emending, I retain the infinitive of the mss.[68]

Bearing in mind what has been established above about the general meaning of δοξάζειν and the context of its appearance in Plutarch, we are, I suggest, faced with a choice between two possible readings:

(1) Ammonius is indeed using B35 as *instructive* but, rather than recommending that his account should be believed *because* it is ἐοικότα τοῖς ἐτύμοισι, he is encouraging his companions to believe *that* it is ἐοικότα τοῖς ἐτύμοισι. Further, the fact that Ammonius goes on to encourage the others to give their own opinions indicates that, for him, believing that *x* is ἐοικότα τοῖς ἐτύμοισι is not the same as believing *x* to be true. It can, at most, indicate a qualified endorsement. On this reading, Ammonius would be saying something along

(1996) 120 retain the infinitive and it is cited as such by LSJ 444. Karsten (1830) 53 seems to be alone in suggesting δεδόξασται 'quod legitur ob verborum nexum'.

66 Lesher (1992) 174. He cites similar parallels at Herodotus 2.33; 2.28, 35; 4.15, 36, 45; 6.55 and points out that such perfect imperatives are also familiar in the summarizing remarks of Aristotle, e.g. *Nicomachean Ethics* 1097a14–15: 'καὶ περὶ μὲν τούτων ἐπὶ τοσοῦτον εἰρήσθω' ('let this be end of the discussion of these matters'). These potential parallels would, if accepted, be evidence in favour of reading the original context of B35 as conclusory.

67 Lesher (1992) 173–4.

68 Lesher (1992) 170. Gentili and Prato (1979) 181 read δεδοξάσθαι as 'infinitivus vi imperativi' citing *Odyssey* 13.307 as a parallel. See Goodwin (1946) sec. 1274: 'The perfect *imperative* generally expresses a command that something shall be *decisive* and *permanent*; as ταῦτα εἰρήσθω, *let this have been said* (i.e. let what has been said be final)' and sec. 1537: 'The infinitive with a subject *accusative* sometimes expresses [. . .] a command, like the third person of the imperative.'

the lines of 'believe my account to be ἐοικότα τοῖς ἐτύμοισι and then tell me what you think on the matter'.

(2) Ammonius is *classifying* his own account as ἐοικότα τοῖς ἐτύμοισι. This reading would be ruled out by adopting the imperative but is perfectly compatible with the infinitive.[69] On this interpretation, Ammonius is saying something like 'I think (i.e. I have judged that) my account is ἐοικότα τοῖς ἐτύμοισι, but tell me what you think on the matter.' In fact, a construal like this, along the lines of 'that's my view, now tell me yours', might be thought a better fit with Ammonius' encouragement to his companions to speak up with their own opinions.

It will once again, I think, prove very difficult to decide between these two readings. Certainly such a choice will be impossible without thinking further about the meaning of ἐοικότα τοῖς ἐτύμοισι. One thing, however, seems to be clear: the Plutarchean context offers no support for reading B35 as an unqualified exhortation to accept ταῦτα as true. Of course, some may object that Plutarch's use of B35 could just as well bear no relation to its meaning in Xenophanes.[70] But, whatever doubts we may have about Plutarch's reliability as a source, any interpretation that is *both* plausibly attributed to Xenophanes *and* sympathetic to the context in which it is cited must surely be preferred. I will argue for such a reading, whereby Xenophanes is both identifying that his account is a plausible candidate for being true and warning that it cannot be known to be true with any certainty. This seems in keeping with the way the fragment is used in *Quaestiones Convivales*, where Ammonius could perfectly well be saying 'You

[69] Assuming that the infinitive arises from the missing Xenophanean context, perhaps as following ὥστε or as part of an indirect statement. Admittedly, the Plutarchean context is not itself an example of indirect speech: ἐπιφωνεῖν is generally employed, as at *Quaest. Conv.* 746b, to introduce a direct quotation or as a verb of exclamation or recitation, rather than as introducing *oratio obliqua*. Of the twelve occurrences of the verb in Plutarch, it is only once (at *Quaest. Plat.* 1046a1 with ὅτι) used in a way that might seem to be introducing direct speech. Such a classificatory reading would also fit Karsten's emendation to δεδόξασται (see n65 above).

[70] Fairbanks (1897) argues that there is good reason to think that Plutarch derived his quotations of Heraclitus, Xenophanes and Parmenides from an intermediate source. He notes (76–7) that Heraclitus B29 is quoted in two different forms at *De Is. et Os.* 370d and *De exil.* 604a but argues that the majority of Plutarch's quotations of verse, particularly of single lines, seem to be accurate, 'though occasionally a question as to the text makes us doubt the accuracy of the copy'.

should think [or 'I do think'] that what I've said about the Muses *might* be true, but why not tell me what you think about them?'

(c) μέν

The truncated state of the fragment makes it impossible to know whether B35's μέν is emphatic or antithetical.[71] Nevertheless, various potential antitheses have been mooted. Those who perceive a connection between this fragment and B34 have suggested that the contrast here, as there, might be between belief and certainty. Thus Lesher imagines the complete thought to be 'let these be accepted, certainly, as like the realities, *but they cannot be known as the clear and certain truth*'.[72] Another possibility is that Xenophanes is emphasizing that ταῦτα are merely *similar to* the truth rather than *actually true*.[73]

In fact, even if no δέ-clause was ever stated explicitly, Xenophanes may still have intended some implicit contrast. It is not uncommon for the μέν *solitarium* to occur 'with words denoting opinion, appearance, or probability, implicitly contrasted with certainty or reality'.[74] It seems likely that, either implicitly or explicitly, B35 represents half of a contrast.[75] Once the sense of the extant verse has been established, it will be useful to reconsider the possibility and nature of such an opposition. For the time being, this issue joins the ever-growing list of those that must be postponed.

71 Note that DK I. 137, Heitsch (1983) 185 and Lesher (1992) 39 combine the two. DK and Heitsch have 'zwar . . . aber' whilst Lesher has 'certainly . . . but'.

72 Lesher (1992) 175 (my emphasis). Also 170. Heitsch (1983) 185 'aber – wo etwa könnte der Gendanke gegangen sein – da wir nur aus Indizien schließen, bleibt eine Unsicherheit'.

73 The possibility is acknowledged and rejected by Lesher (1992) who argues that a denial of truth in B35 would contrast with B34.3's claim 'that someone might succeed *ta malista* in speaking of what is brought to pass, that is, describe exactly what happens'. Even if we accept that B34 implies the possibility of speaking the truth (rather than its impossibility) it is not clear why we should think that B35 is describing such a successful account. One may acknowledge that some people speak accurately without claiming that everything one says is equally successful.

74 Denniston (1954) 380–2. He cites, among others, Herodotus 7.50: δοκέω μὲν οὐδαμῶς ('I don't think there's any way [it can be done]').

75 Although Rivier (1956) 51 suggests that it may be emphatic but not concessive.

(*d*) τοῖς ἐτύμοισι

Is Xenophanes likening ταῦτα to 'truths' or to 'realities'?[76] Is he claiming that his doctrines are somehow similar to truth, or is he asserting that what he says 'corresponds' to the facts of the matter, i.e. is true? Lesher prefers 'realities', a translation which better suits his insistence that Xenophanes is describing a correspondence between his doctrines and reality.[77]

'Truths' is, however, more satisfactory.[78] In fragment B8, we encounter the adverbial form ἐτύμως as meaning 'truly'. Xenophanes offers an estimate of his age accompanied by a *caveat*: εἴπερ ἐγὼ περὶ τῶνδ' οἶδα λέγειν ἐτύμως ('if I know how to speak truly about such things').[79] 'Truths' is also a better translation of τοῖς ἐτύμοισι in the formulae of Homer and Hesiod which I have argued to be the allusive target of B35.[80] Odysseus is not concocting ψεύδεα that are like or representative of reality, since they are by their very nature not like reality, insofar as they are false.[81] He is telling stories which are, for Penelope, like, or indistinguishable from, truths. At *Theogony* 27, the Muses are not warning Hesiod of their ability to produce lies that correspond to reality. They are threatening to tell lies that those without the power to discriminate

76 ἔτυμος can refer to either. See Chantraine (1968) 381 and Cole (1983) 13.

77 Lesher (1992) 171, citing *Odyssey* 19.564–567, Pindar *Olympian* 10.53–55 and Theocritus 12.35–37. Heitsch (1983) 185–6 also prefers 'dem Wirklichen'. According to Lesher, *Odyssey* 19.564–567 is evidence for Homer using τὰ ἔτυμα to mean 'real things' 'when he contrasts dreams that remain unfulfilled (ἀκράαντα) with those having "true issues" (ἔτυμα κραίνουσι)'. However, the contrast here is between 'unfulfilled *words*' (ἔπε' ἀκράαντα), i.e. falsehoods, and τὰ ἔτυμα, suggesting that here too the term could mean something closer to 'truths': 'τῶν οἳ μέν κ' ἔλθωσι διὰ πριστοῦ ἐλέφαντος,/οἵ ῥ' ἐλεφαίρονται, ἔπε' ἀκράαντα φέροντες·/οἳ δὲ διὰ ξεστῶν κεράων ἔλθωσι θύραζε,/οἵ ῥ' ἔτυμα κραίνουσι, βροτῶν ὅτε κέν τις ἴδηται' ('those which come through the gate of sawn ivory deceive, bringing unfulfilled words. But those which come through the gate of polished horn, those dreams come true [sc. LSJ 989], when any mortal sees them').

78 It is also much more widely preferred. See DK 1. 137; Burnet (1930) 121; Gigon (1945) 181; Guthrie (1962) 398; Fränkel (1974) 128; Barnes (1982) 140; KRS 179; McKirahan (1994) 67; Popper (1998) 48; Warren (2007) 51. See also LSJ 704.

79 Diogenes Laertius 9.19.

80 Herodotus 4.195 offers a version of the formula with ἀλήθεια: 'οὕτω ὦν καὶ τὰ ἀπὸ τῆς νήσου τῆς ἐπὶ Λιβύῃ κειμένης οἰκότα ἐστὶ ἀληθείῃ' ('so, what we hear from the island lying off Libya is like the truth').

81 Mogyoródi (2006) 155n102 suggests that Odysseus' story 'gains credibility' because Penelope recognizes that it matches the realities of what Odysseus looked like and wore on his way to Troy, '[t]hus, his fiction becomes a "likely story" because it is based on knowledge of τὰ ἔτυμα'.

will be unable to recognize as such. The unwitting will accept these falsehoods as if they were truths. Further support for reading ἐτύμως as 'truly' is to be found at *Iliad* 10.534, where Nestor asks ψεύσομαι, ἦ ἔτυμον ἐρέω; ('will I lie, or will I speak the truth?').

Of course, the two potential translations need not be viewed as mutually exclusive. ἔτυμος and its cognates are etymologically linked to the verb εἶναι and ἔτυμος accounts are presumably those which describe what really is.[82] If Xenophanes' ταῦτα are ἐοικότα to truths, it may be correct to say that ταῦτα also enjoy some kind of relation to the reality those truths describe. However, it is vital that this vicarious relation should not be confused with correspondence to reality and that Xenophanes should not be assumed to be offering a straightforward truth-claim. The best way to ensure this is to establish in what way ταῦτα are 'like', i.e. ἐοικότα to, truths.

(e) ἐοικότα

Two rival kinds of interpretation have emerged from the above analysis of B35. One sees the fragment as a claim to truth, albeit without certainty, paralleling the apparent message of B34. This interpretation assumes that Xenophanes is describing his ταῦτα as like, i.e. corresponding to, reality.[83] It is a tendency of this kind of reading to attribute the notion of 'plausibility' to B35.[84] Xenophanes, it is claimed, is denying certainty to his account, but claiming 'plausibility' in its place.[85] The alternative interpretation reads B35 as claiming that Xenophanes' ταῦτα are merely *like* the

[82] Krischer (1965) 166.
[83] Guthrie (1962) 396; Rivier (1956) 50; Fränkel (1974) 128; Finkelberg (1990) 131; Lesher (1992) 170 and 175–6; Schofield (1997) 79; Popper (1998) 48; Mogyoródi (2006) 145 and 155.
[84] Thus Fränkel (1974) 128 translates B35: 'let these things be accepted as *plausibly tending* towards what is true' (my emphasis). See also Finkelberg (1990) 131; Hussey (1990) 25; and Mogyoródi (2006) 145 who translates 'Let these [views] be accepted as likely beliefs, similar to realities, (although . . .)' and explains this 'likelihood' in terms of increasing plausibility.
[85] See Lesher (1992) 170 on the inappropriateness of 'plausible' as translation of ἐοικώς in B35.

truth, i.e. not actually true.[86] The only way to decide definitively between these two options is to establish which better suits the meaning of ἐοικώς. Can this term be used to express the kind of correspondence required by those who read B35 as a claim to truth? Or does it represent the idea of 'mere likeness', implying a difference from truth, involved in the latter reading?

Some have attempted to argue that ἐοικώς can express 'correspondence'. Thus Lesher asserts that 'while a likeness represented by the term *eoikōs* can on occasion be only rough or approximate (for example *Iliad* 3.449, where Achilles is likened to a "wild animal"), it can also be quite close (for instance, *Iliad* 2.337, where Nestor complains that the Achaeans are acting "just like foolish children" παισὶν ἐοικότες.../νηπιάχοις.)'[87] Now, even if one were to accept that the likeness adduced between Achilles and a wild animal is 'only rough' whilst that between the Achaeans and children is 'quite close', it is hard to see how the latter could be regarded as a clear-cut case of 'correspondence', such as that which holds between truth and reality.[88]

In fact, as will be extensively argued below, ἐοικώς does describe a particular kind of likeness, namely contingent and potentially specious similarity. Before turning to this demonstration, however, it is worth summarizing what (regrettably little) has so far been established with regard to the meaning of B35. I have argued that the way the fragment is cited in Plutarch militates against reading it as a straightforward endorsement along the lines of 'believe what I have said'. Rather, it represents some kind of claim on the part of Xenophanes *that* his doctrine is *like* the truth. On one reading of the infinitive, this claim could take an instructive form:

ταῦτα δεδοξάσθαι μὲν ἐοικότα τοῖς ἐτύμοισι

Let these [teachings] be believed to be like the truth

[86] Gigon (1945) 19 and 181; Barnes (1982) 140; Morgan (2000) 50.
[87] Lesher (1992) 175.
[88] See Heitsch (1983) 185. He argues that we are not supposed to think of the Achaeans *as* children, but to think about the fact that they behave as children do, so that, at that moment, in some way they are truly 'like children'. Heitsch's position on the overall sense of B35 seems to be a compromise between the two readings described above, and is based on the idea of Xenophanes' teachings being 'as good as true'. He suggests that the sense of the fragment is: 'Das was ich hier ausführe, macht ganz den Eindruck, als wäre es richtig; und deshalb kann und soll man es hinnehmen.'

Construed differently, it could be classificatory:

> These [teachings] have been believed to be like the truth

In fact, both interpretations seem to represent some degree of exhortation. If B35 is intended as instructive, Xenophanes would be offering *explicit* encouragement to his audience to believe that what he says is 'like the truth'. If classificatory, the recommendation would be *implicit*. For I take it that the implication of such a classification would be that, insofar as Xenophanes has judged his account to be like the truth, so too should we. In summary, whatever the strength of the encouragement in B35, it is not for us to believe his doctrines (i.e. to believe them to be true), but to believe the assertion that he makes about their status, i.e. that they are like the truth. In what way are they like the truth? It is, finally, time to investigate the meaning of ἐοικώς.

Poetic similarities

I argued above that Xenophanes' obvious engagement with Homer and Hesiod gives good cause for reading B35 as an intentional allusion to the poetic formula of speaking falsehoods ἐτύμοισιν ὁμοῖα. Bearing this in mind, it is necessary to consider what motivates Xenophanes' alteration of the term for resemblance from ὁμοῖος to ἐοικώς.[89] Analysis of the Homeric usage of ὁμοῖος and ἐοικώς demonstrates that there is an important semantic difference between the two words. For, while both express a relation of similarity, there is a definite disparity between the kinds of resemblance to which they refer. In preferring ἐοικώς to ὁμοῖος, Xenophanes is attributing to his teachings a relationship to truth that is much more specific than mere undefined 'similarity' or 'likeness'.[90] On

[89] Neither Rivier's (1956) 52 claim that the two terms have no semantic equivalence, nor Ioli's (2003) 217n71 assertion that 'dal punto di vista semantico, *omoia* può dunque considerarsi un sinonimo di *eikota* già in età arcaica' is sufficient to render the change insignificant.

[90] The analysis of Homeric ἐοικώς will deal exclusively with the kinds of resemblance expressed by the term and will thus exclude a discussion of the sense 'appropriate to' that the word often carries in Homer. This omission is motivated by the supposition that Xenophanes is replacing one kind of similarity (ὁμοῖος) with another (ἐοικώς). See

the one hand, an understanding of the nature of ὁμοῖος-similarity will clarify what sort of relationship to truth Xenophanes rejects when he emends the formula of Homer and Hesiod. On the other hand, an appreciation of Homeric ἐοικώς-similarity will provide an essential foundation for the interpretation of B35.

ὁμοῖος and ἐοικώς are among the numerous words used to express likeness in Homeric similes.[91] Both terms are found in shorter similes used to make 'quite straightforward *a* = *b* comparison'.[92] Thus, at *Iliad* 17.51–52, the hair of Euphorbus' corpse is said to be ὁμοῖος to that of the Graces:

αἵματί οἱ δεύοντο κόμαι Χαρίτεσσιν ὁμοῖαι
πλοχμοί θ', οἳ χρυσῷ τε καὶ ἀργύρῳ ἐσφήκωντο.

His hair, like that of the Graces, drenched with blood
And his braids too, which were laced with gold and silver.

In the *Odyssey*, the curls of Odysseus' freshly washed tresses are likened to the flowers of the hyacinth:

. . . κὰδ δὲ κάρητος
οὔλας ἧκε κόμας, ὑακινθίνῳ ἄνθει ὁμοίας.[93]

. . . and she made the hair flow down his head
In curls like the flowers of the hyacinth.[94]

ἐοικώς is also found in this kind of brief comparison. At *Iliad* 15.90, Hera is said to look 'like a distraught woman' (ἀτυζομένῃ δὲ ἔοικας), whilst, at *Odyssey* 17.511, Penelope notes of Odysseus 'He is like a man who has done a lot of wandering' (πολυπλάγκτῳ γὰρ ἔοικε). There is, however, a notable disparity in the way that the terms tend to occur. Straightforward comparisons using ὁμοῖος tend to be made in the voice of the poet. On the other hand, those *straightforward* comparisons which employ ἐοικώς and its

also Ioli (2003) 217 who argues that the evidence from Homer suggests that ἐοικότα 'affiancato da un nome di cosa o di persona, debba preferibilmente tradursi con "simile a", e non con "conforme a"'. For a discussion of ἐοικώς as meaning 'appropriate to' see the treatment of Parmenides B8.60 below (68–71).

91 Lee (1964) 62–4.

92 Lee (1964) 48.

93 *Odyssey* 6.230–231; cf. 23. 157–158.

94 See also *Iliad* 5.778–779, where the movement of Athene and Hera is described as 'τρήρωσι πελειάσιν ἴθμαθ' ὁμοῖαι' ('like the gait of timorous doves': reading ἴθματα as an accusative of respect).

cognates are, without exception, found in direct speech.[95] This difference in usage suggests that, whilst ὁμοῖος is used to communicate likenesses that should be taken as objective, i.e. as the poet describes them to be, ἐοικώς expresses a more subjective resemblance, as is perceived by some individual and as may, in the long run, prove to be deceptive. Penelope says that Odysseus looks widely travelled, but she may be wrong. At *Iliad* 11.613–615, when Achilles notes the resemblance of a passing warrior to Machaon, he adds a *caveat*:

> ἤτοι μὲν τά γ' ὄπισθε Μαχάονι πάντα ἔοικε
> τῷ Ἀσκληπιάδῃ, ἀτὰρ οὐκ ἴδον ὄμματα φωτός·
> ἵπποι γάρ με παρήϊξαν πρόσσω μεμαυῖαι.
>
> Indeed, from behind he looked entirely like Machaon,
> Son of Asclepius. But I didn't see his eyes
> Because the horses ran past me at a gallop.

It should be emphasized that the potential error implicit in such ἐοικώς-comparisons is not one regarding the similarity *as such*. The point is not that Penelope thinks both that Odysseus looks like an itinerant and that it may turn out that he doesn't *look like* one after all. Rather, Penelope is asserting a similarity that may or may not be indicative of identity; Odysseus looks as if he has travelled widely and, indeed, it may or may not be the case that he actually has. In contrast, there is no hint of such a possible identity in similes with ὁμοῖος. For, whilst Odysseus' hair really does look like hyacinths (with no hint of speciousness), it would be absurd to suggest that it actually *is* hyacinths.[96]

Where ἐοικώς is used in similes presented in the voice of the poet there is another clear difference from those which employ ὁμοῖος. For while all such ὁμοῖος-similes are of the straightforward $a = b$ type, those with ἐοικώς express a far more general kind of

[95] Further examples of a recognition of resemblance in direct speech are at *Iliad* 2.337 where Nestor speaks; 3.170: Priam; 3.156: the Trojan elders; 3.219: Antenor; 5.800: Athene; 15.90: Themis; *Odyssey* 1.208–209: Athene; 3.124–125; Nestor; 4.141: Helen; 6.187, 243, and 301: Nausicaa; 8.164: Euryalus; 8.166: Odysseus; 10.120: Odysseus; 16.200: Telemachus; 17.416: Odysseus; 17.500: Penelope; 18.128: Odysseus; 19.380–381: Eurycleia; 20.194: Philoetius; 20.227: Odysseus; 24.253–254: Odysseus.

[96] I have identified only one occurrence of a ὁμοῖος-comparison in direct speech. At *Odyssey* 8.14, Athene asserts that Odysseus is like the gods in stature (δέμας ἀθανάτοισιν ὁμοῖος). Even here, the comparison is stated as fact, rather than opinion.

resemblance, best described as 'analogical'. Rather than stating that *a* is like *b*, these 'analogical' similes function via the evocation of indefinite images and ideas. A classic example of this kind of analogical simile is found at *Iliad* 13.754–755:

> Ἦ ῥα, καὶ ὁρμήθη ὄρεϊ νιφόεντι ἐοικὼς
> κεκλήγων, διὰ δὲ Τρώων πέτετ' ἠδ' ἐπικούρων.
>
> So he spoke, and set off like a snowy mountain,
> And shouting out loud, he sped through the Trojans and their allies.

The comparison of Hector to a 'snowy mountain' has long been a source of puzzlement. No attempt to find a specific point of similarity between the dynamic warrior and the wintry land-mass seems quite satisfactory.[97] In fact, such attempts are misguided. Hermann Fränkel's influential treatment of Homeric similes argues that readers are often mistaken in searching for explicit and detailed points of comparison ('Vergleichungspunkt'). Homeric similes are, according to Fränkel, often intended to express or arouse a sentiment ('Stimmung').[98] Lee paraphrases Fränkel's argument:

> We should therefore not always look for a close parallelism between incident and simile: we should rather look at a general picture, and at a parallelism of the emotional background, common to the narrative and the simile: we must try to understand, and to feel, the simile with the mind, ears, and eyes of the Homeric audience.[99]

ἐοικώς-similes are of precisely this kind: indefinite but informative. This is well illustrated by the description of Agamemnon's anger at *Iliad* 1.103–104:

> μένεος δὲ μέγα φρένες ἀμφιμέλαιναι
> πίμπλαντ', ὄσσε δέ οἱ πυρὶ λαμπετόωντι ἐΐκτην.
>
> And his black heart was completely full of hate,
> And his eyes were like burning fire.[100]

Agamemnon's eyes are 'like burning fire' not, one would suppose, because they are glowing red or very hot. Rather, the poetic image

97 Murray (1925) 58–9: 'No subtleties of interpretation seem able to remove the awkwardness of the comparison of a warrior charging upon the foe to a snowy mountain.' See Bradley (1967) on this simile.

98 Fränkel (1921) *passim*.

99 Lee (1964) 47.

100 Cf. *Odyssey* 4.661–662.

of fire expresses his growing and destructive rage. This, at least, is one possible interpretation. The simile functions by allowing each reader to provide their own individual cashing out of its imagery. As Fränkel argues, it expresses an emotion rather than a concrete image.

Another, more extensive, example of this kind of evocative comparison is to be found at *Iliad* 5.87–94:

> θῦνε γὰρ ἂμ πεδίον ποταμῷ πλήθοντι ἐοικὼς
> χειμάρρῳ, ὅς τ' ὦκα ῥέων ἐκέδασσε γεφύρας·
> τὸν δ' οὔτ' ἄρ τε γέφυραι ἐεργμέναι ἰσχανόωσιν,
> οὔτ' ἄρα ἕρκεα ἴσχει ἀλωάων ἐριθηλέων
> ἐλθόντ' ἐξαπίνης ὅτ' ἐπιβρίσῃ Διὸς ὄμβρος·
> πολλὰ δ' ὑπ' αὐτοῦ ἔργα κατήριπε κάλ' αἰζηῶν·
> ὣς ὑπὸ Τυδεΐδῃ πυκιναὶ κλονέοντο φάλαγγες
> Τρώων, οὐδ' ἄρα μιν μίμνον πολέες περ ἐόντες.

> He stormed across the plain like a flooding river in winter,
> Which, fast-flowing, sweeps away the dams.
> The strong-built dams do not check its progress,
> Nor do the walls of the fruitful vineyards hold its sudden coming,
> As the rain of Zeus drives it on.
> Countless fine buildings of men collapse before it.
> Thus were the thick ranks of the Trojans routed by the son of Tydeus,
> Notwithstanding their numbers, they were unable to stop him.

The detailed comparison of Diomedes to a river in spate serves to illustrate the force and speed of his progress against the Trojan troops. The success of the simile derives not from our ability to match up point with point, as if this were one of the '$a = b$ type' comparisons, but from the image as a whole. The irresistible force of the torrent is analogous to that of Diomedes on the battle field. It is in this analogical sense that such ἐοικώς-similes function.[101]

Beyond the similes, both ἐοικώς and ὁμοῖος express specific and differing kinds of resemblance. There are several instances of ὁμοῖος being employed to signify that things are qualitatively

[101] On the analogical aspect of Homeric similes see Lloyd (1966) 190 and Edwards (1991) 35: 'The purpose of a simile is to encourage the listener's imagination by likening something in the narrative of the heroic past to something which is directly within his own experience.'

'the same'. Perhaps the clearest examples are those at *Odyssey* 16.181–182:

> ἀλλοῖός μοι, ξεῖνε, φάνης νέον ἠὲ πάροιθεν,
> ἄλλα δὲ εἵματ' ἔχεις καί τοι χρὼς οὐκέθ' ὁμοῖος.
>
> You seem to me, Stranger, to be different now from how you were before,
> You are dressed differently and your colouring is no longer the same.

and *Iliad* 18.329–330:

> ἄμφω γὰρ πέπρωται ὁμοίην γαῖαν ἐρεῦσαι
> αὐτοῦ ἐνὶ Τροίῃ . . .
>
> For we are both fated to redden the same ground here in Troy . . .

In the first example, ἀλλοῖός is equivalent to οὐκέθ' ὁμοῖος. When Telemachus declares that Odysseus' colouring is οὐκέθ' ὁμοῖος, he is not claiming that it is no longer 'similar' but that it is no longer *the same*.[102] Again, in the example from *Iliad* 18, it is not that Achilles foresees that his blood will redden similar earth to that of Patroclus, but that it will be shed over the *same* battlefield before Troy.[103] In such cases ὁμοῖος conveys a strong sense of similarity, which exceeds mere resemblance and strays towards identity. It seems to express something like sameness of quality or identity in kind. In this respect it is closely connected to another kind of Homeric ὁμοῖος-similarity, namely equality.

'Equal' is by far the most prevalent sense of ὁμοῖος in Homer.[104] At *Iliad* 23.632–633, Nestor reminisces about his past sporting prowess:

[102] See also *Iliad* 18.120 for another example of ὁμοῖος expressing qualitative identity. I take it that the occurrences of the term at *Iliad* 1.278 and *Odyssey* 23.236, which are generally translated 'common', are variations on this idea of sameness.

[103] This example could justifiably be read as an expression of full identity, both qualitative and numerical. See Petersen (1915) 72 who notes that 'ὁμοῖος, which later completely displaces ὁμός, could also at any time be used of complete identity'. Petersen traces the development of ὁμοῖος and other qualitative adjectives of the same type (οἷος, τοῖος, ποῖος) from the genitive plurals of their primitives, citing examples from their Sanskrit equivalents. He also notes that ὁμός could be used of 'sameness of quality, i.e. as a synonym of ὁμοῖος, just as well as of absolute identity'. Cf. *Iliad* 4.437, 15.209, and *Odyssey* 17.563.

[104] I have identified eleven occurrences in the *Iliad* of ὁμοῖος expressing equality (in status or ability) and three more in the *Odyssey*: *Iliad* 2.553; 4.410; 5.440; 9.305; 10.216; 10.437; 12.270; 14.521; 16.53; 17.475; 23.632; *Odyssey* 2.276; 3.120; 19.240.

ἔνθ' οὔ τίς μοι ὁμοῖος ἀνὴρ γένετ', οὔτ' ἄρ' Ἐπειῶν
οὔτ' αὐτῶν Πυλίων οὔτ' Αἰτωλῶν μεγαθύμων.

In those days there was no man equal to me, neither among the Epeians
Nor among the Pylians themselves, nor the great-hearted Aeolians.

At *Odyssey* 19.240, the disguised Odysseus sings his own praises:

... παῦροι γὰρ Ἀχαιῶν ἦσαν ὁμοῖοι.

Few of the Achaeans were his equal.

Equality, like sameness of quality, is a more narrowly defined notion than that of simple similarity. It will be shown below that there is good reason to think Xenophanes is aware of these nuances of meaning and that his terminological tinkering is motivated by this awareness.

ἐοικώς too is used within the Homeric corpus to express a specific kind of similarity, namely that of deceptive appearances and disguises. At *Iliad* 2.20–21, the dream sent by Zeus to Agamemnon appears 'like Nestor, the son of Neleus' ('Νηληΐῳ υἷι ἐοικώς, Νέστορι'). At *Odyssey* 10.278–279, Odysseus describes how he was approached by Hermes 'like a young man' ('νεηνίῃ ἀνδρὶ ἐοικώς').[105] In these cases it is important to note that, although the gods are superficially like humans or animals, their nature remains vitally different, insofar as they are divine.[106] In these

[105] See also *Iliad* 5.64 (Ares disguised as a mortal); 13.357 (Poseidon as a mortal); 14.163 (Poseidon as an old man); 17.323 (Apollo as Periphas); 21.600 (Apollo as Agenor); 24.347 (Hermes as a princely young man); *Odyssey* 4.245 (Odysseus as a beggar).

[106] Ioli (2003) 217 argues that Homer employs ἐοικώς to express a so-called 'metaphorical' resemblance between two realms, especially those of the divine and mortal, citing *Odyssey* 7.208–212: '... οὐ γὰρ ἐγώ γε/ἀθανάτοισιν ἔοικα, τοὶ οὐρανὸν εὐρὺν ἔχουσιν,/οὐ δέμας οὐδὲ φυήν, ἀλλὰ θνητοῖσι βροτοῖσιν./οὕς τινας ὑμεῖς ἴστε μάλιστ' ὀχέοντας ὀϊζὺν/ἀνθρώπων, τοῖσίν κεν ἐν ἄλγεσιν ἰσωσαίμην' ('... for I am not like the immortals, who rule broad heaven, either in body or in stature, but like mortal men. Whichever man you know to put up with the greatest misery, I would liken myself to them in pain').

Whilst Odysseus uses ἐοικώς to describe his (lack of) resemblance to the gods, he likens himself to other miserable men with ἰσωσαίμην. Ioli sees this as evidence that the former term is better suited to likening the unequal realms of human and divine. However, although ἐοικώς is used to describe Odysseus' relation to the gods, it also governs the following clause expressing his resemblance to mortals (ἀλλὰ θνητοῖσι βροτοῖσιν). Thus we see that ἐοικώς can be and is used to express resemblance between items in the same realm, as well as between realms.

cases, appearances really are deceptive, rather than, as with the first kind of ἐοικώς-similarity described above, merely potentially so.

The analogical sense of ἐοικώς identified in the similes and the aspect concerned with disguises are not always easy to separate. Both Buxton and Lloyd note that there is some uncertainty whether the description of the gods as ἐοικώς to animals and birds represents a mere comparison or an actual metamorphosis.[107] *Odyssey* 5.50–54 describes Hermes' journey to Calypso's island:

> Πιερίην δ' ἐπιβὰς ἐξ αἰθέρος ἔμπεσε πόντῳ·
> σεύατ' ἔπειτ' ἐπὶ κῦμα λάρῳ ὄρνιθι ἐοικώς,
> ὅς τε κατὰ δεινοὺς κόλπους ἁλὸς ἀτρυγέτοιο
> ἰχθῦς ἀγρώσσων πυκινὰ πτερὰ δεύεται ἅλμῃ·
> τῷ ἴκελος πολέεσσιν ὀχήσατο κύμασιν Ἑρμῆς.
>
> He went from the heavens onto Pieria and dived towards the sea.
> Then he sped over the swell like a cormorant (λάρῳ ὄρνιθι ἐοικώς)
> Which over the awesome gulfs of the barren sea
> Hunting for fish, dampens its thick plumage in the water.
> Like this (τῷ ἴκελος) Hermes sped across the countless waves.

This passage can be read either as an analogical simile explicating, perhaps, the grace and speed of Hermes' flight, or as an account of metamorphosis, or indeed as both.[108]

ὁμοῖος in Homer expresses objective similarity and relationships of equality or, as it were, sameness of quality. ἐοικώς-similarity, on the other hand, is inherently uncertain or indefinite and even potentially misleading. This uncertainty may result from ignorance, as in deceptive appearances or perceived resemblances, or it may serve the evocative force of a simile. In the case of similes and metamorphoses, ἐοικώς-similarity is analogous or merely partial. This indefinite analogous similarity contrasts with the straightforward resemblance and 'sameness' expressed by ὁμοῖος.

I noted above that two kinds of similarity have been attributed to ἐοικώς in discussions of Xenophanes B35. Some have suggested

[107] Lloyd (1966) 187n1 and Buxton (2004) 143.

[108] Odysseus describes his men's fate at *Odyssey* 10.390 as they are driven out of Circe's hall 'σιάλοισιν ἐοικότας ἐννεώροισιν' ('like nine year old pigs'). This is a clear case of metamorphosis. Less certain is the description of Athene and Apollo at *Iliad* 7.59 sitting in a tree 'ὄρνισιν ἐοικότες αἰγυπιοῖσι' ('like vultures'). The gods may be *disguised* as vultures, but there seems to be analogical value in their being compared to the birds most commonly associated with the battlefield and death.

that it represents a straightforward ‘correspondence’ between truth and reality. Others have argued that it expresses a kind of deficient likeness, implying that some essential disparity remains between ταῦτα and τὰ ἔτυμα. This survey of the Homeric use of ἐοικώς, in demonstrating that the term tends to express an indefinite or potentially specious similarity, seems to favour the latter interpretation. The indefinite aspect of ἐοικώς is ill-suited to expressing straightforward correspondence. It is much closer to the latter sense of deficient similarity. However, as I shall argue below, the best reading is one that combines the two notions, so that ταῦτα are understood as *potentially* corresponding (to truth) with the possibility that this apparent correspondence may be specious.

Xenophanean **ὁμοῖος**

I want to argue for the significance of Xenophanes’ preference for ἐοικώς over ὁμοῖος in fragment B35. He is, I suggest, rejecting the kind of straightforward similarity or equality to truth implied by the latter term in favour of the indefinite similarity conveyed by the former. An examination of those instances where Xenophanes does employ ὁμοῖος will prove useful here. For, as we shall see, there is good reason to think that he uses it in a way that maps onto the sense identified in Homer. And, if this is the case for Xenophanes’ ὁμοῖος, we may feel justified in expecting something similar from his use of ἐοικώς.

Xenophanes employs ὁμοῖος within one of the best-known passages of his poem. Fragment B15 is generally understood to be an attack on the anthropomorphic tendencies of religion:

> ἀλλ’ εἰ χεῖρας ἔχον βόες <ἵπποι τ’> ἠὲ λέοντες
> ἢ γράψαι χείρεσσι καὶ ἔργα τελεῖν ἅπερ ἄνδρες,
> ἵπποι μέν θ’ ἵπποισι βόες δέ τε βουσὶν ὁμοίας
> καί <κε> θεῶν ἰδέας ἔγραφον καὶ σώματ’ ἐποίουν
> τοιαῦθ’ οἷόν περ καὐτοὶ δέμας εἶχον <ἕκαστοι>.[109]

> But if horses or oxen or lions had hands
> or could draw with their hands and accomplish such works as men

[109] Clement *Str.* 5.110. Text following DK.

> horses would draw the figures of gods as the same (ὁμοίας) as horses
> and oxen would draw them as the same as oxen,
> and they would make their bodies of the kind that they each had.

Here, Xenophanes employs a *reductio ad absurdum* to undermine traditional religion. Horses and cows would, if they could, represent their gods in their own image. Humans, in representing *their* gods in *their* own image, are acting just as erroneously and subjectively.[110] B15 is an attack on traditional religion's anthropomorphic depiction of gods.

ὁμοίας in this fragment is generally translated in a relatively unspecific sense of 'like': KRS, for example, translate line 3 as 'horses would draw the forms of the gods like horses'.[111] On this reading, Xenophanes is noting that his herds and, by extension, humans, create gods, or at least images of gods, 'like' themselves. Why should Xenophanes find this so objectionable? The precise nature of the complaint is spelled out in the final lines of the fragment: 'they would make their bodies of the kind that they each had'. The bodies of gods are of the *same kind* (τοιαῦθ' οἷόν) as those possessed by the creators of such images. This relationship is more specific than the indefinite resemblance expressed by those translations which render ὁμοίας as 'like'. In fact, Xenophanes seems to be adducing the sense we saw in Homer of 'sameness' or 'equality'. B15 is not complaining that the images of bovine gods would bear some superficial resemblance to mortal cows (as a portrait of Daisy might resemble the cow in the field) but that the gods of cows would themselves be of the bovine species, just as the gods of horses would be of the equine species. Xenophanes implies that humans represent their gods as the *same* as themselves. The impropriety of such an anthropomorphic tendency is, I think, precisely the point that Xenophanes wishes to emphasize.

110 Schofield (1997) 71 understands B15 as a counter-factual extension of the argument of B16 (see 38 below) designed to deny that gods possess *any* human attributes.

111 KRS 169. The emphasis in translations of B15 tends to be on similarity of appearance, thus reflecting line 3's θεῶν ἰδέας ἔγραφον. Barnes (1982) 92 translates line 3 as 'horses would draw pictures of gods like horses'; Broadie (1999) 209 has 'horses would draw the shapes of gods to look like horses'; Hussey (1972) 13: 'horses would draw the forms of gods like horses'. I read Xenophanes' talk of 'drawing the forms of gods' as representing the anthropomorphic tendency of all areas of religion, not just those of the creation of pictorial representations. It seems likely that Xenophanes also had literary (Homeric) representations of the gods in mind.

Fragment B15's criticism of the human propensity to cast their gods in their own image serves as a complement to B16:

> Αἰθίοπές τε θεοὺς σφετέρους σιμοὺς μέλανάς τε
> Θρῆικές τε γλαυκοὺς καὶ πυρρούς φασι πέλεσθαι.[112]
>
> The Ethiopians say that their gods are snub-nosed and black
> And the Thracians say that theirs are blue-eyed and red-headed.

along with B14:

> ἀλλ' οἱ βροτοὶ δοκέουσι γεννᾶσθαι θεούς,
> τὴν σφετέρην δ' ἐσθῆτα ἔχειν φωνήν τε δέμας τε.[113]
>
> But mortals think that the gods come to be
> And have their clothes and voice and body.

Xenophanes' criticism is not that humans make their gods superficially like themselves but that they make them the same as themselves, even to the point where, as B11 complains, they attribute to them mortal vices:[114]

> Homer and Hesiod have attributed all sorts of behaviour to the gods
> Such as is a matter of reproach and condemnation among mortals:
> Stealing, adultery and swindling one another.

Xenophanes criticizes the inaccuracy of traditional and authoritative accounts of the gods as looking like, behaving like and, to all extents and purposes, being like humans.[115] His choice of

112 Clement *Str.* 7.22. 113 Clement *Str.* 5. 109.

114 Morgan (2000) 50–1 understands Xenophanes as criticizing the poets because they 'attribute to the gods and the world of the divine an excess of correspondence: they make gods exactly like men, and trivially so'. She continues 'poets have lost touch with the metaphoricity of their mythology and [. . .] this leads to facile and immoral comparisons'. Xenophanes may also have objected, as Guthrie (1962) 374 suggests, to the notion that gods were constantly concerned with and indeed involved in human affairs in the manner described throughout Homer. KRS 170 propose that Xenophanes' 'remarkable description [of god] was reached, probably, by taking the very antithesis of the characteristics of a Homeric god'.

115 One might object that Homer's gods are obviously *not* the same as mortals insofar as they are, at the very least, more powerful and live far longer. I take it that this is not, for Xenophanes, sufficient to establish them as anything more than powerful and long-lived mortals, as opposed to suitably *im*-mortal divinities. On this, see Geuss (2005) 131–4. Broadie (1999) 211 speculates that Xenophanes may have been guilty of creating a mind-led god in his *own* image: 'did he construct the conception of god in accordance with what he valued most about himself [i.e. his mind], or was it the other way round?'

ὁμοίας for the likeness relationship under attack is telling. We saw above that, when, as at *Iliad* 2.20–21, the Homeric gods disguise themselves in human or animal form, this deceptive resemblance is generally expressed by ἐοικώς and its cognates. The gods are superficially like certain humans or birds, but in reality their nature is vitally different, insofar as they are divine. Xenophanes, by using ὁμοίας, emphasizes that the potential resemblance between horses and the gods of horses is much more than superficial. It is not merely, as in Homer, that they might appear in the external form of horses, but that they would be 'the same as' or 'equal to', or straightforwardly comparable with mortal horses.[116]

Fragment B23 provides further evidence of Xenophanes' opposition to anthropomorphism:

> εἷς θεός, ἔν τε θεοῖσι καὶ ἀνθρώποισι μέγιστος,
> οὔτι δέμας θνητοῖσιν ὁμοίιος οὐδὲ νόημα.[117]
>
> One god, greatest among gods and men,
> Not at all the same as mortals in body or in thought.[118]

One reading of this fragment, suggested by Clement, takes Xenophanes to be denying that the one god has any body or thought at all (i.e. is dissimilar to humans even to the point that he is incorporeal and, it seems, without thought). Accordingly, Clement introduces Xenophanes' words as showing that god is εἷς καὶ ἀσώματος. With good reason, this interpretation is generally considered to be mistaken.[119] For, elsewhere, Xenophanes seems to conceive of

[116] It is plausible that B15 should be understood, in part, as a criticism of Homeric metamorphoses such as Apollo's and Athene's appearance as vultures at *Iliad* 7.59. Xenophanes imagines that animals would create gods in their own image. What should we think of men who describe their gods not only as sharing their shameful qualities, or even their external form, but also as appearing in the form of beasts? Animals would, according to Xenophanes, imagine their gods as identical to them. Homer outdoes even such foolish herds in imagining his gods in a form *inferior* to himself. Deichgräber (1938) 27n45 suggests that B23 is attacking Homeric descriptions of humans as similar to gods, such as that at *Iliad* 8.305: 'δέμας εἰκυῖα θεῇσι' and *Odyssey* 8.14: 'δέμας ἀθανάτοισιν ὁμοῖος'. I suggest that Xenophanes is primarily concerned with comparisons of the second kind, those rendering mortals ὁμοῖος, i.e. equal to or the same as gods in any respect.

[117] Clement *Str.* 5.109.

[118] 'Not at all the same' should not be read as implying absolute dissimilarity.

[119] See Barnes (1982) 83, who argues that B23 'does not imply, as commentators from Clement onwards have asserted, that god is incorporeal'. Broadie (1999) 211 states

god as possessing both mind and body. Thus, at B24, we are told of the holistic nature of divine thought and perception (presumably implying mind and body with which to think and perceive):

οὖλος ὁρᾶι, οὖλος δὲ νοεῖ, οὖλος δέ τ' ἀκούει.

Whole he sees, whole he thinks, whole he hears.[120]

As with ὁμοίας in B15, ὁμοίιος in B23 is usually translated as non-specifically 'similar' or 'like'.[121] However, reading ὁμοίιος in this underdetermined sense will prove problematic insofar as the translation 'not at all like mortals' seems to imply total dissimilarity between the body and mind of god and that of men. It would be rather unfortunate if Xenophanes were really claiming that there is *no similarity whatever* between god and man in body or in thought. After all, as is noted in the *Protagoras*, any two things will inevitably be alike in *some* respect, even if this is not a sufficient ground for calling the two things 'similar'.[122] Now, one might be tempted to defend the translation 'not at all like mortals' on the grounds that, since similarity and dissimilarity are relative to a genus, Xenophanes could be arguing that, whilst god and men have bodies and minds, these bodies and minds are absolutely dissimilar. Such a move should, I think, be resisted. On the one hand, it seems to assume the disconcerting possibility of having *absolutely* dissimilar members of the same genus. On the other, it overlooks the fact that Xenophanes does seem to think that there are some points of similarity between the bodies and minds of god

that B23 is definite proof against this incorporeal reading, a conclusion which KRS also endorse. Guthrie (1962) 376 asserts that 'there is nothing in [Xenophanes'] remains or the tradition to suggest that he was so far ahead of his time as to have advanced to the notion of incorporeal being, an inherently unlikely supposition'. For a comprehensive discussion of this issue, see Lesher (1992) 96–102.

120 See 10–11 above for a discussion of B25 as an allusion to *Iliad* 1.528–30.

121 Broadie (1999) 210: 'not at all like mortals in body or in thought'; Guthrie (1962) 376: 'in no way like mortals in body'; Lesher (1992) 31: 'not at all like mortals in body or in thought'.

122 *Protagoras* 331d2–e4. In the same way, some minor point of dissimilarity is not sufficient to justify calling two things 'dissimilar': 'but it is not right to call things that have just any similarity "similar", nor to call those having just any dissimilarity "dissimilar", no matter how small the similarity [or dissimilarity]' (ἀλλ' οὐχὶ τὰ ὅμοιόν τι ἔχοντα ὅμοια δίκαιον καλεῖν, οὐδὲ τὰ ἀνόμοιόν τι ἔχοντα ἀνόμοια, κἂν πάνυ σμικρὸν ἔχῃ τὸ ὅμοιον).

and men. For, whilst they may be very different, both god and man apparently possess bodies and minds capable of seeing, thinking and hearing.

Once again, we see that ὁμοίιος is better rendered as expressing a more specific brand of similarity. Thus, LSJ translate ὁμοίιος in B23 'at one with' or 'equal to' (identifying it as a variant of ὁμοῖος). This translation both reflects the Homeric usage of the term and avoids the pitfalls of the more underdetermined 'like'.[123] Xenophanes is claiming that the body and mind of god are *not the same* as those of men.[124] God has a body and thinks but, contrary to what Thracians, Egyptians, horses and Homer might believe, his body and mind are (significantly but not absolutely) dissimilar to those of mortals. B23 thus offers an account of god free from the anthropomorphic mistakes targeted by B15's thought-experiment.[125]

I have attempted to demonstrate that there is good reason to think carefully about what brand of likeness Xenophanes is denying with his use of (variants of) ὁμοῖος in B15 and B23. Xenophanes is not denying that there is any kind of similarity whatever between god and men, rather he is attacking and rejecting those accounts which describe gods as pretty much *the same as* humans. This is a weaker claim than that of absolute dissimilarity but it is also, I think, a more plausible one.

123 LSJ 1224. A parallel use is found at Hesiod *Op.* 182: 'οὐδὲ πατὴρ παίδεσσιν ὁμοίιος οὐδέ τι παῖδες/οὐδὲ ξεῖνος ξεινοδόκῳ καὶ ἑταῖρος ἑταίρῳ,/οὐδὲ κασίγνητος φίλος ἔσσεται, ὡς τὸ πάρος περ' ('a father will not be like his sons, nor sons [like their father], nor guest with host, nor friend with friend, nor will a brother be dear, as he once was'). Although ὁμοῖος occurs more frequently in Homer as a term meaning 'distressing', it obviously does not carry this sense in Xenophanes B23.

124 Thus Warren (2007) 47 translates 'dissimilar from mortals in body and in thought' and argues (48) that, whilst Xenophanes' 'god should not think in the same way that mortals do [. . .] god is not wholly unlike human beings'.

125 Some might think that a denial of identity between god and mortals is a weaker and thus less preferable reading of B23 than a mere denial of similarity. If we say that *x* and *y* have no similarity whatever, we obviously make a much stronger assertion than if we say that *x* and *y* are not completely similar. In the first case we deny that there are *any* points of similarity between the two things, in the second case we only rule out the possibility that the two are *completely alike*, leaving open the possibility that some points of resemblance remain. To say that two things are 'dissimilar' is, as noted in Plato's *Protagoras*, not equivalent to saying that two things share no points of similarity (see n122 above).

Rejecting equality

The analysis of its use in both Homer and Xenophanes supports the supposition that the latter regarded ὁμοῖος as expressing a fairly specific kind of similarity encompassing equality or sameness of quality. I argued above that *Odyssey* 19.203 and *Theogony* 27–28 both imply that their ψεύδεα are indistinguishable from the truth, at least from the point of view of those ignorant of the truth. It is now possible to elaborate on the basis of this indistinguishability. The ignorant are unable to judge between truth and lies because the lies created by Odysseus and the Muses are 'equal' to the truth. They are equal in terms of plausibility, persuasiveness and, perhaps, beauty. Of course, these lies are not the *same* as the truth. For to be the same would entail that they are themselves true. Nevertheless, they are regarded *by their audience* as such and are thus taken to be true. The ὁμοῖος-similarity of Odysseus' ψεύδεα is twofold. On the one hand, Odysseus creates them to be the *equal* of truth in their ability to persuade. On the other hand, they are accepted by those who know no better as the *same* as truth, i.e. as true.

In place of indistinguishability, Xenophanes chooses to attribute to his doctrines a very different kind of similarity to the truth. The analysis of Homeric usage demonstrated that ἐοικώς-similarity is essentially indefinite or uncertain, with the potential to be specious. It is important to distinguish this possibility of deception from that implied by the ψεύδεα which deceive by being ὁμοῖος to truth. For, whilst the capacity for error is an acknowledged aspect of ἐοικώς-similarity, the deceptive power of Odysseus' and the Muses' tall stories derives from the fact that their relationship to truth is of a kind that is assumed to be genuine. The Muses consider their lies to be ὁμοῖος to truth *in terms of persuasiveness*. Their ignorant audience, on the other hand, consider their lies to be ὁμοῖος to truth *in terms of truth*, i.e. they judge them to be true. The Muses themselves, however, might well regard their stories as ἐοικώς to the truth *in terms of truth*, insofar as they appear to be true but are actually false, just as Hermes appears in the guise of a mortal, but is always essentially immortal. An instance of ἐοικώς-similarity will succeed in deceiving if it is taken to be an instance of ὁμοῖος-similarity. By exhorting us to believe that his teachings are ἐοικώς to truth, Xenophanes is, by implication, emphasizing that they should *not* be regarded as ὁμοῖος to truth, i.e. regarded as true. I do not mean to imply that Xenophanes is calling his account untrue. Rather, he is admitting that, although he thinks it may well be true, it cannot be known to be true with any certainty.

ἐοικώς to truth

Three overlapping types of ἐοικώς-similarity were identified in Homer: the analogical similarity found in similes; the potentially erroneous similarity recognized by individuals; and the essentially and intentionally deceptive similarity of gods in disguise as humans and animals. It is time to establish which, if any, of these senses of ἐοικώς best fits with its occurrence in B35.

(a) Analogical similarity

This is a temptingly subtle candidate for the meaning of ἐοικώς in B35. On this reading, Xenophanes would be asserting that some indefinite but informative relationship holds between his doctrines and the truth.[126] His writings are like truth in the same way that Apollo's advent is like the night or Agamemnon's eyes are like fire. The similarity in these analogies is not literal, but rather verges on the metaphorical. By illustrating the attitude or appearance of the heroes and gods in terms of natural and often more familiar imagery, the poet enhances our understanding. I may find it difficult to imagine the consuming wrath of Agamemnon, but I am familiar with the heat, intensity and destructive power of fire. By likening the former to the latter, I can apply my experience of one to the other and thereby increase my understanding.

Could Xenophanes be asserting that his doctrines enjoy this kind of analogical, non-literal similarity to truth? Tempting as I find this possibility, I fear the answer has to be that he could not.

[126] Rivier (1956) 46–7 emphasizes the possibility that B35 is influenced by the informative aspect of ὁμοῖος analogies.

The Homeric analogies function by illustrating the less familiar in terms of the more familiar. By implication, we would have to take Xenophanes' ταῦτα as less familiar than the truths to which they are likened. For our understanding of ταῦτα to be informed by our familiarity with truth would require us to have a pretty fair acquaintance with the latter. Yet the possibility that we could know the truth well enough to be familiar with it is undermined by B34:

> And there has never been any man who has achieved certainty
> Nor will there be anyone who knows about the gods and what I say about everything.
> For even if anyone really managed to enunciate how things are
> He would still not himself have knowledge. Rather, opinion is allotted to all.

Even if an account achieves truth, it can never be known with certainty, i.e. it can never be known to be true.[127] If we are unable to recognize truth with certainty even when, in a best-case scenario, we actually speak it, how can we ever expect to achieve familiarity with truth? Without this familiarity, the analogy of truth and ταῦτα is, at best, distinctly uninformative. It would be the equivalent of attempting to illustrate a close friend's character via a comparison with that of someone we barely knew.

(b) Intentionally deceptive similarity

This kind of reading would take Xenophanes to be asserting that, despite appearances, his account is not actually true. When Hermes is described as νεηνίῃ ἀνδρὶ ἐοικώς, this appearance is deceptive. In reality, he is the immortal Hermes, not a young (mortal) man. If Xenophanes were adducing this kind of likeness, B35 would be an out-and-out warning that his own doctrines are not true, whether they seem convincing or not. The notion that Xenophanes could be calling his own poetry false is, I think, obviously unsatisfactory. In order to salvage such a reading we would need to adjust our understanding of ταῦτα. For, if we took ταῦτα to refer to the doctrines of another author, for instance Homer, it would seem

[127] For further discussion of B34 see, among others, Hussey (1990) 18–22, Lesher (1999) 228–31 and Ioli (2003). Schofield (1997) 78 suggests reading B34 as implying that, whilst truth may be attainable, *clear* truth is not.

quite plausible that Xenophanes could be condemning them as false. This intriguing possibility is undermined by the context of B35 as it is quoted in Plutarch.[128] For there it is clearly intended as reflexive and, in some qualified manner, commendatory. Unless the sense of the fragment had somehow been utterly inverted by the time Plutarch was writing, it is unlikely that the original intention could have been explicitly denunciatory.

(c) Potentially specious similarity

This is a much better candidate for the sense of ἐοικώς in B35. It was shown that the term can function in Homer as expressing a straightforward similarity recognized by some individual but potentially specious. To say that '*x* is ἐοικώς to *y*' in this sense is equivalent to saying '*x* looks as if it may actually *be y* (although it may not be)'. Achilles notes that he thought a passing warrior looked like Machaon, but, since he didn't see his eyes, he can't be sure. Can the expression of similarity in B35 be satisfactorily cashed out in this manner? It seems to me that the answer is a resounding 'yes'. On this reading, Xenophanes would be endorsing his own doctrines as candidates for truth (they look as if they might *be* true) with the implicit *caveat* that they may not be true at all. The similarity between ταῦτα and τὰ ἔτυμα is uncertain, but plausible. If we knew better or had more information about the matter, or perhaps if we were able to test whether the appearance was genuine, we would be able to state that Xenophanes' ταῦτα were ἔτυμα, rather than merely that they were ἐοικότα τοῖς ἐτύμοισι. Likewise Penelope, if she had more information, would be able to state that Odysseus *is* a well-travelled man, rather than just that he looks like one.

As noted above, Hecataeus of Miletus begins his *Genealogies* with a strikingly similar suggestion that the truth of his account is apparent rather than absolutely certain:

> I write these matters as seems to me to be true. For the stories doing the rounds of Greece are many and, in my opinion, ridiculous.[129]

[128] See 21 above. [129] Hecataeus F1a (Jacoby 1,7).

The significance of this parallel lies in the relatively close dating of Hecataeus and Xenophanes.[130] In addition, both authors seem to be engaged in the activity of challenging the unquestioned truth of the poets' accounts.[131] In holding up the poetic authorities' veridicality to scrutiny, it is hardly surprising that both Xenophanes and Hecataeus found the need to question the truth or, at least, the certainty of their own accounts.

This reading of ἐοικώς in B35 as implying an apparent but potentially specious similarity to truth is also more compatible with B34's insistence on uncertainty. B35 echoes the lack of sureness regarding truth voiced in the longer fragment. B34 tells us that, even if we achieved truth, we could never know it as such. B35 represents a claim on Xenophanes' part to have achieved what he believes to be truth, but with the *caveat* that he cannot be certain that this is the case.[132] His doctrines look like truth, but this appearance may be deceptive.

It seems that 'potentially specious similarity' is by far the most satisfactory interpretation of ἐοικώς in B35. This reading fits the Homeric evidence and complements both B34 and the doubts about truth hinted at by Xenophanes' contemporary, Hecataeus. Xenophanes is urging us to believe his account to be possibly but uncertainly true. In this way it seems to fit a 'fallibilist' reading of Xenophanes.[133] Xenophanes is not calling his doctrines untrue, but he is admitting that they could be. In fact, taken in this way, B35 answers the main objection that Lesher levels at the fallibilist interpretation. He argues that 'it is not obvious where

130 See Heidel (1943) on the possible links between the historian and the philosopher. Potentially significant is Heraclitus' connection of the two as the object of his criticism at B40: 'πολυμαθία νόον ἔχειν οὐ διδάσκει· Ἡσίοδον γὰρ ἂν ἐδίδαξε καὶ Πυθαγόρην αὖτις τε Ξενοφάνεά τε καὶ Ἑκαταῖον' ('Learning a lot doesn't teach you to have sense; for it would have taught [i.e. it didn't teach] Hesiod or even Pythagoras or Xenophanes or Hecataeus'). Rivier (1956) 49 questions the value of this parallel.

131 Although, as Classen (1989) 101 notes, Hecataeus appears primarily motivated by the desire to emphasize that his account is *more* plausible than ridiculous tales told by others. Xenophanes, on the other hand, seems to be offering a general description of the nature of human assertions.

132 As will be shown below, these doubts are more fundamental than Guthrie (1962) 396 allows when he attributes them to mere 'modesty and honesty'.

133 Lesher (1992) 164–5. This section forms part of a useful summary of the alternative interpretations that have been offered of B34. Proponents of this fallibilist reading include Guthrie (1962) 396 and Popper (1998) 49.

the ideas of fallibility and a perpetual possibility of error are to be found in fragment B34. "Fallible," "probable," "possibility of error" go far beyond anything found within Xenophanes' text.' The interpretation of B35 that I have developed above identifies precisely this notion of the 'possibility of error' within the term ἐοικώς.

I am aware that some may find my fallibilist Xenophanes too modest for their tastes. They might object that such an admission of potential speciousness could serve only to undermine its proponent, particularly when there are presumably rivals (not least Homer) willing to profess certainty on similar topics.[134] Surely no one wishing to present a persuasive argument could afford to undermine themselves with an admission that their own account could well be false?[135] My answer to such an objection is threefold. First, I see no reason to think that Xenophanes would value persuasiveness more highly than philosophical truth (no matter how uncertain).[136] If he really did believe that his account was a good candidate for truth but possibly erroneous, why should he not say so, even at the risk of being taken by some to have undermined his own position?[137] Second, if it should turn out that Xenophanes is not arguing for the potential speciousness of his own account *alone*, but rather for the inevitable uncertainty of *all* human accounts, he will be no more undermining his own authority than that of everyone else.[138] Third, I am far from the

134 Lesher (1992) 174–5 expresses a concern along these lines: 'Since an author would not normally urge his audience to accept his account while simultaneously demeaning it by describing it as inadequate or inferior, it is difficult to take Xenophanes' comment to mean "Let these be accepted, certainly, they are merely conjectures only resembling how things are".' On my reading, of course, Xenophanes is not urging his audience to 'accept his account' as anything more than possibly true. See Long (1999a) 10 on the agonistic nature of early Greek philosophy, particularly with regard to Xenophanes and Heraclitus. Lloyd (1966) offers a comparative treatment of the extent and importance of adversariality in ancient Greece and China.

135 Of course, on one reading of *Theogony* 27–28 (see 14–15 above), Hesiod makes just this kind of admission.

136 For a discussion of the importance of truthfulness in early Greek philosophy, see Most (1999) 346–8.

137 Indeed, it is not clear that such an admission would have been received in this dismissive fashion. The fact that Parmenides' *Doxa* is, at B8.52, explicitly labelled 'deceptive' (ἀπατηλός) does not seem to have prevented it from being taken seriously by later philosophers (see 73–4 below).

138 As noted by Warren (2007) 50.

first to suggest that Xenophanes' epistemology is of a sceptical bent. Sextus, for example, notes that some have interpreted B34 as expressing a fairly universal scepticism.[139] Whilst such interpretations of Xenophanes may well have been motivated by the sceptical agenda of later authors, their very existence demonstrates that such a reading was not considered obviously absurd.

Xenophanes' fallibilism

I have argued that B35 identifies Xenophanes' account as something that, even if it is potentially deceptive and we can never *know* it to be true, is, at least, possibly true. I now want to offer some tentative suggestions as to the sources of both Xenophanes' pessimism (insofar as he thinks it cannot be known to be true) and his optimism (insofar as he thinks his account might be true). My proposals are necessarily speculative, for they weave together interpretations of several of Xenophanes' most difficult fragments. Of course, each of these fragments is the object of much interpretative debate in its own right and my aim here is not to offer a rigorous treatment of each individually but rather to demonstrate that these fragments can plausibly be read in such a way as to support and, perhaps, to explain the fallibilist position I have attributed to Xenophanes. I will propose that Xenophanes' epistemic pessimism is rooted in his commitment to the cognitive disparity between gods and men, whilst his qualified optimism reflects a confidence in our capacity to reason about the world around us. Finally, I will suggest that Xenophanes' fallibilist position should be read as an explicit challenge to the authority of the poets.

We have already encountered Xenophanes' criticism of those who make gods and humans too similar by giving them the same kind of body and even the same vices.[140] Whilst I argued that Xenophanes is not describing an absolute dissimilarity, it is clear

[139] *Math.* 7.110. See also *Math.* 7.49; Diogenes Laertius (quoting Sotion) 9.20; Hippolytus *Refutation* 1.14; Cicero *Academica* 2.23.74; Pseudo-Plutarch *Misc.* 4 and Timon fragment 59.

[140] See 36–42.

from his positive theological fragments that he is committed to the physical and psychological difference of humans and gods. As we have seen, B23 (along with B11, B15 and B16) rejects sameness or equality between gods and men:

> One god, greatest among gods and men,
> Not at all the same as mortals in body or in thought.

B24 emphasizes the essential difference of god:

> Whole he sees, whole he thinks, whole he hears.

God perceives and thinks as a whole. I take it that this holistic divine perception and cognition is a clarification of how it is that gods are 'not at all the same as mortals in body or in thought'. Indeed, as B25 makes clear, Xenophanes' god is so far removed from human nature that he can engender change without any kind of physical activity:

> But completely without effort he shakes all things with the thought of his mind.

The cognition Xenophanes attributes to god seems to be unlimited in two ways. First, there are no limits within him to circumscribe the extent (or location) of his thought (and perception): he thinks (and perceives) as a whole. Second, it seems that there are no limits to the effective power of his thought: it takes no effort for this god to 'shake all things'.[141]

This much, then, can be established about divine cognition. What of the mortal version from which it differs so dramatically? Whilst B38 is undoubtedly one of Xenophanes' most vexing fragments, it may provide a clue as to the nature of mortal cognition:

> εἰ μὴ χλωρὸν ἔφυσε θεὸς μέλι, πολλὸν ἔφασκον
> γλύσσονα σῦκα πέλεσθαι.[142]
>
> If god had not made yellow honey, they would say
> that figs were much sweeter.

[141] Lesher (1992) 105–6 notes that, whilst Xenophanes offers no explicit ascription of omniscience to his god, B24's repetition of οὖλος 'points in this direction'.

[142] Herodian π. μον. λέξ. 41, 5.

Interpretation of this fragment is notoriously difficult. However, it seems relatively uncontroversial to suggest that it implies the deficiency of (some) mortal opinions. One possible reading is as follows: mortals form opinions about the nature of the world in accordance with their experience. Were they to have different experiences, they would form different opinions. Because humans have experienced both honey and figs, they have come to form the opinion that figs are less sweet (than honey). Had they not tasted honey, they would believe figs to be sweeter than they do now (perhaps because figs would, in the absence of honey, be the *sweetest* thing in the world). My suggestion is that Xenophanes is classifying human cognition as essentially perspectival, insofar as mortal beliefs are always formed in response to specific circumstances or comparisons. In the case described in B38, humans form their opinion about the sweetness of figs from the perspective of those who have experienced honey (and figs). Now, it is conceivable that such perspectival beliefs hit upon the true nature of things, as when humans come to believe that figs are not as sweet as honey. But the limitations on cognition are such that they can never know themselves to have hit upon the truth, because they are always classifying the world from a particular perspective.[143] Humans go wrong if they assert such contextualized opinions as if they were objective knowledge. Rather, they should recognize, as Xenophanes does in B35, that, whilst their assertions may be true, it is possible that they are not. B16 may be an example of such erroneous thinking:

> The Ethiopians say that their gods are snub-nosed and black
> And the Thracians say that theirs are blue-eyed and red-headed.

The fact that mortal beliefs are always contextualized might be seen to encourage this kind of cultural relativism.

[143] Barnes (1982) 142–3 suggests that Xenophanes limits mortals to opinion on the grounds that 'our beliefs – or many of them – are explicable in terms of our circumstances; they do not, therefore, amount to knowledge'. My perspectival reading differs from Barnes's account in two important respects. First, I take Xenophanes to be identifying the deficiency of *all* mortal opinions, rather than 'a very large and important class of beliefs'. Second, whilst such beliefs are always 'explicable in terms of our circumstances', I see no reason to assume that the circumstances in which those opinions are formed should be considered to have 'no connexion with the intrinsic nature [of things]'.

I think we can set the essentially perspectival nature of mortal opinion against B24's description of god as thinking and perceiving as a whole.[144] My suggestion is that Xenophanes' mortals are limited to opinion precisely because they do not possess the unlimited perception and thought of god.[145] I noted above that god's cognition seems to be both internally and externally unlimited.[146] He thinks as a 'whole' and can think about (and thus affect) 'everything'. God is not limited to any particular perspective. Mortal cognition is, I take it, both internally and externally limited. Humans think and perceive in some way less than as a whole and, as I have suggested B38 indicates, only from and about experience within a particular context.

Here I want to emphasize that it is not simply the scope of their experience that limits humans' cognition to opinion. Rather, it seems that Xenophanes identifies this inherent limitation in the *way* that mortals think rather than in *what* they think about. When we think about *x*, we necessarily think about it *from a certain perspective*. It is the nature and circumstance, rather than the scope, of mortal cognition that renders its products uncertain. Even if one unimaginably long-lived mortal were to experience everything, they would still, I take it, be limited to thinking about the totality *perspectivally*. In fact, one possible way of reading the difference between divine and mortal cognition might be as the difference between essentially perspectival opinion and non-perspectival knowledge. One of the contrasts thrown up by the analysis of Homeric ὁμοῖος and ἐοικώς was that, whilst the former tends to describe an objective similarity, the latter, in some cases, expresses a subjective resemblance as it appears to some individual. My tentative suggestion is that Xenophanes' mortals are like the characters in Homer's epic, insofar as they can only describe

144 Mogyoródi (2006) 136–47 argues that humans are limited to opinion (in the realms of natural philosophy and theology) in those assessments of sense experience that attribute an absolute degree of some sensible quality in circumstances where the truth of such an attribution must remain uncertain because of the infinite nature of the evidence (in Xenophanes' infinite cosmos).

145 Mogyoródi (2006) 142–5 contrasts human cognition with the 'synoptic awareness' of god, but appears to imply that god, being himself finite, is incapable of knowledge of the infinite cosmos. See, in particular, 143n70.

146 For discussion of the vexed question whether Xenophanes' god is coextensive with the cosmos, see Finkelberg (1990) and Palmer (1998) 20ff.

contextualized, qualified truths. God, on the other hand, is analogous to the poet, insofar as he is possessed of a synoptic view and thus able to conceive of unqualified truths. Of course, Xenophanes nowhere states that god has objective knowledge, or even that he has knowledge. However, as we have seen, B25 indicates that he is capable of affecting *all things* with his mind.[147]

This idea of the essential difference between human and divine cognition can also be read into B18's denial of revelation:[148]

> οὔτοι ἀπ' ἀρχῆς πάντα θεοὶ θνητοῖσ' ὑπέδειξαν
> ἀλλὰ χρόνῳ ζητοῦντες ἐφευρίσκουσιν ἄμεινον.[149]
>
> The gods have not revealed, from the outset, everything to mortals,
> But, by searching, in time, they discover better.

If I am right in ascribing to Xenophanes the notion that there is a *qualitative* difference between human and divine thought, it is hardly surprising that he rejects the possibility of divine revelation. For, if god thinks synoptically and possesses objective knowledge, whilst humans are limited to perspectival opinion, it's hard to imagine how communication between god and mortal could come about. How, or indeed why, would god chop up his synoptic awareness in order to express it to mortals in a piecemeal fashion?[150]

Having offered some suggestions as to the source of Xenophanes' pessimism, I turn now to the more optimistic implication of B35. For, of course, although Xenophanes thinks that one cannot be certain that one's account is true, he does acknowledge the possibility, in both B34 and, I have argued, B35, that it *might*

147 Of course, if we read B24's νοεῖν as 'know', then Xenophanes does indeed attribute knowledge to god. See Lesher (1992) 103–4.

148 The extent and nature of Xenophanes' rejection of revelation is much debated. Barnes (1982) 140 takes Xenophanes to be allowing some revelation. Lesher (1992) 153–4 reads B18 as a specific criticism of the tendency of mortals to interpret natural phenomena as 'divine intimations to mortals', citing B32's rationalizing account of the rainbow.

149 Stobaeus *Ecl.* 1.8.2.

150 Mogyoródi (2006) 145 makes a similar point, arguing that '[s]o far as [god's] "psychological" constitution is radically different from those of humans, it is not even reasonable for him to reveal himself, nor what he knows, to humans, since they are not able to conceive of him, nor of what he knows'.

be true. In fact, B18 provides perhaps the best evidence for this aspect of Xenophanes' epistemology. For, although Xenophanes rejects coming to know via divine revelation, he offers an alternative: 'searching' (ζήτησις). In fact, so we are told, 'searching' will enable us to 'discover better'. 'Better' than what? My suggestion is that Xenophanes is recommending inquiry over the kind of passive reception of information encouraged by reliance on divine revelation. This inquiry could conceivably include empirical investigation into other cultures (as may have informed B16) or natural phenomena.[151] But I want to suggest that Xenophanes is explicitly recommending the kind of rational inquiry that we see him employing in developing his positive theology.[152] In the theological fragments, he sets out his reasoning about what is and is not appropriate for god and develops his theology accordingly. In B15 and B16, for example, we see Xenophanes employ reasoning to argue against traditional accounts (which tend to claim their authority from their status as divine revelation). B26, meanwhile, gives an example of the kind of 'better' account it is possible to discover if one employs one's reasoning:

> αἰεὶ δ' ἐν ταὐτῶι μίμνει κινούμενος οὐδέν
> οὐδὲ μετέρχεσθαί μιν ἐπιπρέπει ἄλλοτε ἄλληι.[153]
>
> He always remains in the same place, not moving at all
> Nor is it appropriate for him to go to different places at different times.

I propose that B18 presents a contrast between the passive acceptance of so-called divine revelation and the active inquiry that allows us to discover 'better'. Xenophanes is, I take it, asserting his preference for an account developed via rational reflection.[154] It is this quality that makes his own account a possible candidate

[151] As emphasized by Lesher (1992) 154.

[152] Geuss (2005) 131 similarly suggests that, in critiquing anthropomorphism, Xenophanes 'does not appeal to any form of esoteric lore, to intuition, revelation, or the inspiration of the muses, but merely to comparative, empirical observation and to everyday forms of human reasoning'.

[153] Simplicius *Phys.* 23.10.

[154] Mogyoródi (2006) 146 suggests, with reference to Xenophanes' theology, that 'he must be granted some degree of recognition of the imports of metaphysical reasoning'.

for the truth. Xenophanes thinks his doctrines worth taking seriously because they are the product of reasoning. Likewise, we should, one presumes, take seriously any account developed in this fashion, although, of course, we should never regard them as expressing certain truth.

At this point one may wonder why Xenophanes would limit himself to opinion. Presumably, he thinks that he has improved on the culturally contextualized theologies of the Ethiopians and Thracians in his own account of god. If he has succeeded in avoiding such perspectival thinking, might we not think that he has achieved something better than opinion? I think the answer must be that he has indeed improved upon the theologies he criticizes insofar as he has reasoned his way beyond anthropomorphism. However, I take it that the kind of reasoning and inquiry that Xenophanes recommends will result not in an escape from perspective but rather in a *broadening* of perspective. The results of Xenophanes 'searching' are not and never could be synoptic knowledge but they are 'better' than most mortal thinking because they are, in a sense, more comprehensive.

These then are my tentative speculations as to what lies behind the epistemological claim of B35. On the one hand, Xenophanes' denial of certainty may, I have suggested, be rooted in the fact of his own human nature. Being mortal, Xenophanes enjoys an essentially perspectival brand of cognition and is thus limited to opinion. On the other hand, he classifies some varieties of mortal opinions as better than others, so that accounts worked out via rational reflection are superior to those taken to be the result of divine revelation, all the more so since Xenophanes denies the possibility of divine revelation altogether.

Before turning to my conclusion, I want to make one final conjecture about Xenophanes' epistemology. For there is, I think, good reason to interpret it as a relatively explicit attack on those who claim to be inspired and informed by the divine. In denying the possibility of divine revelation and in emphasizing the essential disparity of human and divine cognition, Xenophanes is, I suggest, attacking those who, for example, preface their accounts with a claim to have been informed by the gods. Finally, then, we can see that Xenophanes may be criticizing Homer and Hesiod in part for their claim to have access to the objective and comprehensive certainty that is the province of the divine. Mortals, because of the essential difference in the way they think and perceive, cannot achieve such access.[155] I take it that Xenophanes is not claiming that it is impossible for a poet to speak the truth. Bearing in mind B18's denial of revelation and endorsement of independent reasoning, however, it seems that he thinks it highly unlikely that a poet will tell the truth.

Conclusion

I return to those issues postponed from my analysis of the text of B35:

ταῦτα δεδοξάσθαι μὲν ἐοικότα τοῖς ἐτύμοισι

The first question is the import of δεδοξάσθαι. I have argued against the tendency to read this as a straightforward exhortation to believe Xenophanes' teachings, i.e. to believe them to be true. If there is any explicit encouragement, it is to believe that his account is *like* the truth.

I have also noted that if, as I think we have no good reason not to do, we retain the infinitive of the mss, we are faced with a choice between two interpretations. On one reading, Xenophanes is indeed explicitly *encouraging* his audience to believe his account to be like the truth:

Let these [teachings] be believed to be like the truth

On the other, he is *classifying* it as like the truth:

These [teachings] have been believed to be like the truth

In the end, of course, these two readings are not so far apart. For, presumably any encouragement is predicated on a classification

[155] For an alternative account, see Lesher (2008) 458–70 who argues that Xenophanes is offering a positive epistemology in contrast to what Lesher characterizes as the pessimism of the poets.

and any classification is stated as an implicit encouragement. What matters most is that we correctly specify the content of the belief being either recommended or identified, namely *that* Xenophanes has said something which is ἐοικότα τοῖς ἐτύμοισι. As we have seen, to say that something is like the truth in this sense is to admit that it may not, in the end, be true. Consequently, B35 is as much a warning about the potential speciousness of Xenophanes' account as it is an endorsement of its candidacy for acceptance. We are at one and the same time being encouraged to believe his teachings to be potentially true and warned that we can do no *more* than believe them to be so. Such a reading of B35 fits the epistemological pessimism explicit in B34's claim that 'there has never been any man who has achieved certainty . . . rather, opinion is allotted to all'.

The scope of ταῦτα remains uncertain, even if we accept the plausible suggestion that it corresponds to the subject-matter specified in B34. I have proposed that it is something about the *quality*, rather than the *quantity*, of our thought that limits us to opinion. If I am right, then Xenophanes must be qualifying the status of the entirety of his own account (and, by implication, all rival accounts).

What of the potential antithesis hinted at by μέν? If it ever existed, it seems likely to have contrasted some kind of certitude with the uncertainty expressed by the ἐοικώς of B35. One possibility is that Xenophanes presented a contrast between the uncertainty of mortals and the certainty of god, along the lines of that offered by Alcmaeon:

Ἀλκμαίων Κροτωνιήτης τάδε ἔλεξε Πειρίθου υἱὸς Βροτίνωι καὶ Λέοντι καὶ Βαθύλλωι· περὶ τῶν ἀφανέων, περὶ τῶν θνητῶν σαφήνειαν μὲν θεοὶ ἔχοντι, ὡς δὲ ἀνθρώποις τεκμαίρεσθαι . . .[156]

Alcmaeon of Croton, son of Perithous, uttered these words to Brotinus, Leon, and Bathyllus: 'The gods have certain knowledge about what is unseen and about what is mortal, but so far as men may assume . . . '

Those who read ταῦτα as having a limited scope might expect some kind of contrast between those topics on which we are limited

[156] Alcmaeon B1 (Diogenes Laertius 8.83). Some have suggested a Xenophanean influence in this fragment. See below 96–7.

to opinion and those about which we can claim knowledge ('*these* things are potentially true, but *those* things are certainly true'). On my reading, of course, there are *no* areas about which mortals can claim knowledge for they lack the cognitive capacity which is, for Xenophanes, the privilege of god.

CHAPTER 2

PARMENIDES' ALLUSIVE AMBIGUITY

Introduction

At the beginning of the previous chapter, I suggested that Xenophanes' uncertain biography was in keeping with his pessimistic epistemic outlook. Rightly or wrongly, we tend to think that we know a little bit more about Parmenides.[1] As it happens, this relative familiarity is appropriate to his rather more optimistic epistemology. For Parmenides, in contrast to Xenophanes, certain knowledge is not reserved for the gods alone. In fact, whilst Xenophanes rules out access to god's knowledge, Parmenides presents himself as crossing the barrier between divine and human thought. As has been noted, 'Parmenides' poem is dominated by the conviction that human beings can attain knowledge of reality.'[2] In the opening lines of his poem (B1), Parmenides describes a journey to the presence of a goddess, who makes a promise of enlightenment:

> . . . χρεὼ δέ σε πάντα πυθέσθαι
> ἠμὲν Ἀληθείης εὐπειθέος ἀτρεμὲς ἦτορ
> ἠδὲ βροτῶν δόξας, ταῖς οὐκ ἔνι πίστις ἀληθής.[3]
>
> . . . And it is right that you should learn all things,
> Both the unmoving heart of persuasive truth,
> And the beliefs of mortals, in which there is no true cogency.

Through his meeting with the goddess, Parmenides achieves knowledge.[4] This knowledge is certified as much by the force

[1] Perhaps as a result of his appearance in Plato's *Parmenides*. On the biographical tradition, see Coxon (2009) 39–44. For a discussion of Parmenides' dates, see 93–4.

[2] Coxon (2009) 20.

[3] Sextus Empiricus *Math.* 7.111–114. I follow Gallop (1984) 52 and Mourelatos (2008) 154–8 in preferring Sextus' εὐπειθέος over Simplicius' εὐκυκλέος. See also Jameson (1958).

[4] B1.3 claims that Parmenides is on the route 'that carries the man who knows' (φέρει εἰδότα φῶτα, B1.3).

of the goddess's arguments as by the fact that it is presented as a revelation. On this account, what matters is not whether you think like a human or like a god, but that you think about the right kind of thing. Once one has focussed one's reason on 'what is and cannot not be', one can attain understanding equal to that of the gods.[5]

Parmenides' poem divides relatively neatly into three parts. First is the introductory *Proemium* (B1), in which Parmenides describes his journey towards enlightenment. Fragments B2 to B8 make up the so-called *Aletheia*.[6] This section of the poem, spoken by the goddess, provides the first part of Parmenides' education, explaining the nature of Being as 'ungenerated and imperishable; whole, unique, unmoving, and complete' (B8.3–4). In the third and final section, the *Doxa*, the goddess gives her account of the 'beliefs of mortals' in the form of an extensive cosmology. Although this section seems to have been the longest, relatively little survives.[7]

Most of those who write about Parmenides concentrate on the notorious difficulties of the *Aletheia* and its description of the nature of Being. My focus in this chapter is on the passage marking the transition from the *Aletheia* to the *Doxa*, from B8.50–61. Here, the goddess concludes her description of Being and begins her account of 'mortal beliefs':[8]

ἐν τῶι σοι παύω πιστὸν λόγον ἠδὲ νόημα
ἀμφὶς ἀληθείης· δόξας δ' ἀπὸ τοῦδε βροτείας
μάνθανε κόσμον ἐμῶν ἐπέων ἀπατηλὸν ἀκούων.
μορφὰς γὰρ κατέθεντο δύο γνώμας ὀνομάζειν·
τῶν μίαν οὐ χρεών ἐστιν–ἐν ὧι πεπλανημένοι εἰσίν–
τἀντία δ' ἐκρίναντο δέμας καὶ σήματ' ἔθεντο
χωρὶς ἀπ' ἀλλήλων, τῆι μὲν φλογὸς αἰθέριον πῦρ,
ἤπιον ὄν, μέγ' ἀραιὸν ἐλαφρόν, ἑωυτῶι πάντοσε τωὐτόν,
τῶι δ' ἑτέρωι μὴ τωὐτόν· ἀτὰρ κἀκεῖνο κατ' αὐτό
τἀντία νύκτ' ἀδαῆ, πυκινὸν δέμας ἐμβριθές τε.

5 B2.3: οὐκ ἔστι μὴ εἶναι.

6 Although, as Gallop (1984) 30n11 notes, 'the modern collocations, "Way of Truth [*Aletheia*]" and "Way of Seeming [*Doxa*]," have no textual basis either in the poem or in other ancient sources'.

7 On the textual tradition, see Coxon (2009) 1–6.

8 Which are, as B1.3's reference to the 'man who knows' implies, the beliefs that mortals *tend* to have, rather than those that they necessarily have as a result of their mortal status. See 100–4.

τόν σοι ἐγὼ διάκοσμον ἐοικότα πάντα φατίζω,
ὡς οὐ μή ποτέ τίς σε βροτῶν γνώμη παρελάσσηι.[9]

Here I end my trustworthy discourse and thought
About truth. From this point on learn mortal beliefs,
Listening to the deceitful ordering of my words.
For they have established two forms in their mind to name
Of which it is not right to name one[10] – in which they have erred –
And they have distinguished opposites in body and concocted signs
Separate from one another: here the aetherial fire of flame,
Which is gentle; exceedingly light; the same throughout
But different from the other. Whereas there is one by itself
And opposite: dark night, a dense and heavy body.
I declare to you this ἐοικότα πάντα ordering
So that no opinion of mortals shall ever outstrip you.

The goddess describes the cosmology to follow as a διάκοσμος ἐοικὼς πᾶς. In this chapter, I will attempt to tease out the implications of this label. What does it mean for the goddess to call her cosmology ἐοικώς? What, if anything does this term imply about Parmenides' methodology and epistemology?

Parmenides' philosophy is in hexameter verse, as, of course, are several of the extant fragments of Xenophanes. Some lament this choice for its inherent ambiguities and lack of clarity. To do so is, I think, to miss the point. The fragments are notoriously difficult to interpret and this difficulty is, in part, a result of Parmenides' deliberately allusive and elusive style. These difficulties notwithstanding, there is an 'integral connection between his thought and its mode of expression'.[11] When reading Parmenides, one should not seek to separate what he says from the way he says it. His allusions to other poets are not mere embellishments, nor are his ambiguous vocabulary and syntax accidentally so. Such devices are intended to be philosophically significant and they are at the heart of the account set out below. Since such concerns are central to my interpretation, I will begin with a brief discussion of Parmenides' use of ambiguity and allusion.

9 Simplicius *Phys.* 9.38. Following DK's punctuation.
10 Following Gallop's (1984) translation of this controversial line.
11 Gallop (1984) 5.

Many interpretations have been offered for Parmenides' ἐοικώς. Some see it as a qualified endorsement, others as a warning that the cosmology to follow is specious. I will offer a summary of the four main types of interpretation and argue that the best reading is that which incorporates elements of each. I will go on to present two aspects of Parmenides' use of this term that deserve closer attention than they have previously been afforded. The first is the possibility that Parmenides' vocabulary is influenced by forensic terminology. Several of Parmenides' key terms (σήματα; κρίσις; ἔλεγχος; πίστις) carry forensic connotations. I will argue that this juridical background should inform our understanding of Parmenides' ἐοικώς. It is evidence in favour of taking one aspect of its meaning to be something like the notion of 'plausibility' widely employed in the second half of the fifth century BC. The second is the possibility that Parmenides B8.60 alludes to Xenophanes B35. There is good evidence, in both the doxography and the verbatim fragments, that Parmenides was familiar with Xenophanes' poetry. I will argue that B8.60 is a conscious allusion to Xenophanes and that, as with Xenophanes' allusion to Homer and Hesiod at B35, the significance of the allusion lies in the way that Parmenides alters Xenophanes' formula.

Parmenides' use of ἐοικώς can be usefully compared to his choice of the term πίστις at B1.30 and B8.28. I will argue that, when the goddess claims that her cosmology is ἐοικώς, she is attributing to her account a kind of persuasiveness that is subjectively convincing but ultimately false. This is in opposition to the true, objective cogency attributed to the *Aletheia* via the term πίστις.

I will conclude with some suggestions as to how such a reading can inform our understanding of the relation between the *Aletheia* and the *Doxa*. Here, my conclusions are necessarily limited by the fact that I will not be offering a detailed interpretation of either part. My interest is primarily in the characterization of the *Doxa* as ἐοικώς and what this implies about its relation to the *Aletheia*. The question of the precise import of, in particular, the *Aletheia* would take me far beyond the scope of this book. I will, so far as is possible, be attempting to sidestep many of the issues that have dominated recent scholarship on Parmenides. Most notably, I will not be engaging with the question whether or in what way Parmenides is a monist.[12] I will, of course, be looking at some of the details of the *Aletheia* and offering interpretative suggestions but, in the end, my commitments here do not, I think, go far beyond reading it as an account of 'the unmoving heart of persuasive truth' (B1.29).

Ambiguity and allusion

Anyone attempting to make sense of Parmenides has to face up to the unquestionable obscurity of his poetry. Some have seen his choice of medium as at odds with the philosophical ideal of clear, rational argument. Thus KRS identify a tension between form and content, so that 'the struggle to force novel, difficult and highly abstract philosophical ideas into metrical form frequently results in ineradicable obscurity, especially syntactic obscurity'.[13] Others have been tempted to strip the poetics away entirely. This is the kind of reading offered by Barnes, who, having dismissed Parmenides' decision to present his philosophy in hexameter verse as 'hard to excuse', sets out to clarify the arguments of the *Aletheia*.[14] Without doubt, Barnes's interpretation is far more lucid than Parmenides' verse, but that clarity comes at a price: Parmenides becomes a victim of his own hexameter. Further, whatever philosophical significance he may have intended for his allusions and ambiguities is lost.[15]

An alternative approach embraces the poetics of Parmenides' philosophy. His choice of hexameter was precisely that, a choice.[16] As such it deserves attention, even if not respect. It seems fair to assume that Parmenides was aware of the 'syntactical obscurity' of his verse and I find the suggestion that this obscurity is deliberate rather more palatable than the claim that he could simply do no

[12] For a summary of approaches to Parmenides' monism, see Palmer (2009) 1–50.
[13] KRS 241. [14] Barnes (1982) 155–6. [15] See Osborne (1998).
[16] Lesher (2008) 475–6 proposes an agonistic motivation for Parmenides' choice of verse-form. For the proposal that verse should be considered the default form of philosophical writing for Parmenides, see Osborne (1998).

better.[17] Mourelatos gives a neat explanation of how form and content interact in Parmenides' verse:

> Parmenides uses his keen sense of language to trace out implications at length, to project alternative and related models of his concepts, to establish multiple and systematic connections, and to detect and exploit ambiguity for the purpose of argument and refutation.[18]

This is the kind of reading offered by Barrett, who argues that Parmenides' 'poem offers its own difficulty [. . .] as a key part of its purpose' which is, in one respect, to scrutinize the use of language.[19] The suggestion that Parmenides is importing a degree of conscious ambiguity into his poetry is supported by the fact that the bulk of the poem is presented as a divine revelation. Certain sorts of divine pronouncements, most notably oracles, were notorious for the interpretative demands of their ambiguity.[20] Heraclitus, himself no stranger to deliberate obscurity, offers the following assessment of the Delphic oracle:

> ὁ ἄναξ, οὗ τὸ μαντεῖόν ἐστι τὸ ἐν Δελφοῖς, οὔτε λέγει οὔτε κρύπτει ἀλλὰ σημαίνει.[21]
>
> The lord whose oracle is in Delphi neither declares nor conceals but gives a sign.[22]

This reference to giving a sign (σημαίνει) is telling, for, at B8.2–4, Parmenides' goddess alerts Parmenides to the existence of evidence indicating the nature of Being:[23]

> . . . ταύτηι δ' ἐπὶ σήματ' ἔασι
> πολλὰ μάλ', ὡς ἀγένητον ἐὸν καὶ ἀνώλεθρόν ἐστιν,
> οὖλον μουνογενές τε καὶ ἀτρεμὲς ἠδὲ τελεστόν.[24]
>
> On this [road] there are signs
> Great in number, that what-is is ungenerated and imperishable,
> Whole, unique, unmoving and complete.

[17] Mackenzie (1982) 7 suggests that Parmenides' allusive poetry is particularly suited to 'the gadfly work of dialectic which goads the reader into thinking for himself'.
[18] Mourelatos (2008) 260–1.
[19] Barrett (2004) 267. See Mourelatos (2008) 222–63 on ambiguity in the *Doxa*.
[20] See Stanford (1972) 115–28.
[21] Heraclitus B93 (Plutarch *De Pyth. or.* 404d).
[22] Kahn's (1979) translation.
[23] For a discussion of the forensic connotations of Parmenides' σήματα, see 82–6.
[24] Simplicius *Phys.* 9.144.

The Pythia's utterances are 'signs' that require interpretation.[25] Likewise, Parmenides' goddess gives 'signs' that indicate the nature of Being. Bearing in mind its revelatory context, it is, I think, no accident that Parmenides' poem makes interpretative demands similar to those faced by someone consulting the Delphic oracle. I do not want to claim that there is no way to cut through the ambiguities of Parmenides' hexameters. After all, whilst there may be more than one way to read an oracle, we tend to think that only one turns out to be accurate. However, I do want to emphasize that Parmenides' ambiguities are an integral aspect of his philosophical poem so that, whatever reading one prefers, it should be one that works through, rather than around, those ambiguities.

In this chapter I will propose that there are several viable possibilities for the meaning of ἐοικώς as found in B8.60. My suggestion is that Parmenides may well have intended to adduce more than one sense of the word. I will argue that B8.60 is, in part an allusion to and alteration of Xenophanes B35. The 'highly allusive' nature of Parmenides' poetry is widely recognized. In particular, the Homeric and Hesiodic influences on the poem have been much discussed.[26] The possibility and significance of a Xenophanean influence are rather less well established. This is no doubt due in part to the fragmentary nature of the texts; we will, after all, be hard pressed to recognize an allusion to a text of which we have no knowledge. The subjective nature of the criteria for allusive readings has also served to fuel the interpretative fire. Where one scholar claims a direct allusion, another may see nothing but original thought.

In Chapter 1, I noted that some scholars have resisted the suggestion that Xenophanes could have been significantly influenced by Homer and Hesiod.[27] Similar resistance is found to the proposal that Parmenides took philosophical cues from Xenophanes. Some of those who reject any Xenophanean influence seem mystifyingly intent on insisting that Parmenides should not be read as

[25] On the interpretative demands of such 'signs', see Nagy (1990) 202–22.

[26] Havelock (1958) 135. Mourelatos (2008) 1–46 offers the most comprehensive account of Parmenides' interaction with the Homeric epic form. See also Coxon (2009) 9–18. Pellikaan-Engel (1978) concentrates on the link between Parmenides and Hesiod.

[27] See 10–16.

influenced by *anyone* in any philosophically significant fashion.[28] There seems to be a worry that, if we allow Parmenides' allusiveness to stray beyond some kind of purely literary limits, we will undermine the originality of his epistemological and metaphysical thought. It is as if Parmenides would be somehow diminished were his *philosophy* found to be influenced by a predecessor, especially one who, as with Xenophanes, has been accused of slipping into the canon of ancient philosophers in error.[29] Even those who do acknowledge connections between Xenophanes and Parmenides have sought to downplay their importance. Fränkel, for example, gives with one hand and takes with the other:

> Certainly one can see clearly connections between the theology of Xenophanes and Parmenides' ontological doctrines of Being and Seeming; but in all essentials what Parmenides creates was so new, so important, and so self-contained, that Xenophanes' contribution to it sinks into insignificance.[30]

Parmenides' allusiveness has even been cited as evidence *against* a Xenophanean influence. One suggestion is that the prevalence of *Hesiodic* allusion within the fragments rules against the possibility that Xenophanes might also have any meaningful influence on Parmenides' poem.[31]

Of course, allusion to Hesiod is hardly incompatible with allusion to Xenophanes. After all, I have argued that Xenophanes himself alludes to Hesiod and it is not inconceivable that Parmenides' interest in Homer and Hesiod is prompted by the philosophical poem of Xenophanes. Nor is philosophical originality incompatible with an engagement with the thought of one's predecessors. In fact, the poetic form in which Parmenides presents his new philosophy is, I take it, evidence of his intention to engage with the authority of his predecessors and to present a rival account.

[28] Schofield (2003) 44 notes that 'it is nowadays commonly supposed that Parmenides was a creative genius not much in debt to anyone'.

[29] Cherniss (1951) 18 describes Xenophanes as 'a poet and a rhapsode who has become a figure in the history of Greek philosophy by mistake'. Hussey (1972) 13 also feels that 'Xenophanes is probably not an original thinker.'

[30] Fränkel (1975) 350.

[31] Chalmers (1960) 5, although he does consider the possibility that Parmenides may deliberately be following Xenophanes in writing in verse.

Once we have recognized the allusiveness of Parmenides' poetry, it seems natural to consider its significance.[32]

There is, then, no compelling reason to resist the possibility that Parmenides could be philosophically influenced by his predecessors, his unquestionable originality notwithstanding. In fact, evidence for a connection between Xenophanes and Parmenides is not hard to find. The two are explicitly linked within the doxographical tradition. In addition, as I shall argue below, there are obvious verbal and thematic similarities between the fragments of both philosophers.

Interpretations of ἐοικώς

Translations of B8.60's ἐοικώς fall into four main groups:

(1) 'Similar'
(2) 'Fitting' or 'Appropriate'
(3) 'Specious'
(4) 'Plausible'

Although, as will become clear, there is a certain degree of overlap between these translations, the majority of interpreters argue for a single determinate meaning. One of the difficulties of B8.60–61 is that these lines seem to describe the nature and, in line 61, purpose of the *Doxa*. Such issues are notoriously controversial. In some cases, as we will see, a translation of Parmenides' ἐοικώς is proposed because it fits the interpreter's prior assumptions about the status of the cosmology (and of the *Aletheia*). If we assume, for example, that the cosmology lacks any value at all, we will be more inclined to read ἐοικώς as a pejorative term. My hope is that an investigation of the meaning of ἐοικώς may serve to shed

[32] Morgan (2000) 69 defends Parmenides' choice of writing in verse because it allows him 'to employ subtle forms of echoing and allusion which were perhaps not available in early fifth-century prose' but goes on to suggest that, in practice 'although epic diction lends a sense of familiarity, we do not need to posit specific allusion to understand Parmenides' text'. The suggestion seems to be that it is enough to understand Parmenides' style as allusive in some *general* sense without being concerned about the need to trace specific passages to which we think he might be alluding. Whilst we must accept that the fragmentation of the texts may have placed many potential allusions forever beyond our ken, it seems preferable to consider with care those which we can identify within the poem.

some light on the status and purpose of the *Doxa*. Rather than interpreting ἐοικώς in the light of the *Doxa*, I want to consider what we can learn about the *Doxa* from the fact that the goddess claims it to be ἐοικώς.

(1) *'Similar'*

I begin with the most basic (although perhaps not the simplest) suggestion for the meaning of ἐοικώς. In Chapter 1, I argued that Xenophanes uses ἐοικώς in fragment B35 to describe a particular kind of (potentially specious) similarity to the truth. It has been suggested that Parmenides is also using ἐοικώς to express a likeness relation.[33] In support of this reading, Gomperz cites the description of Apollo at *Iliad* 21.600–601 as a possible parallel:

> αὐτῷ γὰρ ἑκάεργος Ἀγήνορι πάντα ἐοικὼς
> ἔστη πρόσθε ποδῶν, ὃ δ' ἐπέσσυτο ποσσὶ διώκειν·
>
> Resembling Agenor himself in all respects the far-shooting god
> Stood toe-to-toe with [Achilles] and he rushed upon him to pursue him.

There is an obvious difference between this passage and Parmenides B8.60. The *Iliad* passage gives a dative object of comparison: Apollo is like 'Agenor himself' (αὐτῷ . . . Ἀγήνορι). Xenophanes B35 also gives a dative object: his teachings (ταῦτα) are similar to the truth (τοῖς ἐτύμοισι). Parmenides' goddess, in contrast, provides no such object of comparison. Can ἐοικώς carry the sense 'similar' even in the absence of the dative? Gomperz argues that it can, identifying a possible parallel for such a use at Aeschylus *Supplices* 283–284:[34]

> Κύπριος χαρακτὴρ τ' ἐν γυναικείοις τύποις
> εἰκὼς πέπληκται τεκτόνων πρὸς ἀρσένων·
>
> The Cyprian stamp on female forms
> Has been impressed just as it is (i.e. accurately) by male craftsmen.

[33] Gomperz (1924) 17.

[34] The date of the *Supplices* is uncertain, with suggestions ranging from the 490s to the 460s. See Garvie (1969). An earlier date would, of course, lend greater support to Gomperz's thesis that Parmenides might be using the term in the same way. Even a later date would support the thought that the usage was already known before the second half of the fifth century. See Johansen and Whittle (1980) 223–6 for a discussion of the difficulties encountered in interpreting this passage.

Whether the Aeschylean passage provides a parallel or not, the issue of the absent object lingers.[35] Since, 'similar' is a two-place predicate, any statement of similarity is incomplete without such a complement. It is difficult to understand how one could hold *x* to be similar without necessarily holding it to be similar to *y*. After all, unless one already has *y* in mind, one would not be in a position to identify the similarity of *x*. Gomperz himself seems to admit this in suggesting that the διάκοσμος is 'ganz gleich' traditional mortal cosmologies.

One might think that, in the end, the absence of an explicit dative in B8.60 rules against the translation 'similar', but perhaps this need not be the case. Parmenides may be withholding an explicit complement in order to provoke us to consider a variety of alternative options. Perhaps, on hearing the goddess call her cosmology ἐοικώς, one of the many questions we are supposed to ask ourselves is 'similar to what?'[36]

(2) *'Fitting' or 'Appropriate'*

The translation 'appropriate' or 'suitable' seems to have had particular appeal for those seeking to downplay the significance of the *Doxa*.[37] Such a reading is adopted by Owen, for example, in arguing that the *Doxa* represents 'no more than a dialectical device'.[38] For Owen, it seems, the *Doxa* is 'fitting' only insofar as it is appropriate to this purpose.

[35] On the *Supplices* passage, Tucker (1889) 66 agrees with Gomperz, translating εἰκὼς 'to the life'. He does note, however, that others have sought to import the dative τῷ ὑμετέρῳ.

[36] It may be possible to make a similar case for Parmenides' notoriously underdetermined use of εἶναι. Thus, Sedley (1999) 114–15 suggests that, in B2, it may be that no subject is made explicit because 'at this stage we are still investigating the logical behaviour of the verb "to be"'. See also Warren (2007) 83–6.

[37] Proponents include Chalmers (1960) 9, Mansfeld (1964) 146–8, Verdenius (1964) 50–1, Bormann (1971) 47, Cherubin (2005) 10–12, Robbiano (2006) 183–4 and Palmer (2009) 162.

[38] Owen (1960) 49–50. By arguing that the *Doxa* is a 'dialectical device', Owen is challenging claims that Parmenides wrote his poem in the 'broad tradition of Ionian and Italian cosmology' (48).

In support of the translation 'appropriate', Verdenius suggests *Odyssey* 3.124–125 as a textual parallel.[39] Nestor praises Telemachus and reminisces about Odysseus:

> ἦ τοι γὰρ μῦθοί γε ἐοικότες, οὐδέ κε φαίης
> ἄνδρα νεώτερον ὧδε ἐοικότα μυθήσασθαι.

Some translations of this passage render both ἐοικότες in line 124 and ἐοικότα in line 125 as expressing similarity. Thus, for example Rieu translates:

> You talk exactly as he did and I should have sworn no young man could so resemble him in speech.[40]

Verdenius, however, sees no talk of resemblance here. He reads ἐοικότα in line 125 in the sense of 'as is proper' and argues that, from this, 'it follows that in line 124 the word ἐοικότες is used in the absolute sense and does not mean "resembling those of your father", as is often translated'. On this reading, the lines mean something like 'your words are fitting and indeed I have never seen a young man speak so properly'.

One perceived advantage of translating Parmenides' ἐοικώς as 'appropriate' is that, in giving B8.60 a positive spin, it seems in keeping with the apparently optimistic tone of the following line.[41] The goddess is thus approving her cosmology as suitable for the purpose of ensuring that, having heard it, Parmenides will not be 'outstripped' by the opinions of mortals. On this reading, it is only natural that we should ask in what way the *Doxa* is suitable for such a purpose.[42] Verdenius seems to suggest that it is the account's accuracy which makes it appropriate, glossing his translation 'proper' as 'in accordance with the facts'.[43] Cherubin

39 Verdenius (1964) 50–1.

40 Rieu (1946) 53.

41 Verdenius (1964) 50–1 cites the positive tone of line 61 as evidence against translations such as 'probable' or 'specious'. See also Chalmers (1960) 9.

42 See Coxon (2009) 349: 'why should the goddess make a point of labelling her account of the universe simply "fitting"? And why should hearing it place P[armenides] in the special position indicated in the next line?'

43 See also Palmer (2009) 162n34. Palmer cites Helen's announcement at *Odyssey* 4.238–239 (ἦ τοι νῦν δαίνυσθε καθήμενοι ἐν μεγάροισι/καὶ μύθοις τέρπεσθε· ἐοικότα γὰρ καταλέξω) as an example of ἐοικότα carrying a sense along the lines of 'accurate'. Palmer translates 'As you sit now and feast in the great halls, enjoy my story as

proposes that the διάκοσμος is fitting in two ways.[44] First, it 'is analogous to our everyday descriptions of sensory experience', i.e. it is fitting because it is like the kind of things mortals tend to say.[45] Second, it is 'in accord with human capabilities and limitations or lacks'.[46] Cherubin argues that the content of the *Doxa* is fitting for humans precisely because they are humans and should thus expect nothing better. The implication, for Cherubin, is that what is appropriate to mortals is distinguishable from what is appropriate to gods (as I have argued is the case for Xenophanes).[47] Mansfeld, in contrast, suggests that, when the goddess calls her cosmology ἐοικώς, she is referring to the appropriate relations which hold between the two elements that form the foundation of the account.[48] On Mansfeld's reading, it is the subject-matter itself that displays suitability.

The translation 'similar' left us asking 'similar to what?' The translation 'fitting' also raises questions. To what purpose or to whom and in what way does the goddess claim her διάκοσμος to be ἐοικώς?[49]

well – for the things I shall relate are fitting' and suggests that Menelaus' 'subsequent comment at *Od.* 4. 266 that she has told everything κατὰ μοῖραν, "in order" or "rightly", indicates that ἐοικότα here verges on "accurate", that is, in conformity with what actually occurred'. Certainly, one possible translation of ἐοικότα here is 'fitting', but I see no reason to read this as a matter of accuracy. Helen could just as well be claiming that her story is appropriate to the current situation. This seems to be the reading given by Murray (1919) 125, who renders the final clause 'For I will tell what fitteth the time.' Rieu (1946) 70 similarly translates ἐοικότα in line 239 as 'to the point'.

44 Cherubin (2005) 9–12.

45 See also Dalfen (1994) 209–10: 'Die Beschreibung der Welt, wie sie die Göttin jezt als menschliche Weltsicht gibt, ist also "entsprechend", sie gleicht dem, was die Menschen sehen und zu beschreiben versuchen.'

46 Cherubin (2005) 9–12 offers textual parallels for poets employing ἐοικώς to 'speak of that which is appropriate for mortal humans, and [to] contrast this with what is appropriate for immortal gods'. She cites *Odyssey* 5.212–213 and 8.146 and Pindar *Pythian* 3.59–62; *Nemean* 3.19 and 7.58. Cf. Schwabl (1968) 414n19.

47 B1.3's 'εἰδότα φῶτα' tells against such a distinction. See 100–4.

48 Mansfeld (1964) 146–8. He argues that epic grammar demands that the *tertium comparationis* is always to be found in or near the context of the comparison being made.

49 Note that, of Cherubin's examples (see n46 above), *Odyssey* 5.212–213 and 8.146 use ἐοικώς with the accusative plus infinitive to state that it is fitting *that something is the case*. *Nemean* 3.19 has ἐοικώς plus *a dative* (μορφᾷ: 'fitting to his form').

(3) 'Specious'

Whilst those who translate ἐοικώς as 'appropriate' have been encouraged by the positive tone of B8.61, others are more influenced by the goddess's assertion at B8.51–52 that the opinions of mortals are 'deceitful':

> From this point on learn mortal beliefs,
> Listening to the deceitful (ἀπατηλὸν) ordering of my words.

One suggestion is that, as the subject-matter of the cosmology is mere appearances, so the account describing it is 'merely apparent' or 'specious'.[50] Nestle, for example, argues that the διάκοσμος is a false mortal construction standing in opposition to the Being described in the *Aletheia*. In fact, Nestle sees *this* interpretation as in keeping with B8.61: the goddess shares these specious mortal beliefs with Parmenides so that, when presented with them from another source, he will not be distracted from the god-given truth of the *Aletheia*.[51]

In Chapter 1, I suggested that Xenophanes' ἐοικοτα τοῖς ἐτύμοισι should be understood as describing a potentially specious similarity to the truth. This kind of reading of Parmenides' B8.60 offers a reading along these lines of Parmenides' use of ἐοικώς. In this case, however, it is not the perceived similarity to truth that is potentially specious (for no similarity is expressed), rather it is the teachings themselves that are attractive but deceitful. If this is the sense of Parmenides' B8.60, it seems to be the first extant instance of ἐοικώς carrying this meaning.

(4) 'Plausible'

The most widely accepted reading of ἐοικώς is as a qualified recommendation. On this reading, the goddess is recommending her account as 'plausible', 'likely' or 'probable'.

50 See Nestle in Zeller and Nestle (1919) 734, Albertelli (1939) 150 and Capelle (1963) 169.

51 Capelle (1963) 169 also takes B8.61 as evidence that the goddess regards the διάκοσμος which she presents to be false. He suggests that it needs to be presented so that it will not impress Parmenides if he hears it from another source.

In discussing the translation 'similar', I suggested that Parmenides might be withholding an explicit complement for ἐοικώς in order to provoke his audience into considering a variety of options. For some, Xenophanes B35 suggests an obvious candidate for consideration: the truth (τοῖς ἐτύμοισι).[52] Perhaps the goddess is claiming that the *Doxa* is 'likely' insofar as it is (implicitly) like the truth.

On this interpretation, whatever epistemological likelihood the *Doxa* possesses would be a result of the similarity that holds either between the cosmology itself and the truth or between its subject-matter and that of the *Aletheia*.[53]

Others have dismissed the need for even an implicit dative, arguing that B8.60 is an early occurrence of the simple participle carrying the sense 'plausible'.[54] Some dispute the claim that ἐοικώς has already developed this sense.[55] Pindar's *Pythian* 1 (*c.*470 BC), however, may support such a reading:[56]

ναυσιφορήτοις δ' ἀνδράσι πρώτα χάρις
ἐς πλόον ἀρχομένοις πομπαῖον ἐλθεῖν
οὖρον· ἐοικότα γάρ
καὶ τελευτᾷ φερτέρου νόστου τυχεῖν.

First Blessing for sailors
When setting out on a voyage is the coming of a favourable wind,
Since it augurs well [literally: for it is likely that there will occur] for a more prosperous return at the end.[57]

52 Cornford (1939) 46 understands τοῖς ἐτύμοισι as implicit within B8.60, citing Xenophanes as a parallel. Hussey (1990) 35 and Morgan (2000) 85 both read ἐοικότα as 'likely' in the sense of 'like the truth' importing truth into their (and the goddess's) accounts. I take it that O'Brien's (1987) 45 'looks good enough' is a version of this idea of similarity to the truth, since it is offered as a translation of the French term 'vraisemblance'. Hussey notes a persistent connection between the notion of likelihood and the family of words for resemblance.

53 Thus Coxon (2009) 351 suggests that the *Doxa* is 'likely' because it is 'as *like* the one reality as is possible for a dualist order'.

54 Including Heitsch (1974) 416, Frère (1987) 202, Sedley (1999) 123 and Hermann (2004) 153. Long (1963) 96 reads the term as meaning '"probable" carrying an allusion to εἰκός, as distinct from what is the case of necessity'.

55 Verdenius (1964) 50–1 objects that 'it is not likely that ἐοικώς at this period already had the meaning we find in Plato's term εἰκὼς λόγος'. See also Mansfeld (1964) 146. This assumption is questioned by Guthrie (1965) 51.

56 Gildersleeve (1890) 240 proposes a date of 474 BC or later; Kirkwood (1982) 125 suggests 470 BC.

57 Translation from Race (1986) 40. The dependence of τυχεῖν on ἐοικότα emphasizes that this is an occurrence of the impersonal use of the participle to mean 'likely', as does the

If we accept the translation 'plausible', either as the result of some implied similarity to the truth, or simply because we think this is what ἐοικώς has come to mean, certain questions necessarily follow. Is the goddess *recommending* her account as plausible? Lesher, for example, takes the term to be a positive endorsement of an account, albeit one limited to plausibility because of the lack of certainty available about its subject-matter.[58] As we have seen, this kind of positive interpretation seems to fit B8.61, but it is less in keeping with the assertion that the account is 'deceitful' at B8.53. Does the goddess expect Parmenides to find the account plausible, even after she has labelled it 'deceitful'?

We may be tempted to think that a divine claim of plausibility is more or less equivalent to a straightforward recommendation of her cosmology as at least possibly true. But, of course, the label 'deceitful' seems to indicate that it is, in fact, false.[59] Is it the case that the goddess requires Parmenides to accept *both* that '*x* is a plausible account' in the sense of '*x* may be true' *and* that '*x* is a deceitful account' in the sense of '*x* is false'? One way of avoiding this potential inconsistency is to introduce a distinction between objective truth and falsehood and subjective plausibility. It would be quite consistent for Parmenides to hold that '*x* is plausible' in the sense of '*x* may be believed to be true by some other (less discerning) individuals' and that '*x* is false'. Such a position is tenable because plausibility can be understood as a subjective quality of accounts distinct from their objective truth or falsehood.[60] This kind of distinction allows for an account to be both plausible and false. The sailors of *Pythian* 1, for example, may well believe that fine weather at the beginning of their voyage gives hope for a successful completion to their trip and it may be a matter of fact that this is how things generally do turn out.[61]

idea underlying the passage that things that begin well are likely to finish in the same way.

58 Lesher (1992) 240–1.

59 Popper (1998) 26–32 argues that, for *x* to be like the truth, *x* must be other than the truth. He thus sees B8.60 itself as, in part, a claim that the account to follow is false.

60 Morgan (2000) 85, for example, claims that the account is deceptive precisely because it resembles the truth.

61 Thus it seems to be an example of 'probability' rather than 'plausibility' (or a plausible account of probable events).

However, if we were to substitute 'mortals who know nothing' (B6.4: βροτοὶ εἰδότες οὐδὲν) for Pindar's sailors and to describe one of their widely held beliefs, such as that 'it both is and is not', we would be describing a belief that is at once plausible, insofar as it is considered to be so by mortals, and false (according to the account of the *Aletheia*).[62] Such a belief will be subjectively plausible but objectively false.

Ambiguity in B8.60–61

Many discussions of B8.60 assume that ἐοικώς should have one determinate meaning. Others, however, suggest that the word may combine more than one of the senses suggested above. So, for example, those who read τοῖς ἐτύμοισι as an implicit dative are deriving the sense 'plausible' from that of 'similar (to the truth)'. Another example of this kind of composite reading is offered by Wilamowitz, who suggests that Parmenides' ἐοικώς indicates that the διάκοσμος is both 'plausible' and 'only apparent'.[63] On this reading, ἐοικώς expresses both the persuasive quality of the account and the status of its subject-matter as nothing other than appearances. Similarly, Mourelatos identifies a 'play of negative against positive meanings' in Parmenides' ἐοικώς.[64] He suggests that both the sense of 'probable' and that of 'seeming, apparent' are present: 'to the uninitiated mortals it means the first; to the goddess and the Kouros, the second'.[65] Mourelatos presents his reading of B8.60 within the context of a more general discussion

[62] Reinhardt (1916) 26 argues that B8.60's ἐοικώς indicates that, although the account is false, it is persuasive insofar as it possesses consistency and obviousness ('Folgerichtigkeit und Augensheinlichkeit').

[63] Wilamowitz (1899) 204–5. He translates διάκοσμον ἐοικότα πάντα as 'eine [Weltordnung], die ganz scheinbar ist' and expands on his translation 'die zwar nur eine Meinung, also trüglich ist, aber eine in sich geschlossene und durchaus wahrscheinliche'.

[64] Mourelatos (2008) 231. See also Austin (1986) 166n30: 'nothing prevents the ironic demotion of a plausibility word when applied to the cosmos of mortals. [The translation of ἐοικότα as] "Semblance" is intended to reflect both sides of the irony.'

[65] Guthrie (1965) 50 and Curd (1998) 102 both translate 'likely-seeming'. KRS 256 gives 'The whole ordering of these I tell you as seems fitting.' DK 1.240 have 'wahrscheinlich-einleuchtende'. Even Owen (1960), despite his choice of 'fitting' as the best translation (50), goes on (54) to argue that, although completely false, the account given is intended as the 'most complete and *plausible* system' (my italics).

of the ambiguity of the language of the *Doxa*.[66] He suggests that B8.52 warns not only 'that δόξαι are deceptive but further that the *arrangement* or the context in which the goddess' words appear may assign to them multiple or conflicting meanings'.[67] In fact, the ambiguity of B8.60 is not limited to the meaning of ἐοικώς. Let us look again at the phrase διάκοσμον ἐοικότα πάντα. It is not clear whether διάκοσμος refers to the ordering of the account itself or to the ordering of the subject-matter described. In fact, it may refer to both.[68] Similarly the scope of πάντα is unclear. The goddess may be claiming that her *entire* account or subject-matter is ἐοικώς.[69] Equally, she may be claiming that her account or subject-matter is *entirely* ἐοικώς.[70] She may even be asserting that her *entire* account or subject-matter is *entirely* ἐοικώς.[71] Some will prefer to translate such ambiguities away; I see no reason to think that they are unintentional on Parmenides' part. It seems perfectly possible that Parmenides intended his use of ἐοικώς to be equivocal and that this ambiguity is philosophically significant.

At this point, it is worth returning to *Odyssey* 3.124–125, cited as an Homeric parallel for ἐοικώς as meaning 'fitting' or 'appropriate':

> ἦ τοι γὰρ μῦθοί γε ἐοικότες, οὐδέ κε φαίης
> ἄνδρα νεώτερον ὧδε ἐοικότα μυθήσασθαι.

As noted above, Verdenius reads Menelaus' use of ἐοικότα and ἐοικότες as divorced from any notion of resemblance. However, the broader context of these lines indicates that, in praising Telemachus, Nestor is thinking about the degree to which the young man resembles his father:

66 Mourelatos (2008) 222–63.
67 Mourelatos (2008) 227.
68 See Wilamowitz (1899) 204–5. Graham (2006) 169 notes the ambiguity of B8.52's κόσμος.
69 Some, including Diels (1897) 41, Verdenius (1964) 51, KRS 256, Gallop (1984) 75 and Mourelatos (2008) 230, take πάντα as masculine accusative singular, qualifying διάκοσμος. Thus Gallop (1984) 75 translates 'All this arrangement I proclaim to you as a plausible.'
70 A reading preferred by Wilamowitz (1899) 204–5, Cornford (1933) 108, O'Brien (1987) 45 and Coxon (2009) 78. Coxon translates 'This order of things I declare to you to be likely in its entirety.' He (351) argues that the claim of '"complete" likeliness' at B8.60 is anticipated by the occurrence of πάντα at B1.32 (διὰ παντὸς πάντα περῶντα).
71 Palmer (2009) 162 offers yet another alternative with his translation of διάκοσμον ἐοικότα πάντα as 'ordering of things, entire and fitting'.

ἔνθ' οὔ τίς ποτε μῆτιν ὁμοιωθήμεναι ἄντην
ἤθελ', ἐπεὶ μάλα πολλὸν ἐνίκα δῖος Ὀδυσσεὺς
παντοίοισι δόλοισι, πατὴρ τεός, εἰ ἐτεόν γε
κείνου ἔκγονός ἐσσι· σέβας μ' ἔχει εἰσορόωντα.
ἦ τοι γὰρ μῦθοί γε ἐοικότες, οὐδέ κε φαίης
ἄνδρα νεώτερον ὧδε ἐοικότα μυθήσασθαι.
ἔνθ' ἦ τοι εἷος μὲν ἐγὼ καὶ δῖος Ὀδυσσεὺς
οὔτε ποτ' εἰν ἀγορῇ δίχ' ἐβάζομεν οὔτ' ἐνὶ βουλῇ,
ἀλλ' ἕνα θυμὸν ἔχοντε νόῳ καὶ ἐπίφρονι βουλῇ
φραζόμεθ' Ἀργείοισιν ὅπως ὄχ' ἄριστα γένοιτο.

There, no one ever wanted to compete with his cunning,
Since noble Odysseus, your father, was pre-eminent in every sort of trick,
If you really are his son; I'm dumbstruck as I look at you.
ἦ τοι γὰρ μῦθοί γε ἐοικότες, οὐδέ κε φαίης
ἄνδρα νεώτερον ὧδε ἐοικότα μυθήσασθαι.
In all the years there, noble Odysseus and I
Never disagreed in the assembly or in the council
But with common purpose, with sense and wise counsel,
We advised the Argives what would be best.

Some commentators have suggested that Nestor is here acknowledging both that Telemachus speaks in a way similar to his father and that he speaks in an appropriate fashion.[72] On this reading Homer is adducing both these potential meanings in quick succession to produce a 'subtle transition' between Telemachus' similarity to Odysseus and the suitability of his speech.[73]

[72] See Heubeck and West (1981) 288–9: 'Nestore fonde, piuttosto confusamente, due concetti: (1) il modo di parlare di Telemaco è sorprendentemente simile a quello di Odisseo; (2) è simile a ciò che dovrebbe essere, cioè notevolmente assennato per un giovane... La circostanza che il modo di parlare simile a quello di Odisseo sarebbe di fatto conveniente e appropriato facilita la confusione.' See also Stanford (1959) 254.

[73] Hayman (1866) 72 suggests that Nestor makes a 'subtle transition' between Telemachus' similarity to Odysseus and the suitability of his speech because 'to take both ἐοικότες and ἐοικότα [...] in sense of "suitable" seems lame and tautological, and evacuates γε of its force, which is, "your words *at any rate* are like his", referring to the doubt of his sonship just before stated; and to take them both in sense of "like", i.e. like Odysseus' way of speaking, would leave σέβας μ' ἔχει κ.τ.λ. without due force'. Merry and Riddell (1886) 103–4 go so far as to suggest that both ἐοικότες and ἐοικότα be read as hurriedly expressing a 'familiar sentiment' with the dative understood, citing *Odyssey* 4.140 and 19.380 as support. They understand the lines to mean 'Thy manner is like his [...] you would not expect a young man to speak so like his *elder*, unless the two were *father and son*.'

As I hope is clear from the summaries above, none of the suggested translations of Parmenides' ἐοικώς is obviously unacceptable. Even where we think the syntax is incompatible with a particular sense, there is no reason to rule out the possibility that Parmenides could be alluding to such a usage. In fact, I will argue for an interpretation of B8.60 that incorporates aspects of each of these suggested senses. As we have seen, there is reason to think that, in the *Odyssey* passage above, Homer's verse slides between potential meanings of ἐοικώς within the space of a few lines. My suggestion is that Parmenides offers one instance of ἐοικώς which, in itself, slides between multiple meanings or, perhaps better, is intended to prompt us to think of the variety of different possible senses of the word.[74]

Those who seek to rule out a particular sense tend to do so on one of two grounds. The first is that ἐοικώς has not yet developed a particular meaning at the time of Parmenides' *floruit*. This kind of objection is rather rickety, based as it is on speculations about dating and assumptions that the interpretation of ἐοικώς in other texts is more secure. The second is that, unless it appears in a particular grammatical context, ἐοικώς cannot carry a particular sense. Verdenius, for example argues that ἐοικώς cannot, 'at this period', carry the sense 'probable' (or 'specious') without a dative.[75] Even if this is correct, as those who accept *Pythian* 1 as a parallel would deny, it seems quite possible that Parmenides could be alluding to the sense it carries with the dative even in the absence of an explicit complement. In the previous chapter, I argued that Xenophanes B35 both alludes to and alters the poetic formula ἐτύμοισι ὁμοῖα familiar from Homer and Hesiod. In fact, the significance of the allusion is indicated by the alteration of term for likeness. Similarly, I take it that the lack of a dative at Parmenides B8.60 need be no obstacle to reading this line as an allusion to occurrences of the term with a dative such as that at Xenophanes B35. Indeed, as I will argue below, there is good reason to think that Parmenides may be alluding to Xenophanes, if only to correct his epistemological pessimism.

[74] See Tarán (1965) 212 and 226n59.

[75] Verdenius (1964) 50–1.

The summary of different translations given above has raised many questions. In what follows, I will focus on two. First, I will consider the degree to which Parmenides' ἐοικώς incorporates a notion of plausibility or probability. Here, a discussion of some of Parmenides' other significant terms will prove valuable. I will argue that several of these terms are forensic in tone (if not in meaning) and that this 'proto-rhetorical' aspect of Parmenides' language should inform our understanding of the meaning of ἐοικώς at B8.60. Second, I will investigate the nature and degree of Parmenides' engagement with Xenophanes. My aim is to offer a consistent and constructive interpretation of several passages which seem to allude to Xenophanes. I hope to show that such a reading can enhance our understanding of Parmenides' epistemological originality.

Before investigating the possible 'plausibility' of Parmenides' ἐοικώς, it is worth looking, albeit briefly, at the development of this sense of the word, which, of course, comes to be of fundamental philosophical importance in the fifth century BC.

A short history of plausibility

According to both Plato and Aristotle, the Sicilians Corax and Tisias theorized about arguments from probability. At *Phaedrus* 273b3–d6, Socrates gives an account of an argument from probability attributed to Tisias:[76]

Τοῦτο δή, ὡς ἔοικε, σοφὸν εὑρὼν ἅμα καὶ τεχνικὸν ἔγραψεν ὡς ἐάν τις ἀσθενὴς καὶ ἀνδρικὸς ἰσχυρὸν καὶ δειλὸν συγκόψας, ἱμάτιον ἤ τι ἄλλο ἀφελόμενος, εἰς δικαστήριον ἄγηται, δεῖ δὴ τἀληθὲς μηδέτερον λέγειν, ἀλλὰ τὸν μὲν δειλὸν μὴ ὑπὸ μόνου φάναι τοῦ ἀνδρικοῦ συγκεκόφθαι, τὸν δὲ τοῦτο μὲν ἐλέγχειν ὡς μόνω ἤστην, ἐκείνῳ δὲ καταχρήσασθαι τῷ 'Πῶς δ' ἂν ἐγω τοιόσδε τοιῷδε ἐπεχείρησα;' ὁ δ' οὐκ ἐρεῖ δὴ τὴν ἑαυτοῦ κάκην, ἀλλά τι ἄλλο ψεύδεσθαι ἐπιχειρῶν τάχ' ἂν ἔλεγχόν πῃ παραδοίη τῷ ἀντιδίκῳ. καὶ περὶ τἄλλα δὴ τοιαῦτ' ἄττα ἐστὶ τὰ τέχνῃ λεγόμενα.

It's likely that it was when he discovered this wise and skilful technique that he wrote that if a feisty weakling is sued for mugging a cowardly muscle-man and

[76] Aristotle attributes the same example of an argument from probability to Corax at *Rhetoric* 2.24.1402a.

> stealing his cloak or something, neither should tell the truth. The coward should say that the feisty man had help to beat him up and the latter should retort that they were alone and employ that common tactic: how could someone like me attack someone like that? The muscle-man will not admit to his cowardice, but will concoct some other lie, and may thus help his opponent to refute him. And in other cases the tactics will be much the same.

Although the dates for these early rhetoricians are uncertain, there is some (very late) evidence that Corax was active in politics in Syracuse in the first half of the fifth century.[77] It is tempting to suggest that Parmenides felt the influence of this emerging interest in rhetoric, especially when one considers the relative geographical proximity of Syracuse and Elea. One obvious objection to such a suggestion is that Corax seems to have been active late in Parmenides' life (if one follows Plato's dating of the latter) or even after his death (according to Diogenes Laertius). Of course, if Tisias and Corax are not originators of such arguments, this need not be a problem. In considering the hypothetical case of the brave weakling and cowardly muscle-man attributed to Tisias in the *Phaedrus*, Gagarin argues that Tisias' originality must have been in offering a *particular kind* of argument from probability, because 'if this is all that Tisias' teaching about probability amounted to, it would not have won recognition for originality, since probability arguments had long been known and used'.[78]

According to Gagarin, the earliest example of an explicit argument for probability is to be found in the Homeric *Hymn to Hermes*. Although its date is disputed, it is generally placed around the turn of the sixth and fifth centuries BC. Hermes steals Apollo's cattle and Apollo demands retribution. Hauled up for judgement before Zeus, Hermes appeals to the implausibility of his behaving in such a manner. For, he says, he is a mere babe and thus incapable of cattle-rustling:

> οὐδὲ βοῶν ἐλατῆρι καρταιῷ φωτὶ ἔοικα,
> οὐδ' ἐμὸν ἔργον τοῦτο, πάρος δέ μοι ἄλλα μέμμηλεν.[79]
>
> But I am not like a cattle-rustler or a strong man,
> And this is not my work, rather other things are my concern.

77 Cicero *Brutus* 2.46. 78 Gagarin (1994) 51. 79 *Hymn to Hermes* 265–266.

Here, ἔοικα refers explicitly to similarity. But Hermes' claim that he is not like a 'cattle-rustler' also seems to be adducing the notion of appropriateness. The sense of the argument seems to be that it is *implausible* for Hermes to have behaved in a manner so *unsuited to* (or unlike) that of an infant. On this construal, the passage fits Aristotle's description of 'probability' in the *Rhetoric*:

τὸ μὲν γὰρ εἰκός ἐστι τὸ ὡς ἐπὶ τὸ πολὺ γινόμενον, οὐχ ἁπλῶς δὲ καθάπερ ὁρίζονταί τινες, ἀλλὰ τὸ περὶ τὰ ἐνδεχόμενα ἄλλως ἔχειν, οὕτως ἔχον πρὸς ἐκεῖνο πρὸς ὃ εἰκὸς ὡς τὸ καθόλου πρὸς τὸ κατὰ μέρος.[80]

τὸ εἰκός is what happens for the most part, not simply so, as some define it, but with regard to things which could turn out otherwise, standing in relation to that in connection to which it is probable as the universal stands to the particular.

εἰκός is cashed out in terms of frequency, so that the probable is that which is *likely* to happen. In Hermes' argument, 'what happens for the most part' is that cattle-thieves, not babies, steal cattle. Of course, despite the apparent improbability of such an occurrence, Hermes has stolen, cooked and eaten Apollo's herd. Hermes' defence is based on what is proper for or appropriate to someone like himself. Here, we see notions of what is plausible and what is appropriate combined within what is ἐοικώς. I shall argue below that something similar is happening at Parmenides B8.60–61. For now, however, I turn to the task of drawing out what I take to be the forensic connotations of some of Parmenides' key terms. Such juridical undertones are, I take it, evidence in favour of reading 'plausible' as one of the possible intended meanings of ἐοικώς.

Forensic vocabulary in the fragments

The fragments themselves provide good reason to suspect that Parmenides might be employing terminology of the type later found in forensic and deliberative rhetoric. Many of the key terms employed by the goddess in the *Aletheia* have a rhetorical or forensic connotation: σήματα, κρίσις, δίκη, ἔλεγχος, πίστις and, I suggest,

80 *Rhetoric* 1.2.1357a34–b1.

ἐοικώς.[81] Taking any one of these words in isolation, it is difficult to defend a 'forensic' interpretation, but taken together they make a strong case for a potential influence from rhetoric.[82] This is not to say that Parmenides is writing about rhetoric in any specific sense. I merely want to suggest that his choice of vocabulary and its intended meaning may be influenced by the language of rhetoric. If this is the case, then an awareness of this rhetorical background will enhance our understanding of his poem, and of the use of ἐοικώς in particular.

(i) Δίκη

Justice appears twice in Parmenides' poem. Her first appearance is at B1.13–14 as Parmenides describes his journey towards the gates of Night and Day:

> αὐταὶ δ' αἰθέριαι πλῆνται μεγάλοισι θυρέτροις·
> τῶν δὲ Δίκη πολύποινος ἔχει κληῖδας ἀμοιβούς.
>
> The etherial gates themselves are filled by great doors
> For which stern Justice holds the keys of retribution.

At B8.13–15 we are told how Justice controls Being:

> . . . τοῦ εἵνεκεν οὔτε γενέσθαι
> οὔτ' ὄλλυσθαι ἀνῆκε Δίκη χαλάσασα πέδησιν,
> ἀλλ' ἔχει·
>
> . . . for the sake of which neither Coming-to-be
> Nor passing away has Justice allowed by loosening her shackles,
> But she keeps it.

As Mourelatos notes, Parmenides' Justice 'is not assessed by any court'.[83] Parmenides is not describing the everyday justice of the mortal world; this is cosmic justice.[84] Nevertheless, the importance

81 Note that nearly all occur in some form in Aristotle's *Rhetoric*.

82 Heidel (1912–1913) 718 suggests that, at B8.12 following, Parmenides is inspired by 'an action at law in which the issue is drawn and judgement is rendered'. Mourelatos (2008) 150 acknowledges that 'the figure of Justice and the recurrent idea of a κρίσις, "decision," make Heidel's translation [of πίστις as "the force of evidence, *or* of proof"] attractive. But one must concede that the juridical vocabulary in Parmenides is too general to sustain the specific image of action in court.'

83 Mourelatos (2008) 152.

84 Coxon (2009) 277 suggests an Homeric influence here.

of this notion of Justice supports the suggestion that the poem as a whole is influenced by the language of the law court.[85] The fact that Justice controls Being affects the language to be used of Being. A system directed by Justice will rightly be described in the language of justice and deliberation.[86]

Aetius identifies the goddess of B12, who 'steers all things' in the cosmos described by the *Doxa*, as Justice:

τῶν δὲ συμμιγῶν τὴν μεσαιτάτην ἁπάσαις τοκέα πάσης κινήσεως καὶ γενέσεως ὑπάρχειν, ἥντινα καὶ δαίμονα κυβερνῆτιν καὶ κληιδοῦχον ἐπονομάζει Δίκην τε καὶ ἀνάγκην.[87]

The innermost of the mixed rings is parent of all movement and Coming-to-be for all of them, which he calls the 'steering goddess', 'key-carrier', 'Justice' and 'Necessity'.

This identification, if it is correct, establishes a parallel between the *Aletheia* and the *Doxa*. In the *Aletheia*, Justice holds Being, in the *Doxa*, she directs Coming-to-be and Passing-away.[88] This is not the only similarity between the language of these parts of the poem, as will become clear.[89]

(ii) σήματα

There are three occurrences of the word in the verbatim fragments: at B8.2–4, B8.55 and B10.1–2.

[85] So, for example, Coxon (2009) 320 reads B8.13–16 as 'an extended judicial metaphor expressive of logical necessity'.

[86] Anaximander B1. ἐξ ὧν δὲ ἡ γένεσίς ἐστι τοῖς οὖσι, καὶ τὴν φθορὰν εἰς ταῦτα γίνεσθαι 'κατὰ τὸ χρεών. διδόναι γὰρ αὐτὰ δίκην καὶ τίσιν ἀλλήλοις τῆς ἀδικίας κατὰ τὴν τοῦ χρόνου τάξιν', ποιητικωτέροις οὕτως ὀνόμασιν αὐτὰ λέγων·

[87] Aetius II.7.1.12–16 following DG 335 in reading ἁπάσαις τοκέα in preference to DK 224 ἁπάσαις <ἀρχήν>τε καὶ <αἰτίαν>.

[88] Not forgetting the Justice of the *Proemium*, who might be thought a third wheel. There is, as has been noted by Woodbury (1966) and Havelock (1978) 268–70, good reason to identify the goddess of the *Doxa* with the Justice of the *Proemium* (an identification supported by Aetius' κληιδοῦχον).

[89] The suggestive similarities between the language of the *Aletheia* and *Doxa* have long been noted. See Mansfeld (1964) 122–221 for an extensive discussion. Mourelatos (2008) 247–53 presents a tabulation of the 'similarities-with-a-difference' between the *Aletheia* and *Doxa*.

For Aristotle, σημεῖον is a term for a piece of evidence employed in argument, literally 'a sign'.[90] Mourelatos denies the possibility that σήματα might have a related meaning for Parmenides, arguing that 'the syntax of the passage [at B8.2–4] makes Parmenides' "signs" into something physical' such as a 'marking on the route'.[91] The goddess states that 'there are many signs along the way' and Mourelatos understands this to mean that there are many '*signposts*' along the route that we follow with the goddess.[92]

Despite his preference for this physical construal, Mourelatos admits that 'proofs' is a possible translation of σήματα, and that the word occurs with this sense in Homer.[93] There, it occurs only infrequently as referring to a physical sign (other than a grave mound). It does occur in this sense at, for example, *Iliad* 10.466 where it refers to a marker set up by Odysseus to remind him where he has left his booty. On one occasion, it is used as if to refer to the kind of 'signpost' suggested by Mourelatos. At *Iliad* 23.326ff., Nestor advises his son, Antilochus, on how best to complete the chariot race in which he is about to take part. He begins:

> σῆμα δέ τοι ἐρέω μάλ' ἀριφραδές, οὐδέ σε λήσει.
>
> I'll describe a clear sign that you can't miss.

He then goes on to explain that Antilochus should look out for the stump of a tree lying on the course which will be a marker and guide for the path of his chariot:

> ἤ τευ σῆμα βροτοῖο πάλαι κατατεθνηῶτος,
> ἦ τό γε νύσσα τέτυκτο ἐπὶ προτέρων ἀνθρώπων.
>
> Either it is a tomb of some long-dead fellow
> Or it was made a turning-post by previous generations.

90 *Rhetoric* 1.2.1357a22–33. See also Antiphon *Tetralogies* 1.4.10.

91 Mourelatos (2008) 25n40. He cites the reference to the stars as σήματα at B10.2 as evidence that Parmenides is familiar with the use of the term to refer to the stars as signposts for sailors. In fact, the most frequent Homeric meaning for σῆμα is tomb and it seems unlikely that it carries this sense for Parmenides.

92 See also Barrett (2004) 275–7. McKirahan (2008) provides a detailed discussion of the σήματα of the *Aletheia*.

93 Cf. Boeder (1962) 154.

The stump may be either a tomb or Mourelatos' 'signpost'. Note, however, that it is νύσσα rather than σῆμα, that actually refers to the 'signpost'.[94]

Elsewhere in Homer and Hesiod, σῆμα is frequently used to refer to divine portents, most often to the thunder of Zeus.[95] The fact that the σήματα in Parmenides' poem are described by a goddess might suggest that he is alluding, in part, to this kind of divine portent.

One final sort of Homeric σήματα, which anticipates the sense it carries in the *Rhetoric*, may inform Parmenides' usage. In book 23 of the *Odyssey*, Penelope is confronted by a man claiming to be her husband. Apparently suspicious of his claim, she tests him, asking him to give evidence to prove his identity. Indeed, even before she has made this demand, Eurycleia has attempted to persuade her with such evidence:

> θυμὸς δέ τοι αἰὲν ἄπιστος.
> ἀλλ' ἄγε τοι καὶ σῆμα ἀριφραδὲς ἄλλο τι εἴπω,
> οὐλήν, τήν ποτέ μιν σῦς ἤλασε λευκῷ ὀδόντι.[96]
>
> You have a suspicious mind.
> But come and I'll tell you another obvious sign,
> A scar, which a boar inflicted on him with its white tusk.

Eurycleia assumes that her evidence will dissolve Penelope's natural suspicion (θυμὸς... ἄπιστος). At 23.109–110, Penelope demands that Odysseus prove himself:

> ἔστι γὰρ ἥμιν
> σήμαθ', ἃ δὴ καὶ νῶϊ κεκρυμμένα ἴδμεν ἀπ' ἄλλων.[97]
>
> For we have signs, that are hidden from others and only we two know.

94 The only similar occurrence is of the verb being used to describe 'showing the way' at *Odyssey* 12.25–26 where Circe declares to the departing Odysseus that she will show him the way 'and point out each sign (ἕκαστα σημανέω)'.

95 E.g. *Odyssey* 21.413; *Iliad* 2.308; 4.381; 8.171; 13.244. In Hesiod, it appears to take on the meaning of 'signal' rather than specifically 'portent', as at *Erga* 450, where the cry of the crane is described as a signal for men to begin their ploughing. At *Odyssey* 20.111 and *Iliad* 6.176–178, it refers to some sort of 'code', a sense which might also have some influence on Parmenides' use, bearing in mind what seems to be the deliberate ambiguity and obscurity of his poetry. See Barrett (2004) 275ff. He argues that Parmenides is exploiting the ambiguous nature of σήματα as 'divine signs' which require careful scrutiny and often do not 'refer in a straightforward manner'.

96 *Odyssey* 23.72–74.

97 See also *Odyssey* 21.217; 23.203, 206; 24.329, 346.

Penelope is asking for evidence that the apparent stranger in front of her possesses the privileged knowledge that she shares with her husband.

I suggest that Parmenides is employing the term σήματα in a similar fashion at B8.2–4 and 55 (and perhaps even at B10.1–2). Such a reading need not and indeed should not exclude the possibility that the word carries other senses *at the same time*. There is no reason that σήματα cannot mean or allude to the notions of 'proofs', 'signposts', and 'portents' simultaneously. At B8.2–4 the syntax supports the idea that we are being alerted to proofs *that* something is the case:

> ταύτηι δ' ἐπὶ σήματ' ἔασι
> πολλὰ μάλ', ὡς ἀγένητον ἐὸν καὶ ἀνώλεθρόν ἐστιν,
> οὖλον μουνογενές τε καὶ ἀτρεμὲς ἠδὲ τελεστόν.
>
> On this [road] there are signs
> Great in number, *that* what-is is ungenerated and imperishable,
> Whole, unique, unmoving and complete.

It is possible to make a similar case for the occurrence of σήματα at B8.55–59:

> And they have distinguished opposites in body and concocted signs (σήματ' ἔθεντο)
> Separate from one another: here the aetherial fire of flame,
> Which is gentle; exceedingly light; the same throughout
> But different from the other. Whereas there is one by itself
> And opposite: dark night, a dense and heavy body

The goddess tells us that mortals have distinguished (or 'chosen': ἐκρίναντο) opposites and 'set up signs' (σήματ' ἔθεντο) 'apart from one another'. These 'signs' are then glossed as characteristics of the chosen opposites. It is possible to read these 'signs' or 'characteristics' in the (not necessarily exclusive) sense of 'proofs'. On this reading, mortals have made the misguided choice of an arbitrary pair of opposites and then concocted evidence (σήματ' ἔθεντο) to support that choice in the form of apparent physical phenomena. This fabricated 'evidence' is sufficient to convince them that they are right, despite the fact that they have literally made it up themselves.[98] B8.55 thus elaborates on the condemnation of mortals at B8.38–41:

> . . . τῶι πάντ' ὀνόμασται,[99]
> ὅσσα βροτοὶ κατέθεντο πεποιθότες εἶναι ἀληθῆ,
> γίγνεσθαί τε καὶ ὄλλυσθαι, εἶναί τε καὶ οὐχί,
> καὶ τόπον ἀλλάσσειν διά τε χρόα φανὸν ἀμείβειν.

> . . . in this way it has been named all things
> That mortals have set down, trusting them to be true:
> Coming-to-be and passing away, being and not being
> And changing place and altering bright colour.

Above, I identified two roles for Justice, one in the *Aletheia* and the other in the *Doxa*. Here we have another parallel between these two parts of the poem insofar as the goddess refers to two sets of σήματα.[100] The first is those 'signs' at B8.2–4 which she describes as evidence of the nature of Being. The second set at B8.55 is those signs that mortals have fabricated to suit their erroneous thinking.[101]

(iii) κρίσις

In Homer, the most frequent use of κρίσις and its cognates is to signify an act of choice, in the sense of the selection of certain members of a group. So the majority of Homeric occurrences describe the selection of smaller bands of men from the mass of troops.[102]

For my purposes, the most interesting passages are those which demonstrate that κρίσις has already developed a judicial sense. *Iliad* 16.384–394, for example, describes Hector's pursuit of Patroclus. The noise of their galloping horses is compared to a storm:

98 Barrett (2004) 283 reads B8.38–41 as a claim that mortals have 'decided' (κατέθεντο) on the names they have established, i.e. that the process of naming shows itself to be entirely conventional.

99 I follow, among others, KRS 252, Gallop (1984) 70 and Mourelatos (2008) 180–5 in preferring ὀνόμασται to ὄνομα ἔσται.

100 As noted by Mourelatos (2008) 250.

101 I take it that the σήματα of B10 are similarly fabricated.

102 E.g. *Odyssey* 4.408, 530; 9.90, 195; 10.102; 24.108; *Iliad* 13.129; 19.193. It is occasionally used to describe an arrangement or marshalling of troops, as at *Iliad* 2.446 and 16.199.

ὡς δ' ὑπὸ λαίλαπι πᾶσα κελαινὴ βέβριθε χθὼν
ἤματ' ὀπωρινῷ, ὅτε λαβρότατον χέει ὕδωρ
Ζεύς, ὅτε δή ῥ' ἄνδρεσσι κοτεσσάμενος χαλεπήνῃ,
οἳ βίῃ εἰν ἀγορῇ σκολιὰς κρίνωσι θέμιστας,
ἐκ δὲ δίκην ἐλάσωσι θεῶν ὄπιν οὐκ ἀλέγοντες·

And just as the whole black earth is compacted by the storm
On a day in late summer, when Zeus forcefully pours down rain,
When he develops a vicious grudge against men
Who make crooked decisions with force in the agora
And drive justice out paying no heed to the gods . . .

The evidence for early Greek legal proceedings is scarce indeed. This passage, at the very least, implies that some kind of 'system' existed to be abused. It also indicates that the verb κρίνω can, even at this stage, describe an act of judging or deciding that is in some sense legal.[103]

Another example of this 'judicial' usage is found at *Odyssey* 12.438–441, where Odysseus describes his wait for Charybdis to regurgitate his raft:

ἐελδομένῳ δέ μοι ἦλθον,
ὄψ'· ἦμος δ' ἐπὶ δόρπον ἀνὴρ ἀγορῆθεν ἀνέστη
κρίνων νείκεα πολλὰ δικαζομένων αἰζηῶν,
τῆμος δὴ τά γε δοῦρα Χαρύβδιος ἐξεφαάνθη.

Finally it came to me.
At the time when the man leaves court for dinner
Having decided the numerous disputes the youths have brought
That was the time that the raft appeared out of Charybdis.

Again we see the forensic connotations carried by κρίσις in Homer. That such a meaning is already evident serves to support the suggestion that Parmenides is employing the term in a similar sense or, perhaps better, that this judicial notion informs the sense intended by Parmenides.

Just as there are two sets of σήματα, one proving the nature of Being, the other 'proving' the beliefs of mortals, so there are two kinds of κρίσις to be found in the fragments. In fact, we have one κρίσις describing a choice to be made and, consequently,

[103] Ebert (1983) 185–9 argues that early uses of κρίνειν describe acts of 'deciding' (between options or about a case) rather than 'judging'.

two alternative choices that have been made (one correct and one incorrect). First, at B7.5–6 the goddess exhorts Parmenides to make a κρίσις:

> . . . κρῖναι δὲ λόγωι πολύδηριν ἔλεγχον
> ἐξ ἐμέθεν ῥηθέντα.[104]

> . . . decide (κρῖναι) by discourse the controversial testing (ἔλεγχον) spoken by me.[105]

At B8.15–18, the goddess states that a 'decision', apparently that κρίσις she encouraged in B7, has now been made:

> . . . ἡ δὲ κρίσις περὶ τούτων ἐν τῶιδ' ἔστιν·
> ἔστιν ἢ οὐκ ἔστιν· κέκριται δ' οὖν, ὥσπερ ἀνάγκη,
> τὴν μὲν ἐᾶν ἀνόητον ἀνώνυμον (οὐ γὰρ ἀληθής
> ἔστιν ὁδός), τὴν δ' ὥστε πέλειν καὶ ἐτήτυμον εἶναι.

> . . . the decision about these things is in regard to this:
> It is or it is not; and so, it has been decided, as is necessary,
> To let alone the unthinkable, unnameable (for the road
> Is not real), and that the other is and is true.

In this case, both the mention of Δίκη in the preceding lines and the syntax of the passage suggest that here too the term κρίσις means 'decision' and κέκριται something like 'it has been decided'.

As noted above, at B8.55–56 we are told of the κρίσις made by mortals in positing their duality of forms:

> And they have distinguished (ἐκρίναντο) opposites in body and concocted signs
> Separate from one another

The mortals have made an arbitrary and erroneous choice of opposites. Having made this false choice, they go on to concoct evidence (σήματ' ἔθεντο) in favour of that choice. This concocted and arbitrary decision should be contrasted with that of B8.15–18. That decision is a result of the σήματα presented by the goddess rather than requiring that σήματα be fabricated in support of it. Some might object that, here, κρίσις does not seem to carry any obvious

104 Sextus Empiricus *Math.* 7.144.

105 The presence of ἔλεγχον in the line suggests that the most natural translation of κρῖναι is 'decide'. See Coxon (2009) 311.

judicial or forensic connotations. Rather, it looks like the kind of act of selection noted above as a common Homeric use of the term. This need not be a problem for my interpretation. I am not claiming that Parmenides always uses κρίσις (or any of the other key terms I discuss) in an explicitly and exclusively judicial sense. I simply want to suggest that there is good reason to think that this kind of forensic language is one possible influence.

(iv) ἔλεγχος

I suggested above that the meaning of κρίσις at B7.5–6 is informed by its conjunction with ἔλεγχος:

> ... decide (κρῖναι) by discourse the controversial testing (ἔλεγχον) spoken by me ...

Parmenides' use of the term ἔλεγχος is discussed in detail by Lesher, who traces its development from an origin as a term of disgrace (*Theogony* 26–27) to its Homeric meaning of a disgrace explicitly linked to failure in an athletic or military contest.[106] In Pindar, it comes to designate the test or contest itself, as at *Nemean* 8.20–21:

> πολλὰ γὰρ πολλᾷ λέλεκται, νεαρὰ δ' ἐξευρόντα δόμεν βασάνῳ
> ἐς ἔλεγχον, ἅπας κίνδυνος.[107]

> For many things have been said in many ways but, discovering new ones, to put them to the touchstone
> For testing, is utter peril.

Lesher demonstrates that, by the fifth century BC, ἔλεγχος was commonly used to refer to the test of a person's truthfulness or character. Further, he suggests that we see 'in Aeschylus' plays the first signs of a "legalized" idea of *elenchos*, the "cross-examination" or testing of a person to determine his truthfulness or innocence'.[108] If such a sense is present in Aeschylus, I see no reason to deny that Parmenides is working with a similarly 'legalized' idea of ἔλεγχος. As before, I am not suggesting that

[106] Lesher (1984) 1–30. He cites *Iliad* 11.312–315 and *Odyssey* 21.424–425.
[107] Also *Olympian* 4.17–18 and *Nemean* 3.15–17.
[108] Lesher (1984) 6, citing *Eumenides* 433 and *The Libation Bearers* 851.

Parmenides is using the term in an explicitly forensic sense. That is clearly not the case. Rather, I want to claim that, taken together with σήματα and κρίσις in the context of an account dominated by Δίκη, there is good reason to read ἔλεγχος as carrying at least a forensic undertone.

I have been emphasizing the apparent parallels between the *Doxa* and the *Aletheia*: two kinds of controlling Δίκη, two sets of σήματα, two opposed types of κρίσις. The *Doxa* lacks any explicit reference to an ἔλεγχος of its own to match that of the *Aletheia*.[109] Of course, it may be that a correlate of the *Aletheia*'s ἔλεγχος was to be found in the missing sections of the *Doxa*. One might think that B6, although it lacks an explicit reference to an ἔλεγχος, provides a disproof of mortal beliefs to match the proof of the nature of Being described by the goddess. Presumably such a disproof would be a case of putting such beliefs 'to the touchstone for testing' and, of course, finding them to be false. Another possibility is that the content of the *Doxa* is opposed to that of the *Aletheia* (whatever may have preceded the occurrence of the term at B7) insofar as it has undergone no such process of testing. Indeed, one might think that the content of the *Doxa* cannot be tested in such a way because this would lead to its immediate rejection. We have seen the arbitrary nature of both the evidence and the 'decision' constructed by mortals and recounted in the *Doxa*. These are the results of muddle-headed thinking which does not 'decide by discourse' and, perhaps, does not test itself with a process of ἔλεγχος.

(v) πίστις

πίστις occurs three times in the extant fragments.[110] At B1.30, it is used to explain what is lacking from mortal beliefs:

[109] Those who, *contra* Lesher, understand the ἔλεγχος of B7.5 to be a refutation or testing of mortal opinions such as those set out in the *Doxa* would, I take it, argue that there is in fact, no ἔλεγχος in the *Aletheia* to match that of the *Doxa*. One possibility is that ἔλεγχος can be understood as carrying the twofold sense of *both* refutation (of mortal opinions) *and* testing to prove worthwhile (of the truth).

[110] See Ch. 4 for the suggestion that Parmenides' πίστις is an allusive target of *Timaeus* 29c3.

> . . . And it is right that you should learn all things,
> Both the unmoving heart of persuasive truth
> And the beliefs of mortals, in which there is no true πίστις.

At B8.12, the goddess refers to the 'strength of πίστις':

> οὐδέ ποτ' ἐκ μὴ ἐόντος ἐφήσει πίστιος ἰσχύς
> γίγνεσθαί τι παρ' αὐτό·
>
> Nor from What-is-not will the strength of πίστις ever allow
> Anything to come to be beside it.

B8.28 describes the impossibility of Coming-to-be and Passing-away:

> αὐτὰρ ἀκίνητον μεγάλων ἐν πείρασι δεσμῶν
> ἔστιν ἄναρχον ἄπαυστον, ἐπεὶ γένεσις καὶ ὄλεθρος
> τῆλε μάλ' ἐπλάχθησαν, ἀπῶσε δὲ πίστις ἀληθής.
>
> And unchanging in the limits of great fetters
> It is without beginning and without end, since Coming-to-be and Passing-away
> Have been driven far away, and true πίστις has expelled them.

Heidel suggests an explicitly juridical interpretation, taking the term to mean 'such evidence or proof as may be adduced in court, a meaning which the word quite regularly bore in legal argumentation'.[111] Of course, πίστις certainly does come to be a rhetorical term and, just as with the other words discussed above, I think there is good reason to see a forensic influence on Parmenides' language.[112] Some have objected that Parmenides is probably not employing the explicit metaphor of a trial.[113] It may be right to reject an *explicit* metaphor but Parmenides' use of these various forensic terms certainly points towards an *implicit* engagement with such a context. Below, I will propose that Parmenides' ἐοικώς should also be read as carrying forensic connotations. I

[111] Heidel (1912–1913) 718. He cites the terms κρίσις and σήματα in support of his forensic reading.

[112] Aristotle explains πίστις as referring to a kind of rhetorical ἀπόδειξις based in persuasion rather than science.

[113] Mourelatos (2008) 150 and Lesher (1984) 17. Although Mourelatos surely cannot be right to claim that the translation '"true evidence" seems tautological' since evidence can often be used to deceive, as we saw in the case of Hermes' defence against the charges of Apollo. He points to his youth and his weakness as evidence against the fact that he could have stolen the cattle but this evidence is, of course, contrary to the truth.

will also suggest that ἐοικώς can be usefully compared to πίστις ἀληθής. Bearing this in mind, it is worth taking the time to consider Parmenides' use of πίστις in a little more detail.

Parmenides' πίστις is quite often translated as 'conviction'. Coxon, for example, takes it to describe a cognitive state, glossing its occurrence at B1.30 as 'the certainty resulting from the persuasion which reality exercises on the mind by causing it to reason deductively'.[114]

There is an alternative reading which is, I think, more in keeping with the way πίστις seems to work in B8. As Coxon describes it, πίστις is the cognitive state which results from reasoning or argument. B8.12 and B8.28, however, describe πίστις as what explains why Being is as it is. I take this to mean that it is what *justifies* the results of deductive reasoning rather than, as Coxon has it, the (justified) results themselves. When the goddess claims that true πίστις has driven away Coming-to-be and Passing-away, she is adducing something like the logical force of her arguments. There is no room for Coming-to-be and Passing-away in her account of Being, because rational argument shows them to be impossible. Bearing this in mind, I want to suggest that Parmenides' πίστις should be understood as persuasive force that an account holds, rather than as the persuasion that it induces. I think the qualification ἀληθής is significant here. I take it to indicate that the persuasive force of the *Aletheia* is genuine, i.e. that it justifies the acceptance of the account of the *Aletheia*.[115] πίστις ἀληθής represents the objective persuasive force exerted by the arguments of the *Aletheia*. As such, one suitable translation, which seems to capture the sense of compulsion identifiable at B8.12 and 28, might be 'genuine cogency'.[116]

It is worth noting that this kind of interpretation fits both the occurrences of πίστις in B8's description of Being and its

[114] Coxon (2009) 284.

[115] As Palmer (2009) 92 explains in his discussion of πίστις ἀληθής: 'confidence, trust, and assurance are "true" when they are the kind that will not be disappointed'.

[116] Mourelatos (2008) 136–63 discusses the term in detail and suggests (140) that πίστις could be translated in several ways, e.g. 'warranty', 'promise', 'commitment', 'good faith', 'compliance' or 'reliability'. He finally (204) settles on 'faith'/'fidelity' so that B1.30 is taken to mean that 'the things accredited by mortals have "no true faith in them"'.

appearance at B1.30. In the latter case, the goddess is asserting that mortal beliefs, i.e. the accounts that mortals construct for themselves, lack any kind of 'genuine cogency'. For all that mortals may tend to believe such things, they have no justification for doing so. At B8.39, the goddess asserts that mortals establish everything for themselves 'trusting (πεποιθότες) them to be true'. The content of mortal beliefs is thought by humans to be persuasive and worth believing. Mortals think that their cosmologies are true, trust in them and find them to be persuasive when in fact they are lacking in any real cogency. How can there be no conviction in these beliefs when mortals do indeed find them to be convincing? It must be that this is what is convincing for mortals, i.e. *subjectively* trustworthy. This stands in opposition to what is *truly* convincing, i.e. what convinces those who think rightly.

I will argue below that this distinction between accounts possessing real cogency (πίστις ἀληθής) and those with only subjective appeal is central to the significance of Parmenides' use of ἐοικώς. Before I do so, I want to make a case for reading Parmenides as consciously engaged with the philosophical poetry of Xenophanes. Parmenides is, in part, attempting to correct Xenophanes' fallibilist position.

Allusion to Xenophanes

I argued above that there is no good reason to resist the possibility that Parmenides is philosophically influenced by his predecessors. In fact, authors from Plato onwards suggest some kind of association between Parmenides and Xenophanes.[117] The evidence of the texts themselves also supports some kind of connection.

(i) The doxographical tradition

The dates of both Xenophanes and Parmenides are notoriously uncertain. In the case of the former, we must settle for a vague

[117] One might even suggest that, if Parmenides considered himself to have any predecessor in the genre of 'philosophical poetry', it would be Xenophanes rather than Hesiod or Homer.

birth-date around the beginning of the sixth century.[118] His own description of his longevity may justify the assumption that he lived some way into the next century.[119] For Parmenides, we have inherited two competing traditions: on the one hand, Diogenes Laertius' claim that Parmenides 'flourished' in the sixty-ninth Olympiad dates his birth somewhere around 540 BC;[120] on the other hand, Plato's *Parmenides*, by describing a meeting between a sixty-five-year-old Parmenides and a very young Socrates in *c*.450 BC, dates the birth of the older man to around 515 BC.[121] It is generally felt that Diogenes Laertius is making an arbitrary attempt to establish a date for Parmenides forty years after the foundation of Elea, a point in time connected by Apollodorus (Diogenes' source) to the *floruit* of Xenophanes.[122] The evidence of the *Parmenides* seems to be more widely preferred.

These vague possible dates obviously cannot be used either to prove or to rule out direct contact between Parmenides and Xenophanes. Nonetheless, the ancient *testimonia* claim Parmenides was a pupil of Xenophanes. At *Metaphysics* A5 986b21, Aristotle criticizes Xenophanes:

Ξενοφάνης δὲ πρῶτος τούτων ἑνίσας (ὁ γὰρ Παρμενίδης τούτου λέγεται γενέσθαι μαθητής) οὐθὲν διεσαφήνισεν.[123]

Xenophanes, the first of the monists (for Parmenides is said to have been his pupil), made nothing clear.

This relationship is seconded by Theophrastus, as cited by Simplicius:

[118] Both KRS 164 and Lesher (1992) 3 suggest 570–560 BC.

[119] Xenophanes B8 (Diogenes Laertius 9.19) makes the impressive claim that he had reached at least the age of ninety-two.

[120] Diogenes Laertius 9.21–23.

[121] *Parmenides* 127a–c.

[122] KRS 240. Mansfeld (1990a) 64–8 argues that Plato is presenting a 'pseudo-precise' date which recognizes the debt of influence to Parmenides but does not represent an accurate chronology.

[123] Guthrie (1965) 2 argues that Aristotle is qualifying this suggested relationship by attributing it to others. On this reading λέγεται would mean 'they say . . . but it probably isn't the case'. If such a reading is accepted it is unclear why Aristotle bothers to mention the possibility at all. Finkelberg (1990) 105n8 counters that 'λέγεται is regularly used in references to an established, known fact'.

μίαν δὲ τὴν ἀρχὴν ἤτοι ἓν τὸ ὂν καὶ πᾶν καὶ οὔτε πεπερασμένον οὔτε ἄπειρον οὔτε κινούμενον οὔτε ἠρεμοῦν Ξενοφάνην τὸν Κολοφώνιον τὸν Παρμενίδου διδάσκαλον ὑποτίθεσθαί φησιν ὁ Θεόφραστος . . .[124]

Theophrastus says that Xenophanes of Colophon, the teacher of Parmenides, suggests that the principle is one or that Being and the universe are one, neither limited nor unlimited, neither moving nor at rest . . .

Those who reject a significant connection between Xenophanes and Parmenides dismiss such claims as founded on a misunderstanding of a passage from Plato's *Sophist*:

τὸ δὲ παρ' ἡμῖν Ἐλεατικὸν ἔθνος, ἀπὸ Ξενοφάνους τε καὶ ἔτι πρόσθεν ἀρξάμενον, ὡς ἑνὸς ὄντος τῶν πάντων καλουμένων οὕτω διεξέρχεται τοῖς μύθοις.[125]

And the Eleatic tribe in our parts, who originate with Xenophanes or even before, spread their stories that what is called 'all things' is one.

Of course, the verity of the Stranger's claim here is more or less impossible to establish.[126] Those who doubt it tend to read this passage as ironic.[127] However, even if the *Sophist* passage is not claiming a direct relationship, it is not obvious that this justifies dismissing Aristotle's claim. To do so requires us to assume that the *Sophist* is Aristotle's only source, that Aristotle failed to get the joke and that he embellished the Stranger's claim that Xenophanes was an Eleatic into an assertion that he was Parmenides' teacher.[128]

124 Simplicius *Phys.* 22, 26.

125 *Sophist* 242d4–6. This is only the second occurrence of Ἐλεατικόν (apparently coined by Plato) to refer to the Eleatic school, as opposed to Ἐλεατής (Elean). The first is at *Phaedrus* 261d6–8.

126 It is possible that, as KRS 165 suggest, 'this remark was not necessarily intended as a serious historical judgement [. . .] as is confirmed by the addition of the words καὶ ἔτι πρόσθεν'. See Finkelberg (1990) 111n28. A consideration often overlooked by those seeking to explain away the comment of the Stranger of Elea is that he is precisely that, *from Elea*. The link between Xenophanes and Parmenides is presented as a tradition internal to Elea or perhaps even to the Eleatic school. Plato may be joking, but the question remains what the joke is. Is he poking fun at figures such as the Stranger, who may have had a tendency to represent themselves as part of a tradition going back to Xenophanes and even before?

127 See, for example, Burnet (1930) 127 and Jaeger (1947) 54n65.

128 Finkelberg (1990) 111n28 summarizes this uncharitable reading: 'with slight variations, the popular explanation runs along the following lines: in relating Xenophanes to the "Eleatic tribe" Plato was possibly joking; Aristotle probably took this remark too seriously, while Theophrastus, of course, only repeated his master's opinion'. He goes on to show how open to objection such an account must be: 'But what of the possibility that one of the actors in this comedy of doxographic errors misread his part, – for

Theophrastus and Aristotle may well be elaborating the conceptual connection of the *Sophist* into a direct apprenticeship but it is also possible that they are describing a genuine tradition. It would, I think, be misguided to attempt to argue that Xenophanes and Parmenides must have met. A less controversial suggestion is that Parmenides had access to the text or (perhaps better) content of Xenophanes' work.[129] Indeed, further evidence in favour of this possibility might be found in the tradition that has Xenophanes travelling to Sicily and being involved in the foundation of Elea.[130]

Elsewhere, we find evidence that Xenophanes was known to other philosophers. Heraclitus, whose *floruit* Diogenes Laertius dates to 504–501 BC, is clearly aware of Xenophanes:[131]

πολυμαθία νόον ἔχειν οὐ διδάσκει· Ἡσίοδον γὰρ ἂν ἐδίδαξε καὶ Πυθαγόρην αὖτίς τε Ξενοφάνεά τε καὶ Ἑκαταῖον.[132]

Learning a lot doesn't teach you to have sense. For it would have taught Hesiod or even Pythagoras or Xenophanes or Hecataeus.

Alcmaeon B1 may also show the influence of Xenophanes. Both share a scepticism regarding the human potential for certainty:[133]

περὶ τῶν ἀφανέων, περὶ τῶν θνητῶν σαφήνειαν μὲν θεοὶ ἔχοντι, ὡς δὲ ἀνθρώποις τεκμαίρεσθαι . . . [134]

The gods have certainty about what is unseen and about what is mortal, but so far as men may assume . . .

example, Plato was serious, Aristotle was not a credulous simpleton, or Theophrastus disappointingly consulted Xenophanes' verse.' Schofield (2003) 45 points out that those who insist that Parmenides and Xenophanes should be kept utterly separate are at odds with Plato and Aristotle.

129 One puzzling aspect of the standard dismissive interpretations of these *testimonia* is their insistence that any Xenophanean influence on Parmenides must be predicated on a master-pupil relationship.

130 Of course, this evidence is open to the same kind of objections as those linking Xenophanes and Parmenides, and might be dismissed as a later development in the same tradition. The fact remains that there is a tradition of Xenophanes' involvement with Elea, as Diogenes Laertius 9.18ff. demonstrates.

131 Diogenes Laertius 9.1.

132 Heraclitus B40 (Diogenes Laertius 9.1). Hussey (1990) 35n69 offers the intriguing suggestion that Heraclitus B47 is punning on ἐοικώς: μὴ εἰκῆ περὶ τῶν μεγίστων συμβαλλώμεθα. If this is Heraclitus' intention here, it might be evidence that Xenophanes B35 has already established an influence.

133 See 56–7.

134 Diogenes Laertius 8.83.

Alcmaeon is generally dated to the first half of the fifth century.[135] If both Alcmaeon and Heraclitus were aware of Xenophanes, I see no good reason to insist that he was unknown to Parmenides.[136]

In the end, however, the best evidence for Xenophanes' influence on Parmenides is to be found in the extant fragments.

(ii) The evidence of the texts

For all that allusions are difficult things to prove, I am by no means the first person to suggest a connection between Xenophanes' theology and Parmenides' metaphysics.[137] It has even been claimed that Xenophanes' god is the 'immediate pattern' for Parmenides' Being.[138] The first potential parallel is to be found in the stability of the *descripta*:

αἰεὶ δ' ἐν ταὐτῶι μίμνει κινούμενος οὐδέν
οὐδὲ μετέρχεσθαί μιν ἐπιπρέπει ἄλλοτε ἄλλῃι.

(Xen. B26)

αὐτὰρ **ἀκίνητον** μεγάλων ἐν πείρασι δεσμῶν
ἔστιν ἄναρχον ἄπαυστον, ἐπεὶ γένεσις καὶ ὄλεθρος
τῆλε μάλ' ἐπλάχθησαν, ἀπῶσε δὲ πίστις ἀληθής.
ταὐτόν τ' ἐν ταὐτῶι τε μένον καθ' ἑαυτό τε κεῖται
χοὔτως ἔμπεδον αὖθι μένει· κρατερὴ γὰρ Ἀνάγκη
πείρατος ἐν δεσμοῖσιν ἔχει, τό μιν ἀμφὶς ἐέργει,
οὕνεκεν **οὐκ ἀτελεύτητον τὸ ἐὸν θέμις εἶναι·**
ἔστι γὰρ οὐκ ἐπιδευές· μὴ ἐὸν δ' ἂν παντὸς ἐδεῖτο.

135 KRS 339 are circumspect in suggesting that Alcmaeon 'perhaps wrote in the early fifth century'. Longrigg (1993) 51 proposes the second quarter of the fifth century. Guthrie (1962) 357–8 offers a date of some time after 510 BC.

136 Inwood (2001) 23 has no such reticence in suggesting that Empedocles was influenced by Xenophanes: 'Geographical proximity and a probable allusion [at Empedocles B39] show that Xenophanes' popular poetry was familiar to Empedocles.' Inwood also argues that Empedocles' 'vivid and fantastic image of divinity as a limbless "thought-organ" unmistakably links him to Xenophanes' theology, just as surely as the unified cosmic sphere reveals the influence of Parmenides' description of the one being'.

137 The similarity is recognized as significant by, among others, Guthrie (1965) 2, Fränkel (1975) 350, KRS 241 (although the relation is dismissed as 'superficial' at 165), Popper (1998) 17 and 121n58, Lesher (1999) 230, Palmer (1999) 193, Schofield (2003) 44 and Coxon (2009) 327.

138 Coxon (2009) 297.

He always remains in the same place, not moving at all
Nor is it appropriate for him to go to different places at different times.

(Parm. B8.26–33)
And unmoving in the limits of great fetters
It is without beginning and without end, since Coming-to-be and passing-away
Have been driven far away, and true cogency has expelled them
Remaining the same and in the same it lies by itself
And thus stands fast. For powerful Necessity
Holds it in bonds of limit, circumscribing it,
Because it is not right that Being is incomplete
For it does not lack; Not Being would lack everything.

Xenophanes' god does not move, for to do so would not be fitting (οὐδὲ . . . ἐπιπρέπει). Likewise, the motionlessness of Parmenides' Being is connected to the completeness dictated by what is right (θέμις). In fact, as has been noted, Parmenides' use of the term ἀκίνητον and the phrase ταὐτόν τ' ἐν ταὐτῶι τε μένον look very much like a 'reformulation' of Xenophanes' description of god in B26. Indeed, for Coxon, Parmenides B8.29 is 'the most substantial ground in the extant fragments of both writers for treating [Xenophanes] as in any sense his [sc. Parmenides] precursor'.[139] There are, I think, further grounds for positing a Xenophanean influence on Parmenides. Both Xenophanes' god and Parmenides' Being are in some sense 'whole' (οὖλος):

οὖλος ὁρᾶι, οὖλος δὲ νοεῖ, οὖλος δέ τ'ἀκούει.
(Xen. B24)

. . . μόνος δ' ἔτι μῦθος ὁδοῖο
λείπεται ὡς ἔστιν· ταύτηι δ' ἐπὶ σήματ' ἔασι
πολλὰ μάλ', ὡς ἀγένητον ἐὸν καὶ ἀνώλεθρόν ἐστιν,
οὖλον μουνογενές τε καὶ ἀτρεμὲς ἠδὲ τελεστόν
οὐδέ ποτ' ἦν οὐδ' ἔσται, ἐπεὶ νῦν ἔστιν ὁμοῦ πᾶν,
ἕν, συνεχές.
(Parm. B8.1–6)

139 For Coxon (2009) 329, the difference between the two phrases is important: '[Parmenides'] transformation of Xenophanes' view however is more significant than his imitation of it. His substitution of ταὐτόν for Xenophanes' αἰεὶ is itself significant; P[armenides] uses αἰεί only of temporal duration (fr.15), never of the now which characterizes Being.'

Whole he sees, whole he thinks, whole he hears.

. . . only the story of the road
That is still remains; on this there are signs
Great in number, *that* what-is is ungenerated and imperishable,
Whole, unique, unmoving and complete.
It never was nor will be, since it is now all the same,
One, continuous.

The similarity here is not limited to the wholeness of the two *descripta*. Note that Parmenides' Being is both 'whole' and 'unique' (μουνογενές). Now, whilst no straightforward parallel for the latter word appears in Xenophanes, B23 does seem to describe a unique god, insofar as he describes his god as 'one' and 'greatest':

εἷς θεός, ἔν τε θεοῖσι καὶ ἀνθρώποισι μέγιστος,
οὔτι δέμας θνητοῖσιν ὁμοίιος οὐδὲ νόημα.[140]

One god, greatest among gods and men,
Not at all the same as mortals in body or in thought.

The *combination* of 'whole' and 'unique' (οὖλον μουνογενές) in Parmenides B8.4 can also plausibly be read as evidence for a Xenophanean influence.[141] The formula 'whole, unique' can be taken as evidence of the homogeneity of Parmenides' Being.[142] Similarly, Xenophanes B24's description of god's perception ('whole he sees') seems to imply that god is some kind of common sensorium, with the further implication that he is homogeneous.[143]

Taken individually, these potential parallels may be thought insufficient to establish a connection between Xenophanes and

[140] Clement *Str.* 5.109.

[141] I follow Coxon in preferring the text of the beginning of B8.4 attested by Simplicius, Clement and Philoponus (see DK 235) against that of Plutarch *adv. Col.* 1114C: ἐστι γὰρ οὐλομελές. Plutarch's text would provide better evidence of a link with Xenophanes. Popper (1998) 75 argues (in reference to B16) that Parmenides' μέλος is properly understood as a sense organ rather than as a limb. If this is the case and Parmenides describes his Being as some kind of 'whole-sense-organ', the similarity to Xenophanes' god, which senses and thinks as a whole, is striking (implying that this reading of the text may have been influenced by a wish to produce a link to Xenophanes B24). The same connection can be made for the emendation suggested by Wilson (1970) 32–4 and adopted by Gallop (1984) 64: οὖλον μουνομελές.

[142] As can B8.22's description of Being as 'all the same' (πᾶν ἔστιν ὁμοῖον).

[143] Finkelberg (1990) 117–21 states that homogeneity is not an attribute of Xenophanes' god 'on its own merits' but an 'implicit corollary' of the fact that it perceives as a whole. He goes on to argue that the doxographic attribution of homogeneity to Xenophanes' god is the result of a 'Parmenidizing' reading.

Parmenides. Taken together and in the light of the doxographical tradition linking the two, they provide rather good evidence that Parmenides was somehow engaged with and influenced by Xenophanes' theological teachings.[144] In the next section, I will pursue the possibility that Parmenides may also be engaged with Xenophanes' epistemological teachings. This possibility seems all the more likely when one bears in mind that, for Xenophanes, epistemology is inseparable from theology. It would, I think, be rather difficult for Parmenides to react to Xenophanes' talk of god without simultaneously getting to grips with his talk of knowledge and opinion. I want to suggest that Parmenides is attempting to engage with and correct Xenophanes' epistemic pessimism with a view to reading B8.60's use of ἐοικώς as, in part, a critical allusion to Xenophanes B35.[145]

Corrective epistemology

In the previous chapter, I noted that Xenophanes limits humans to opinions. I argued that this limitation is not, as some have suggested, applicable only to questions of theology and natural science. Mortals are, by their very nature, incapable of achieving certainty about anything. Of course, Xenophanes B34 does pick out theology as an area about which no man can ever know and, as we have just seen, Parmenides' Being shares many of the significant qualities of Xenophanes' god: it is stable, whole and unique. Nonetheless, Parmenides' epistemological outlook is rather more positive, albeit only in certain respects. The goddess promises Parmenides that he will learn the truth about Being (B1.28–32). Throughout her exposition, she directs his thinking towards its proper object, with the implication that choosing the correct route of inquiry (B6.3), employing reason to judge her testing (ἔλεγχος: B7.5) and recognizing her evidence (σήματα) for the nature of Being (B8.2) will bring Parmenides knowledge. Engaging his mind in this way elevates him to the status of the 'man who knows'

144 Palmer (2009) 350 suggests it would be 'perverse' not to admit some kind of influence.

145 For an alternative account of Parmenides' response to Xenophanes' epistemology, see Mogyoródi (2006) 154–7.

(B1.3: εἰδότα φῶτα). For Parmenides, human nature need be no obstacle to knowledge because his emphasis is not on the nature of the 'knower' but on the nature of what can be known.[146]

In this way, Parmenides demonstrates a greater optimism than Xenophanes with regard to mortals' capacity to have certainty. If they focus their reasoning on the nature of what is and cannot not be (B2.3), they too can learn the 'steadfast heart of persuasive truth'. Such optimism is, however, limited. Whilst mortals may have the capacity to reason their way to certainty (if they reason about the right sort of thing), they *tend* to stray onto the wrong path, populated as it is by unsuitable objects of cognition (B8.38–41; 53–59). In fact, both Parmenides and Xenophanes attribute opinion to mortals and, in both cases, those opinions are set over Coming-to-be rather than Being:

ἀλλ' οἱ **βροτοὶ** δοκέουσι **γεννᾶσθαι** θεούς,
τὴν σφετέρην δ' ἐσθῆτα ἔχειν φωνήν τε δέμας τε.
(Xen. B14)

. . . τῶι πάντ' ὀνόμασται,
ὅσσα **βροτοὶ** κατέθεντο πεποιθότες εἶναι ἀληθῆ,
γίγνεσθαί τε καὶ ὄλλυσθαι, εἶναί τε καὶ οὐχί,
καὶ τόπον ἀλλάσσειν διά τε χρόα φανὸν ἀμείβειν.
(Parm. B8.38–40)

Xenophanes claims that mortals have opinion (δοκέουσι) about the Coming-to-be (γεννᾶσθαι) of the gods. The introductory ἀλλά, when read against the theological fragments B23–36, implies that such beliefs are false. Likewise, Parmenides' mortals have mere opinion about the objects they set up for themselves as real. B1.30 tells us that such beliefs are lacking in truth.[147] Parmenides'

[146] Coxon (2009) 19: 'Xenophanes however claimed for his theology no higher certainty than that of belief founded on moral or religious fitness, and denied that human beings can have knowledge of the divine. Parmenides sought to counter his scepticism by considering the nature of assertion and by showing that the characteristics which Xenophanes ascribed conjecturally to God, together with others, must be asserted of a transcendent subject not "probably" but necessarily and that, so far from human beings having no knowledge but only belief about such a reality, it was the only subject of which knowledge was possible. Parmenides' affirmation of the possibility of human knowledge enabled him to reformulate in turn the criterion of right belief as that which was "like the truth" in a different sense from that envisaged by Xenophanes.'

[147] The possibility that there is a more direct relation between the two texts is supported by the fact that, in addition to their thematic similarity, the term βροτοί occurs in the same position in both hexameters. LSJ 331 define βροτός as 'mortal man', whose mortality is conceptually opposed to that of an ἀθάνατος or θεός. Both Xenophanes and Parmenides use the term as shorthand for the limitations placed on man's epistemological potential.

mortals have opinions because they think about the wrong sort of things. If they were to think (rightly) about the right sort of things, i.e. about the unchanging, unqualified Being described in the *Aletheia*, they could achieve certain knowledge. In this, Parmenides' object-centred epistemology differs from the subject-centred pessimism of his predecessor. For Xenophanes, mortals have beliefs about Coming-to-be *because* they are mortal. I suggested in Chapter 1 that this is because they are limited to thinking about anything *from a certain perspective* in a way that god is not. For Parmenides, mortals have *false* beliefs about Coming-to-be *because* those beliefs are *about* Coming-to-be, rather than because their human nature forces them to think about anything in a particular way. Indeed, I take it that the *Aletheia* represents the goddess's encouragement to Parmenides to think about Being in the right way. Xenophanes claims that one's nature restricts the kind of cognition one can have; Parmenides presents the possibility of knowledge as dictated by the object about which one thinks.

The difference between these two epistemologies is best illustrated by their divergent attitudes towards revelation and inquiry. As I argued in the previous chapter, Xenophanes denies divine revelation and sets up inquiry as a route to discovering 'better' (B18).[148] It is inquiry alone that promises (limited) epistemological progress. Parmenides' goddess also champions inquiry but, of course, insofar as she is a goddess, this recommendation is presented as a revelation:

οὔτοι ἀπ' ἀρχῆς πάντα θεοὶ θνητοῖσ' ὑπέδειξαν,
ἀλλὰ χρόνωι ζητοῦντες ἐφευρίσκουσιν ἄμεινον.
(Xen. B18)
The gods have not revealed, from the outset, everything to mortals,
But, by searching, in time, they discover better.

εἰ δ' ἄγ' ἐγὼν ἐρέω, κόμισαι δὲ σὺ μῦθον ἀκούσας,
αἵπερ ὁδοὶ μοῦναι διζήσιός εἰσι νοῆσαι·
(Parm. B2.1–2)[149]
Come, I'll tell you, and you listen and pay heed to my words,
Which are the only roads of inquiry to be thought.

The revelatory framework of Parmenides' poem can be read as a relatively optimistic response to Xenophanes' epistemic

However, whilst Xenophanes assumes that it is the nature of βροτοί to have beliefs rather than knowledge, Parmenides makes clear that these limitations are self-imposed and unnecessary.

148 See 52–5. 149 Simplicius *Phys.* 9.116. See also B6.3; B7.2.

pessimism.[150] Xenophanes attributes to mortals a necessary lack of certainty whilst Parmenides, by reinstating divine revelation, is offering the possibility of certainty for those humans who think rightly about Being. Here again, we see the difference between Xenophanes' subject-centred and Parmenides' object-centred epistemologies.[151] For Xenophanes to reject revelation, as he does at B18, is to reinforce the claim that mortals have no access to certainty. Revelation, as the medium of communication between gods and men, represents the possibility that divine knowledge is in some sense accessible for mortals. To allow revelation would thus serve to undermine Xenophanes' total separation of divine and human cognition. According to Xenophanes, such epistemological traffic is not possible and, accordingly, revelation is denied. Parmenides appears to have no such qualms about the possibility of interaction between human and divine understanding.

I want to suggest that Parmenides is deliberately collapsing the division between revelation and inquiry set up by Xenophanes.[152] By incorporating talk of inquiry within a revelatory framework, he demonstrates that, since the proper objects of inquiry are the same for god and man, our mortal nature need be no bar to knowledge. The truth expressed by the goddess in the *Aletheia* is what should properly be regarded as true by mortals, for all that they tend to

150 Lesher (2008) 473–4 appears to read Parmenides as championing active inquiry over the passive acceptance of revelation. If I am right to suggest (see 63) that revelation often requires a certain degree of interpretation, we can see how Parmenides might think inquiry and revelation fit together.

151 One interesting, if speculative, comparison can be made with regard to the way that the two philosophers employ the term τετελεσμένον. At B34.3, Xenophanes employs the Homeric formula τετελεσμένον εἰπών to express the idea that mortals, even if they hit upon the truth, could not know that their belief has been fulfilled and thus is true. At B8.42, Parmenides describes Being: αὐτὰρ ἐπεὶ πεῖρας πύματον, τετελεσμένον ἐστί (I follow DK and Mourelatos (2008) 123n24 in retaining the comma after ἐστί and thus taking this clause as a separate idea from that beginning πάντοθεν). Perhaps, by labelling his object of knowledge 'completed', Parmenides is echoing the Xenophanean claim that the object of certainty is that which is known to be completed. He is claiming that his Being is τετελεσμένον and that we are able to share in the knowledge of this completion possessed by the goddess. Such completed entities are correctly set under knowledge rather than belief, but that is not to say that they must be beyond the cognitive scope of mortals.

152 Guthrie (1965) 51 argues that Parmenides' divine teacher is an evocation of Hesiod's muses. See also Morgan (2000) 68. There is an important enough difference between the multiple muses and this singular goddess to suggest that Parmenides is deliberately altering the Hesiodic model.

convince themselves of other 'truths' (B8.39–41). Insofar as this truth is objective, we can follow the goddess in recognizing it as such. The truth is no different in the human and divine realms.[153] In fact, humans do *tend* to have no more than belief, but that is not to say that they *can* have no more than belief. Parmenides' truth may be expressed by a goddess, but her interaction with Parmenides symbolizes his rejection of the limits attributed to human nature by Xenophanes.[154]

Of course, in one respect, Xenophanes might be thought more optimistic than Parmenides. Xenophanes B34 and B35, as I argued in Chapter 1, indicate that humans, although limited to belief, may well hit upon the truth. B35 classifies (or recommends) Xenophanes' teachings as plausible but necessarily uncertain candidates for the truth. Parmenides, in contrast, appears to claim that the majority of human beliefs, because they are set over something other than what is and cannot not be, are false (B1.30; 8.51–52). Xenophanes offers us the possibility of achieving the truth about Coming-to-be; Parmenides appears to deny that there is such a thing. What Xenophanes denies us is the opportunity to *know* that we have achieved the truth; Parmenides offers such certainty, but only in thinking about Being. Xenophanes offers mortals (nothing more than) a partial success in their intellectual endeavours whilst Parmenides champions human epistemological potential, if not their general cognitive tendencies.[155]

Conclusion

I have argued for the importance of two aspects of Parmenides' poem. First, several of his key terms carry forensic connotations.

153 Chalmers (1960) 21 claims that the gap between the two worlds, in the sphere of both epistemology and metaphysics, is bridged by divine agency. This is partly true, insofar as divine agency is the means of bridging the gap set up by Xenophanes but with the ultimate intention of showing that gap to be non-existent.

154 Schofield (2003) 61 proposes that Parmenides' regards his goddess as representing the 'logical space' in which he can consider and express radically differing perspectives. See also Schofield (1987) 356–9. Sedley (1999) 114 suggests that the goddess represents the divine viewpoint which Parmenides has attained for himself through argument.

155 See Graham (2006) 176.

Second, the doxographical and textual evidence supports reading Parmenides as critically engaged with Xenophanes' philosophy. In making my case, I may seem to have strayed rather far from my avowed aim of investigating the meaning of Parmenides' use of ἐοικώς. In fact, as I now hope to show, both aspects can usefully inform our understanding of B8.60–61.

In summarizing the various possible interpretations of Parmenides' ἐοικώς, I argued that the lack of an explicit dative need not rule against the suggestion that B8.60 is, in part, an allusion to Xenophanes B35. The fact that Parmenides' description of Being seems to carry explicit echoes of Xenophanes' positive theological fragments is, I take it, evidence in favour of such an allusive reading of B8.60. Indeed, if Parmenides B8.60 is alluding to Xenophanes B35, the import of the allusion may well be located in the way that Parmenides alters the Xenophanean formula. It may be, as I suggested above, that the *absence* of a dative is itself significant. Further, bearing the Xenophanean background in mind, it may be that the absence of the *specific* dative τοῖς ἐτύμοισι is important here. On this kind of interpretation, Parmenides is alluding to Xenophanes' claim that his account is similar to the truth, i.e. to Xenophanes' suggestion that his teachings are possibly but uncertainly true. However, by withholding the complement τοῖς ἐτύμοισι, Parmenides is indicating that his cosmology *does not* possess this kind of similarity to the truth.

Some may wonder why Parmenides would want to allude to a relationship to truth that he denies for his own account. My answer is twofold. First, I take it that this is intended as a criticism of Xenophanes' claim that it may be possible to hit upon the truth (albeit necessarily uncertain truth) about Coming-to-be. Parmenides' omission of τοῖς ἐτύμοισι indicates his belief, *contra* Xenophanes, that truth is only achievable if one thinks about the right kind of object, namely Being. Second, it may be that Parmenides is emphasizing, via his allusion to Xenophanes B35, the clear similarities that hold between the *Aletheia* and the *Doxa*. In discussing the forensic connotations of Parmenides' vocabulary, I noted a tendency for a term to be employed in both parts of the poem. Thus we have a Justice of the *Aletheia* (who holds Being) and a Justice of the *Doxa* (who directs Coming-to-be and

Passing-away). Similarly, we have two sets of σήματα and two kinds of κρίσις. There seems to be a relationship of 'similarity-with-a-difference', as Mourelatos has called it, between the *Aletheia* and the *Doxa*, whereby aspects of the account of Being are echoed and altered in the cosmology.[156] My suggestion is that Parmenides' ἐοικώς, in alluding to Xenophanes' claim that his account is similar to the truth, is indeed describing the similarity between the *Aletheia* and the *Doxa*. However, by omitting τοῖς ἐτύμοισι, Parmenides is simultaneously indicating the unbridgeable difference between these two parts of his poem. For, whilst the *Doxa* may be in some sense similar to the *Aletheia*, it can never itself be true, since it describes Coming-to-be rather than Being.[157]

What of the forensic influence? I have noted that the use of ἐοικώς in connection with arguments from probability can be traced back to the Homeric *Hymn to Hermes*. I have also suggested that Pindar's *Pythian* 1 may provide a possible, roughly contemporaneous parallel for ἐοικώς carrying the sense 'plausible'. The juridical connotations of Parmenides' Δίκη, σήματα, κρίσις, ἔλεγχος and πίστις encourage me to propose that his ἐοικώς is similarly informed. So, in addition to its representing an allusion to Xenophanes B35's 'similar', I read Parmenides' ἐοικώς as incorporating the rhetorical sense 'plausible'.

In cashing out this Parmenidean plausibility, it will be useful to bear in mind both the Xenophanean and the forensic backgrounds. When discussing the translation 'plausible' above, I noted that there seems to be some inconsistency in the fact that the goddess both warns Parmenides that the *Doxa* is deceitful and seems to recommend it as plausible. I suggested that this apparent inconsistency can be dissolved by reading the plausibility of the *Doxa* as subjective. It is now possible to consider this subjectivity in a little more detail. The goddess's claim that the cosmology is ἐοικώς is not an assertion that Parmenides should himself find it plausible and thus come to believe it. The goddess is not labelling the account objectively trustworthy. Rather, she is indicating that the cosmology to be offered is plausible to some, perhaps most, mortals. This is, of course, not equivalent to the claim that it *should* be found

156 See Mourelatos (2008) 222–63.

157 On the similarity see 111–12.

plausible or to a recommendation that Parmenides should believe it to be true.[158] Thus, the goddess's assertions of the deceptiveness and the plausibility of her account stand together. Parmenides can recognize that the *Doxa* is plausible to some and that it deceives some without himself being persuaded and deceived by it.

I have argued that there are two sets of evidence (σήματα) in Parmenides' poem and that one set, i.e. that mentioned at B8.55, is claimed to be fabricated by mortals to support their arbitrary choice of a particular pair of opposites. My suggestion is that the plausibility of the διάκοσμος which sets out such fabricated evidence is the kind of subjective persuasiveness possessed by accounts concocted in this way. The διάκοσμος ἐοικὼς πᾶς of the *Doxa* is plausible to those people who think, as Xenophanes does, that one can speak the truth about Coming-to-be. It is the kind of account that would be found plausible by wrong-headed mortals. It is not the kind of account that right-thinking mortals such as Parmenides should find persuasive.

It will be useful here to draw a contrast between the πίστις ἀληθής denied to mortal beliefs in the *Proemium* and the claim that the account of these beliefs is ἐοικώς. I have suggested that πίστις ἀληθής should be read as expressing the genuine cogency possessed by deductive arguments about the nature of Being. What is ἐοικώς, however, is *plausible* but *deceptive*. Cosmologies such as that of the *Doxa* possess this latter type of subjective plausibility but lack any kind of genuine cogency. With the *Doxa*, then, the goddess is giving a plausible account of typical mortal beliefs which stands in opposition to the properly convincing and cogent argument of the *Aletheia*. On this reading, ἐοικώς is not a word of recommendation. The *Doxa* may be a subjectively plausible cosmology. It may even be the most subjectively plausible of such cosmologies. It would not, however, be found convincing by anyone who understands the truth as set out by the goddess. We, if we have knowledge, should not be persuaded by the *Doxa* or by any such cosmologies because they do not possess such genuine

158 Heitsch (1974) 416 suggests that the *Doxa* is *subjectively* deceptive but *objectively* plausible. On my reading, it is both *subjectively* deceptive and *subjectively* plausible. It deceives only those whom it persuades. Parmenides and those who, like him, have followed the proofs of the *Aletheia* will find the *Doxa* neither plausible nor deceptive.

cogency. Such accounts do not justify the faith that mortals place in them. They are merely subjectively plausible and thus, for all that they may possess the power to persuade, i.e. to deceive, those who are ignorant, they should not persuade those who recognize them as no more than specious fabrications.

I take it to be a point in favour of this reading that it sets up a connection between the end of the *Proemium* and the end of the *Aletheia*. At B1.31, as we have seen, the goddess proclaims that the opinions of mortals contain no 'genuine cogency' (πίστις ἀληθής). Later, at B8.28, we are told that this 'genuine cogency' has expelled Coming-to-be and Passing-away. So, 'genuine cogency' is a quality possessed by the arguments of the *Aletheia*, whilst the quality of being ἐοικώς belongs to the 'opinions' of mortals. How are we to understand this contrast? Well perhaps we can think of πίστις ἀληθής and ἐοικώς as a pair of forensic terms. 'Genuine cogency' is a quality possessed by arguments which present genuine evidence and which reason from this evidence to justified and certain conclusions; 'plausibility' is a quality possessed by arguments in support of which one needs to cook up the evidence and which are trusted to be true despite their lack of proof.[159]

On this reading, Parmenides would be drawing a distinction analogous to the *nomos–phusis* contrast familiar from the second half of the fifth century BC.[160] The *Aletheia* describes Being and what truly exists. The *Doxa* gives an account of the kind of beliefs mortals set up as conventions irrespective of this truth. The goddess is condemning mortals for privileging convention over nature, plausibility over truth.

A similar attitude towards human beliefs can be identified in Heraclitus B1:

τοῦ δὲ λόγου τοῦδ' ἐόντος ἀεὶ ἀξύνετοι γίνονται ἄνθρωποι καὶ πρόσθεν ἢ ἀκοῦσαι καὶ ἀκούσαντες τὸ πρῶτον· γινομένων γὰρ πάντων κατὰ τὸν λόγον τόνδε ἀπείροισιν ἐοίκασι, πειρώμενοι καὶ ἐπέων καὶ ἔργων τοιούτων, ὁκοίων

[159] At *Rhetoric* 1.1.1355a3–18, Aristotle presents probability arguments as a subset of πίστεις. Even if this schema predates Aristotle, the suggested contrast can stand. It may be that both πίστις ἀληθής and ἐοικώς are subsets of unqualified πίστις.

[160] See Kerferd (1981) 111–30. Note his assertion (111) that 'central to the meaning of the term [*phusis*] is the static concept of "the way things are"'. Being in the *Aletheia* is both static and, of course, 'the way things are'.

ἐγὼ διηγεῦμαι κατὰ φύσιν διαιρέων ἕκαστον καὶ φράζων ὅκως ἔχει. τοὺς δὲ ἄλλους ἀνθρώπους λανθάνει ὁκόσα ἐγερθέντες ποιοῦσιν, ὅκωσπερ ὁκόσα εὕδοντες ἐπιλανθάνονται.[161]

Although this account holds forever, men ever fail to comprehend, both before hearing it and once they have heard. Although all things come to pass in accordance with this account, men are like the untried when they try such words and works as I set forth, distinguishing each according to its nature and telling how it is. But other men are oblivious of what they do awake, just as they are forgetful of what they do asleep.[162]

Kahn interprets λόγος as referring both to Heraclitus' subjective account, as expressed in his own words, and to the eternal, objective truth represented by those words.[163] Whereas Heraclitus claims to give a correct account, contrasting it to what Kahn calls the 'incompetent response of mankind', Parmenides' goddess gives both the truth (in the *Aletheia*) and the 'incompetent response' (in the *Doxa*). I argued above that, for Parmenides, mortality is no barrier to certainty (as long as one considers the appropriate object, namely Being). In this regard at least, Heraclitus offers a similarly optimistic epistemology. Some men are oblivious to what they do when awake but others, such as Heraclitus, can see reality as it is.[164]

Insofar as I read Parmenides' ἐοικώς as multifaceted, it accommodates each of the various translations that have been offered elsewhere: 'similar', 'plausible', 'specious' and 'appropriate'. I see no reason to rule against any of these possibilities and, in fact, it seems perfectly conceivable that Parmenides is adducing aspects of each. As a critique of Xenophanes' claim that we can achieve truth about Coming-to-be, it alludes to the sense 'similar'. On the one hand, the absence of the dative τοὶς ἐτύμοισι indicates the lack of truth in the *Doxa*. On the other hand, the allusion to Xenophanes' formula may point towards the fact that there are similarities-with-differences between the *Doxa* and the *Aletheia*. Via this allusion, Parmenides' ἐοικώς expresses that the *Doxa* is

161 Sextus Empiricus *Math.* 7.132.

162 Kahn's (1979) translation.

163 Kahn (1979) 96–100.

164 Kahn (1979) 99 describes the 'almost pathetic epistemic isolation of a man trying to convey the vision of an obvious and immediate truth to men who stagger past, unable to notice what they are doing all day long'.

both *similar* to the truth of the *Aletheia*, insofar as it shares terminology, and *different* from the truth, insofar as it is not true. This occurrence of ἐοικώς also, I have argued, incorporates the sense 'plausible'. This plausibility is the persuasive appeal it has to those people who privilege the unsatisfactory evidence of sense-perception as described in the *Doxa*, as opposed to the cogency of the arguments presented in the *Aletheia*.[165] Since the plausibility of the *Doxa* does not result from its truth, but merely its subjective appeal to wrong-headed mortals, room can also be found for the sense 'specious'. The account appeals to mortals only because they have the wrong end of the stick about the cosmos.

In some respects, I am arguing for an interpretation of Parmenides' ἐοίκως that is very similar to Mourelatos' claim that it indicates that the *Doxa* is 'probable' to 'uninitiated mortals' but 'seeming' (in the sense of 'specious') to the goddess and Parmenides.[166] In fact, my reading of B8.60 seeks to unite this interpretation with another aspect of Mourelatos' account of the *Doxa*, namely the suggestion that it bears a relation of 'similarity-with-a-difference' to the *Aletheia*.[167] As far as I am aware, Mourelatos does not draw an explicit connection between the description of the *Doxa* as ἐοικώς and its relation to the *Aletheia*. My claim is that reading B8.60 as an allusion to Xenophanes allows us to do so.

What of the translation 'appropriate'? This too can be incorporated into the sense of Parmenides' ἐοικώς. It may be that the *Doxa* is appropriate insofar as it is representative of the kind of cosmologies that mortals produce.[168] Or it may be that it is appropriate to the purpose for which the goddess exhorts Parmenides to listen to her cosmology, namely that hearing it will ensure that he is not 'outstripped' by any mortal opinion. Of course, this suggestion raises the notoriously difficult question of the purpose of the *Doxa*.[169] How will hearing a cosmology that is plausible but

[165] B7 seems to suggest that sense-perception is the source of mortal error.
[166] See 74–5. [167] See 106.
[168] Which is not to say that it is simply a systematic account of contemporary cosmologies, as suggested by Burnet (1930) 185–7.
[169] See, for example, Long (1963), Mackenzie (1982) and Graham (2006) 172–4 for discussion of the purpose of the *Doxa*.

specious, like the truth but not itself true, ensure that Parmenides is not 'outstripped'? Why does the goddess devote the majority of her poem to the falsehoods of the *Doxa*? I have argued that the meaning of Parmenides' ἐοικώς is multifaceted. If I am right about this, it should be possible to explain the purpose of the *Doxa* in a way that takes account of this ambiguity.

B8.61 implies that hearing the cosmology of the *Doxa* will act as some kind of prophylactic. The *Doxa* is an extended cosmology along the lines of those that mortals tend to produce to suit their own wrong-headed preferences.[170] It seems clear that Parmenides is intended to learn something from this account. But what more is there to learn beyond the nature of Being as has been described in the *Aletheia*? Perhaps hearing the *Doxa* will serve to reinforce the truth of the *Aletheia*. One possibility is that recognizing and tracing the *Doxa*'s relationship of 'similarity-with-a-difference' to the *Aletheia* will be in some sense educative.[171] It may be that, in assessing in what ways the *Doxa* systematically diverges from the *Aletheia*, Parmenides can both reaffirm the arguments of the *Aletheia* and increase his understanding of how and why mortals tend to err. If the *Doxa* is 'appropriate' insofar as it is the best account possible, it may be that Parmenides is being asked to recognize where even this best account fails. One suggestion is that the cosmology of the *Doxa* goes wrong only in positing one too many things, so that there are two basic principles rather than one.[172] On this reading, the *Doxa* is as much like the *Aletheia* as a pluralist cosmology can get (it is only wrong by one) whilst also being different from the *Aletheia* (it is false).

It is worth flagging up one notable case of 'similarity-with-a-difference' between the subject-matter of the *Aletheia* and that of the *Doxa*. At B8.29–34, the goddess describes the unchanging nature of Being:

> ταὐτόν τ' ἐν ταὐτῶι τε μένον καθ' ἑαυτό τε κεῖται
> χοὔτως ἔμπεδον αὖθι μένει· κρατερὴ γὰρ Ἀνάγκη

[170] Mourelatos (2008) 240 suggests that the *Doxa* is designed simultaneously to appeal to those mortals who know no better and to explain their wrong-headedness to Parmenides.

[171] Mourelatos (2008) 261 calls the *Doxa* a 'commentary' on the *Aletheia*.

[172] See Owen (1960) 54 and Sedley (1999) 123–5.

πείρατος ἐν δεσμοῖσιν ἔχει, τό μιν ἀμφὶς ἐέργει,
οὕνεκεν οὐκ ἀτελεύτητον τὸ ἐὸν θέμις εἶναι.

Remaining the same and in the same it lies by itself
And thus stands fast. For powerful Necessity
Holds it in bonds of limit, circumscribing it,
Because it is not right that Being is incomplete.

The language of B10.5–7's promise of cosmological instruction is strikingly similar:

... εἰδήσεις δὲ καὶ οὐρανὸν ἀμφὶς ἔχοντα
ἔνθεν ἔφυ τε καὶ ὥς μιν ἄγους' ἐπέδησεν Ἀνάγκη
πείρατ' ἔχειν ἄστρων.[173]

And you will know the surrounding sky
Whence it came to be and how Necessity guided it and bound it
To hold the limits of the stars.

In the *Aletheia*, the goddess explains that Necessity dictates that Being is complete and thus 'holds it in the bonds of limit' (πείρατος ἐν δεσμοῖσιν ἔχει). In the *Doxa*, we are told that Necessity has caused the sky 'to hold the limits of the stars' (πείρατ' ἔχειν ἄστρων). There are clear parallels between these two passages, but there are also obvious differences. For whilst B8 describes an *unchanging* entity bound and circumscribed by Necessity itself, B10 describes how Necessity has caused the sky to *come to be* the thing which surrounds and limits the cosmos. This is, I think, the kind of 'similarity-with-a-difference' signified by Parmenides' use of ἐοίκως. How one seeks to interpret this kind of parallel will, of course, depend on one's reading of the metaphysics of the *Aletheia*.[174] For my purposes, what is significant is that the multifaceted sense of ἐοίκως provides a framework within which one should consider the relation between the details and language of the *Doxa* and the *Aletheia*.

173 Clement *Str*. 5.14, 138.

174 See, for example, Palmer (2009) 183 who emphasizes the similarities between the two passages, arguing that they 'strongly suggest that the two [i.e. Being and the cosmos] are coterminous and, therefore, that What Is and the perceptible cosmos are envisioned as occupying the same space'. See Coxon (2009) 356–7 for the suggestion that B10 represents Parmenides' 'derivation of physical from metaphysical and logical necessity'.

On the one hand, then, Parmenides will learn what it is that mortals tend to find plausible, i.e. the kind of accounts they tend to produce. On the other hand, he will learn what is wrong with such accounts, i.e. why they are merely specious. In a sense, the unjustified plausibility of the *Doxa* provides an instructive contrast to the genuine cogency of the *Aletheia*. On this reading, B8.60–61 represents an exhortation along the following lines: 'I will present the following cosmology as a fitting example of the kind of account that mortals tend to regard as plausible. I do so in order that you may, by recognizing its speciousness, understand that and why such accounts should hold no appeal for you, a man who knows the truth.'

CHAPTER 3

PLATO'S *TIMAEUS*

Introduction

Plato's *Timaeus* opens with a conversation between Socrates and three companions, Critias, Timaeus and Hermocrates. This group are meeting for the second day in a row. On the previous day, Socrates described the best kind of constitution and citizen.[1] He also, it seems, assigned homework to his audience; today, he expects them to repay his speech with their own. At 19c2–8, Socrates expresses his desire to hear a speech describing his theoretical city 'in competition with other cities'. The three companions have conspired and worked out a plan for their response. In the section 21a7–26e1, Critias gives a précis of his intended offering of a 'Solonic' story of Athens at war with the erstwhile power of Atlantis. Before he gives this account in full, however, Critias announces that Timaeus is to give his own speech:

ἔδοξεν γὰρ ἡμῖν Τίμαιον μέν, ἅτε ὄντα ἀστρονομικώτατον ἡμῶν καὶ περὶ φύσεως τοῦ παντὸς εἰδέναι μάλιστα ἔργον πεποιημένον, πρῶτον λέγειν ἀρχόμενον ἀπὸ τῆς τοῦ κόσμου γενέσεως, τελευτᾶν δὲ εἰς ἀνθρώπων φύσιν·

We thought that Timaeus, as the best astronomer among us and someone who has made it his particular business to know about the nature of the universe, should speak first, beginning from the Coming-to-be of the cosmos, and ending with the nature of man.

From 27c1 onwards, with the exception of one brief interjection from Socrates at 29d4–6, the *Timaeus* is a cosmological monologue. Timaeus presents a description of the cosmos' creation by a divine craftsman, a Demiurge, as a likeness of an eternal model. He sets out his reasons for thinking that the cosmos has come into

[1] As has often been noted, his summary of this description, from 17c6–19a9, is notably reminiscent of the *Republic*. See Ch. 4 n24.

being in this way in the *proemium* of his cosmology (29b1–d3).[2] There, he also makes a notorious claim about the status of his cosmology. Timaeus claims first that the status of accounts is related to the status of their subject-matter. He goes on to note, frustratingly briefly, that his own account, being of a likeness (εἰκών), will be 'likely' (εἰκώς):

τούτων δὲ ὑπαρχόντων αὖ πᾶσα ἀνάγκη τόνδε τὸν κόσμον εἰκόνα τινὸς εἶναι. μέγιστον δὴ παντὸς ἄρξασθαι κατὰ φύσιν ἀρχήν. ὧδε οὖν περί τε εἰκόνος καὶ περὶ τοῦ παραδείγματος αὐτῆς διοριστέον, ὡς ἄρα τοὺς λόγους, ὧνπέρ εἰσιν ἐξηγηταί, τούτων αὐτῶν καὶ συγγενεῖς ὄντας· τοῦ μὲν οὖν μονίμου καὶ βεβαίου καὶ μετὰ νοῦ καταφανοῦς μονίμους καὶ ἀμεταπτώτους, καθ' ὅσον[3] τε καὶ ἀνελέγκτοις προσήκει λόγοις εἶναι καὶ ἀνικήτοις, τούτου δὲ[4] μηδὲν ἐλλείπειν·[5] τοὺς δὲ τοῦ πρὸς μὲν ἐκεῖνο ἀπεικασθέντος, ὄντος δὲ εἰκόνος εἰκότας ἀνὰ λόγον τε ἐκείνων ὄντας·[6] ὅτιπερ πρὸς γένεσιν οὐσία, τοῦτο πρὸς πίστιν ἀλήθεια. ἐὰν

2 Socrates refers to Timaeus' introduction as a προοίμιον at 29d4–6.

3 Following Archer-Hind (1888) 88–9 in adopting the text of the Vienna MS (Y) and omitting οἷόν, which he suggests 'may have arisen from a duplication of ὅσον'. He suggests that 'some corruption has clearly found its way into this sentence' but that, by the omission of οἷόν, it 'becomes perfectly grammatical'. Archer-Hind translates: 'therefore of that which is abiding and sure and discoverable by the aid of reason the words too must be abiding and unchanging and so far as it lies in words to be incontrovertible and immovable, they must in no wise fall short of this'. In contrast, Cornford (1937) 23 renders Burnet's text (retaining οἷόν) with an explicit parenthesis: 'an account of that which is abiding and stable and discoverable by the aid of reason will itself be abiding and unchangeable (so far as it is possible and it lies in the nature of an account to be incontrovertible and irrefutable, there must be no falling short of that)...' Mourelatos (2010) emphasizes what he takes to be the parenthetical nature of this clause.

4 Reading, with P, δὲ rather than δεῖ. See 119–27 below for further discussion of the prescriptive nature of Timaeus' words.

5 Stallbaum (1888) 117–18 has: τοῦ μὲν οὖν μονίμου καὶ βεβαίου καὶ μετὰ νοῦ καταφανοῦς μονίμους καὶ ἀμεταπτώτους καὶ καθ'ὅσον οἷον τε ἀνελέγκτους προσήκει λόγους εἶναι καὶ ἀκινήτους, τούτου δὲ μηδὲν ἐλλείπειν· Cook Wilson (1889) 102–3 notes that Stallbaum takes τούτου δὲ μηδὲν ἐλλείπειν as referring to 'the whole condition μονίμους καὶ ἀμεταπτώτους καὶ ἀνελέγκτους καὶ ἀκινήτους εἶναι'. But Cook Wilson argues, 'we get an excellent sense if τούτου refers to μονίμου καὶ βεβαίου. "The arguments which deal with what is lasting and stable, must in no way be inadequate to it (τούτου δὲ μηδὲν ἐλλείπειν), but be themselves like it, lasting and stable (μονίμους καὶ βεβαίους)."' Cook Wilson translates the sentence as explicitly prescriptive ('must') but follows Stallbaum in preferring δὲ to δεῖ. He also suggests that the genitives μονίμου καὶ βεβαίου are governed not by τοὺς λόγους in the previous clause, but by ἐξηγηταί. On this reading, the accounts' status as exegetes of their subject-matter would, I take it, be of central explanatory value to the fact that they share the qualities of their subject-matter. Taylor (1928) 74 rightly rejects this reading.

6 Archer-Hind (1888) 88 (following Stallbaum): τοὺς δὲ τοῦ πρὸς μὲν ἐκεῖνο ἀπεικασθέντος, ὄντος δὲ εἰκόνος, εἰκότας ἀνὰ λόγον τε ἐκείνων ὄντας. The extra commas formally separate the likeness and likelihood to which Timaeus refers. The proximity of εἰκών and εἰκώς indicates a significant connection between the two ideas, as reflected in

οὖν, ὦ Σώκρατες, πολλὰ πολλῶν πέρι, θεῶν καὶ τῆς τοῦ παντὸς γενέσεως, μὴ δυνατοὶ γιγνώμεθα πάντῃ πάντως αὐτοὺς ἑαυτοῖς ὁμολογουμένους λόγους καὶ ἀπηκριβωμένους ἀποδοῦναι, μὴ θαυμάσῃς· ἀλλ' ἐὰν ἄρα μηδενὸς ἧττον παρεχώμεθα εἰκότας, ἀγαπᾶν χρή, μεμνημένους ὡς ὁ λέγων ἐγὼ ὑμεῖς τε οἱ κριταὶ φύσιν ἀνθρωπίνην ἔχομεν, ὥστε περὶ τούτων τὸν εἰκότα μῦθον ἀποδεχομένους πρέπει τούτου μηδὲν ἔτι πέρα ζητεῖν.

These things being so, it is necessarily the case that this cosmos is an image of something. It is of the utmost importance to start everything from its natural starting point. And so, with regard to both an image and its model, this distinction should be drawn: that accounts are kin of the subject-matter of which they are interpreters. So, accounts of what is permanent and stable and evident with the help of reason are stable and permanent, insofar as it is appropriate for accounts to achieve irrefutability and incontrovertibility and not to fall short of this standard, but accounts of that which is created to be like that [which is stable and unchanging], being of a likeness,[7] are likely and stand in proportion to those others.[8] As Being is to Coming-to-be so truth is to convincingness. So if, Socrates, we turn out frequently to be unable to produce accounts on a variety of topics, namely the gods and the coming-to-be of the universe, which are entirely mutually consistent and accurate in every way, don't be surprised. But if we supply accounts no less likely than any other's[9] we should be content, bearing in mind that I as a speaker and you, sitting in judgement, possess a human nature, so that it is fitting that we should accept the likely story about these matters and search for nothing more.

Can the link between εἰκών and εἰκώς be anything more than a philosophically insignificant pun? There seems to be no obvious reason to think that an account of a likeness should be classed

Archer-Hind's own translation: 'but those [accounts] which deal with that which is made in the image of the former and which is a likeness *must* be likely and duly corresponding with their object' (my emphasis).

7 The genitive participle ὄντος εἰκόνος is sometimes taken as causal. Zeyl (2000) 15 translates 'since they are accounts of what is a likeness'. Brisson (2001) 117 has 'parce qu'il s'agit d'une copie'.

8 Taylor (1928) 74 and Archer-Hind (1888) understand ἐκείνων as referring to the subject-matter of likely accounts. A preferable alternative, which reflects the tendency of ἐκεῖνος to mean 'the former', is to read ἐκείνων as the stable accounts. Certainly, the plural ἐκείνων is more satisfactorily taken as referring to the plural stable accounts of b7 than the singular subject-matter of c1–2.

9 Following Burnyeat's (2005) 148n13 suggestion that μηδενὸς should be read as masculine. Burnyeat is influenced by the possibility that this line, in connection with the reference to mortality, provides an echo of Parmenides' goddess's assertion that she offers her plausible ordering 'so that no opinion of mortals shall ever outstrip you'. The possibility that Timaeus' *proemium* alludes to Parmenides is one for which I will argue in Ch. 4.

as 'likely' or 'plausible' in contrast to the stability and transparency to reason attributed to accounts of stable originals. Rowe has expressed what looks, at first glance, to be the most immediate problem with Timaeus' link between likeness and likelihood:

> why should something's being an *eikôn* of something else entail that any account of that something must be no more than an *eikôs* account of it (the something)? If I make a drawing of a person, then it seems just as possible to give an accurate and truthful account of the drawing, as it does of the subject of the drawing.[10]

Clearly, Rowe is correct. It is indeed possible for one to make statements about the portrait of Simmias that are at least as accurate as those that one can make about Simmias himself. One can, for example, describe the portrait's colouring and dimensions with as much accuracy as one can state that Simmias is a character in Plato's *Phaedo* and is long dead.[11]

In order to understand why Plato has Timaeus make this seemingly odd methodological and epistemological claim, and thus to save him from the charge of indulging in empty word-games, we need to consider the meaning of the term εἰκώς as it is used in the *Timaeus*. In the discussion above, I translated εἰκώς as 'likely', which, when paired with 'likeness', happily reflects the semantic connection between εἰκώς and εἰκών that Plato clearly wants to exploit.[12] Much remains to be said, however, about what this so-called 'likelihood' actually is. Is εἰκώς being used in some technical and specifically Platonic sense?[13] Is it similar to Xenophanes B35 in claiming that his account is potentially true but lacking in certainty? Or does it echo Parmenides' denigration of cosmology as possessing no more than subjective persuasiveness?

10 Rowe (2003) 28.

11 Note that the accuracy of such statements about a likeness will be independent of the accuracy of the likeness *qua* representation.

12 Meyer-Abich (1973) 23 champions the translation 'likeness-likely' as similar to the German idea that 'Natur' must be described by a 'natürliche' account. He goes on to suggest that εἰκώς combines the senses 'plausible' and 'natural'. I assume that the latter emphasizes the status of the account as about the physical world. See Burnyeat (2005) 146–7 for further discussion of the suitability of various translations. Patterson (1985) 30–1 notes that the term εἰκών is used by Plato to refer to all kinds of images, including comparisons and similes.

13 Howald (1922) 67 asserts that the term is undoubtedly technical, developed by Plato as part of a broader project of establishing a philosophical terminology.

With the aim of clarifying the nature of the connection between εἰκών and εἰκώς, I will begin with an analysis of Timaeus' methodological *proemium*. What sense can be made of Timaeus' claim that accounts are συγγενεῖς of their subject-matter? I will argue that it is the status of the subject-matter as a likeness, rather than as changing and unstable Coming-to-be, that is significant for the likelihood of an εἰκώς λόγος.[14] I will also support the view that Timaeus is setting positive standards at which those who seek to describe the cosmos should aim, rather than diagnosing the deficiency of such accounts.[15] In this chapter, my treatment of Timaeus' methodological comments will focus on the first half of the passage, from 29b1 to 29c2. In the chapter that follows, I will turn to the section which runs from 29c3 to 29d3, in which Timaeus describes the relation between accounts of the stable model and those of its likeness and introduces the notion of a 'likely' μῦθος. Before attempting any explication of this second passage, it is necessary to have a clear understanding of the likelihood-claim to which it is connected.

I will consider three kinds of interpretation of Timaeus' claim to likelihood. The first two treat εἰκώς as expressing a deficiency, either of certainty or of truth. The last is a more positive reading but, I think, fails to pay sufficient attention to the link between likeness and likelihood explicitly set up by Timaeus.

I will go on to propose that, in the *Timaeus*, Plato employs εἰκώς in an original and technical manner founded in the term's etymological link to εἰκών. I want to suggest that this etymological connection is evidence in favour of a more positive interpretation of εἰκώς than has generally been considered. I do not want to insist that Timaeus' εἰκώς can never be read as expressing the traditional sense of 'likely' as a synonym of 'plausible'. However, I do want

[14] I follow Vlastos (1965a) 380–3 and Rowe (2003) 27 in reading the label εἰκώς as more significant than the fact that Timaeus also calls it a μῦθος (at, for example, 29d2 and 68d2). The 'mythic' status of Timaeus' cosmology has excited much interest. See, for example, Morgan (2000) 271–81. For the purposes of the present discussion, the text justifies considering the εἰκότες accounts to which Timaeus refers as λόγοι, since the distinction (διοριστέον) drawn at 29b3ff. is explicitly between two kinds of λόγοι, and not between λόγοι and μῦθοι. The significance of the label μῦθος will be scrutinized in Ch. 4.

[15] Following Burnyeat (2005). See 137–9 below.

to argue that it should also be understood as 'likely' *primarily* in a sense fundamentally informed by the connection to εἰκών. In Chapter 2, I argued that Parmenides' use of εἰκώς is complex and ambiguous. It would, of course, be perverse to deny that Plato is equally capable of such subtlety and complexity. The aim of this chapter, however, is simply to offer an adequate explanation of Timaeus' association of 'likeness' and 'likelihood'.[16] I will argue that interpreters of the *Timaeus* have been led astray by the hostility that Plato demonstrates towards τὸ εἰκός in dialogues such as the *Phaedrus* and *Theaetetus*. Rather than signalling that his account is somehow deficient, Timaeus' εἰκώς-claim should be understood as indicating, at least primarily, that it *successfully* relates the status of its *descriptum* as a likeness. For an account to be 'likely' in this sense is for it adequately to explain the nature of its subject-matter as having been likened to a model. An εἰκώς account will thus explain the way in which the likeness has been influenced by the nature of the model. I will go on to examine some of the passages, other than the *proemium*, in which Timaeus refers to his cosmology as εἰκώς and argue that these instances can profitably be read as reminders that Timaeus is, in giving a likely account, aiming to offer an account of the cosmos *as a likeness*.

Finally, I will suggest that this interpretation of Timaeus' εἰκώς-claim reflects a Platonic desire to emphasize the positive relation that holds between the perceptible world and the intelligible realm. Rather than driving a wedge between the two worlds, Plato is seeking to emphasize the value of the cosmos as modelled on the Forms.

The συγγενεῖς-relation

Fundamental to the εἰκών–εἰκώς connection established by Timaeus is his assertion that accounts are kin (συγγενεῖς) of

[16] On my interpretation, any plausibility possessed by the account will derive from, rather than coincide with, its status as 'likely'. Thus, an account of a portrait will be likely if it succeeds in describing the portrait as a likeness of its model. The account will be plausible only if this 'likely' account is perceived as convincing. Just as an account can, and often is, true, but nevertheless judged implausible, so an account might succeed in being likely without convincing anyone that it should be accepted.

their subject-matter. This is a strange suggestion that has attracted nowhere near as much attention as it deserves.[17] I hope to clarify it in two ways. The first involves a scrutiny of the context in which Timaeus presents the συγγενεῖς-claim. The second is via a consideration of potential Platonic parallels adducing a link between the status of a λόγος and that which it describes.

The συγγενεῖς-claim is immediately preceded by the assertion that 'with regard to both an image and its model, this distinction should be drawn' (ὧδε οὖν περί τε εἰκόνος καὶ περὶ τοῦ παραδείγματος αὐτῆς διοριστέον).[18] It is worth emphasizing that the distinction (or, as Zeyl translates, 'specification') to be made is with reference to the likeness and its paradigm, rather than to Being and Coming-to-be. Also worth noting is that this distinction looks to be prescriptive rather than descriptive. Timaeus is not saying that accounts are classified according to their subject-matter but that the status of the *descriptum* as either likeness or model will or, rather, should influence the status of the description.

The prescriptive nature of the συγγενεῖς-claim is made clear by the manner in which the distinction is introduced by the assertion that 'it is of the utmost importance to start everything from its natural starting point' (μέγιστον δὴ παντὸς ἄρξασθαι κατὰ φύσιν ἀρχήν).[19] Some have taken this 'natural starting point' to refer to the distinction itself. On this reading the sense of the passage is

[17] As Burnyeat (2005) 149 notes, interpreters, once they have translated the line, tend to 'proceed as if nothing extraordinary has been said'. See, for example, Morgan (2000) 271 who, notwithstanding her interest in the adequacy of language to express reality, simply asserts that 'words are interpreters, related to what they describe'.

[18] The most satisfactory reading of this verbal adjective is 'the distinction must be made', i.e. between accounts of the image and those of its model. This sense is clearly preferable to Bury's (1929) 53 'we must affirm'. Taylor (1928) 74 has 'we must lay it down that discourses are akin in character to that which they expound'. Throughout the *Timaeus*, cognates of διορίζω are used to refer to acts of either mental or physical 'distinguishing'. At 54b, for example, we are told that greater accuracy is required about the elements than has previously been offered: τὸ δὴ πρόσθεν ἀσαφῶς ῥηθὲν νῦν μᾶλλον διοριστέον. See also 38c6, 45a5, 51b7, 52c1, 68e6 and 69e6.

[19] Taylor (1928) 73–4 notes that two readings of this line are possible. The first takes it to be a fairly specific claim: 'most important in the whole matter is to start from the natural beginning'. Proclus *In Timaeum* 1, 337–338, however, understands it as more generally applicable: 'the most important thing in every case is to start from the natural beginning' (with παντὸς depending on ἄρξασθαι). Since Timaeus is, as Taylor notes, presenting a 'general rule of method', the latter reading is preferable. Cicero *Timaeus* 157b also opts for the general reading: 'difficillimum autem est in omni conquisitione rationis exordium.'

something along the lines of: 'The most important thing in every case is to start from the natural beginning. In this case the natural beginning is to make the following distinction . . .'[20] Now, on this interpretation, it is unclear why Timaeus would regard his distinction as the natural (κατὰ φύσιν) starting point for his cosmology. My preference, therefore, is for a reading that makes more of the description of the starting point as 'natural'.[21] I take the lines to mean 'The most important thing in every case is to start from (or identify) the natural beginning. We must make the following distinction in order to ensure that we recognize what are the natural starting points for different kinds of accounts. A stable object is the starting point of a stable account . . .' Read in this fashion, 29b2–5 acts as an exhortation to pay attention to the nature of the things we describe and to ensure that our accounts share that nature. I thus follow Burnyeat in reading Timaeus' *proemium* as a prescription for how to compose accounts rather than a classification of already existing λόγοι:[22] We should aim, when talking about a likeness, to produce an account which shares the status of its subject-matter, i.e. which is 'likely'. Burnyeat writes:

Stability and irrefutability are not automatic consequences of the accounts' having a stable and unchanging subject matter. Rather, they are standards the accounts are expected to live up to. The point is not that you cannot go wrong when expounding a stable unchanging subject matter, e.g. that you cannot make a

20 Burnyeat (2005) 149 prefers this reading: 'Now in any matter it is most important to begin at the natural beginning. Accordingly [i.e. this is our beginning], we should make the following distinction concerning a likeness and its model.'

21 The need to begin one's enquiries with a consideration of the nature of the subject-matter is first signalled by Timaeus at 28b4–7. He begins his cosmology by noting that the cosmos has come-to-be. 29b1ff. restates the need to consider the nature of the subject-matter in the light of the preceding argument that it has come-to-be by being modelled on an eternal paradigm.

22 Burnyeat (2005) 150 follows Burnet in reading δεῖ rather than δὲ. He translates accordingly: 'On the one hand, accounts exegetic of that which is permanent and stable and manifest to reason are themselves permanent and unchangeable: to the extent that it is possible and fitting for accounts to be irrefutable and invincible, there ought [δεῖ] to be no falling short of this.' Burnyeat emphasizes the δεῖ in order to make his case for a prescriptive reading. This emphasis is perhaps unnecessary once we realize that Timaeus is describing the necessary link between the subject-matter and a *successful* description of those things. It is not true that every attempt to describe a stable entity will be irrefutable, but a wholly successful description would be. Correspondingly, a *successful* description of a likeness will be likely, which is to say that a necessary condition of successfully describing a likeness is that the account is likely.

mistake in mathematics (like the slave in the *Meno*) or when talking about the Forms (like Socrates in the *Parmenides*). Of course you can. But you ought not to. If you do, you are falling short of the standards required for successful exegesis *of such things* [. . .] Being εἰκώς will not be an automatic consequence of undertaking the exegesis of the likeness, still less a depressing consequence of speaking about the physical world at all. Rather, it will be an *aspiration* that Timaeus' discourse will try to live up to, as a standard to judge it by.

I agree with Burnyeat that 'being εἰκώς will not be an automatic consequence of undertaking the exegesis of the likeness'. It will, rather, be a necessary condition of producing a successful account of a likeness. Stability and irrefutability will likewise be necessary conditions of a successful account of what is stable and unchanging.[23]

It remains to be seen just what counts as a successful likely account of a likeness. Before proceeding, however, it is worth briefly considering the description of λόγοι as both συγγενεῖς and ἐξηγηταί. Proclus takes the συγγενεῖς-connection between the account and its subject-matter to be obvious, stating that 'it is necessary that an account is of the same kind (ὅμοιον) as things. For it couldn't interpret (ἐξηγήσαιτο) the nature of things other than by being akin (συγγενῶς) to them.'[24] Unfortunately, the matter is not as straightforward as Proclus suggests. Burnyeat notes that 'exegete' everywhere else in Plato refers to a person, rather than an account. In the *Laws*, for example, the term refers to those who interpret the laws, in particular the religious laws of the state.[25] Influenced by this fact, Burnyeat argues that the use of the term ἐξηγηταί signifies that the accounts Timaeus is discussing 'are very special accounts personified as the exegetes who expound or explain the unobvious significance of an object like a dream, ritual or oracle which does not bear its meaning on its surface, because it comes from, or has some important connection with, the divine'.[26]

[23] Of course, Timaeus' *caveat* at 29b7–c1 suggests that such a stable account may be impossible to achieve.

[24] Proclus *In Timaeum* 1, 341. He seems to understand this relation as causal.

[25] See, for example, *Laws* 759c7 and 775a2. See also *Republic* 4, 427c2–3 and *Euthyphro* 4c8.

[26] Note, however, that ἐξηγούμενοι occurs at *Cratylus* 407b1 as describing an act more like literary interpretation than divine explanation (although, admittedly, the poetry being interpreted is about Athene).

Burnyeat's spiritual emphasis is attractive and I can offer no better explanation of Plato's choice of terminology.[27] However, the description of λόγοι as συγγενεῖς further complicates the matter. This term too signifies a personification of the accounts: they are the 'kin' of their subject-matter.[28] It is difficult to see how these notions of kinship and divine interpretation are intended to work together. Perhaps we need say no more than that Plato is personifying the λόγοι and deliberately proclaiming a strong connection between their status and that of their subject-matter.[29]

What is the nature of this connection? Here are two possible ways of reading the συγγενεῖς-claim. A weak reading of 29b4–5 takes it as doing little more than acknowledging that accounts are about their subject-matter and, as such, can be described in a way that reflects this relationship. For example, a treatise about horses can be labelled 'equine' whilst a description of a painting can be called 'artistic'. The label applied to the account reflects its subject-matter and thus is informative of the account's nature. However, it is only informative in a qualified sense, insofar as it indicates no more than what the account is about. An 'equine' account is not 'equine' in the same sense as its subject-matter; it does not eat oats or neigh. Equally, a treatise about art can be described as 'artistic', but, in itself, may be less than aesthetically pleasing. So perhaps all that Timaeus implies by his claim that accounts are συγγενεῖς of their subject-matter is something along these lines: λόγοι of stable subjects can be described as 'stable' insofar as they are about what is stable, whilst those about likenesses can be described as 'likely', implying nothing more about their natures than that they are about likenesses.[30]

[27] For a secularized interpretation, see Betegh (2010) 216–17.

[28] LSJ 1659–60: συγγενής with the genitive tends to express blood-kinship (being the kin of) rather than merely being 'akin to' or 'of like kind'. Thus Gregory (2000) 251 translates: 'accounts [. . .] will be of the same family as the things they expound'. For a similar usage see 31a1, where Timaeus notes the kinship that holds between the Living Thing that is the cosmos and those living things that it contains. Blood-kinship is a much stronger relationship than the merely being 'akin to'. Compare the use of συγγενεῖς with the dative at 47b8, d2, and 90c8.

[29] See *Phaedo* 89b9–c1 for another example of the personification of λόγοι.

[30] Plato has fun with this kind of weak relation at *Euthydemus* 284d–285a. Ctesippus claims that those who speak the truth are those who speak about the things *as they are*, so that the good speak 'ill' (κακῶς) of 'the evil' (τοὺς κακούς), Euthydemus wonders if

Such a weak reading of 29b4–5 would, I take it, render Timaeus' claim to likelihood non-contentious. On this line of interpretation, he is asserting nothing more than that his account is about something, namely a likeness. He is not claiming that accounts of likenesses are uncertain. Indeed, he is not making any kind of claim about its epistemological status or veridicality and thus is not open to the kind of criticism set out above.[31]

When one considers the way that Timaeus talks about the stable and permanent accounts of stable subjects, it soon becomes clear that such a reading is too weak. For, at 29b7–c1, he makes it clear that he is describing a relation between the nature of the stable subject-matter and the nature of its description. The label 'stable and permanent' (μονίμους καὶ ἀμεταπτώτους) is not applied to such λόγοι simply as indicative of their subject-matter but rather as descriptive of their own nature as stable and permanent. This point is made explicit by the qualification that Timaeus offers to the effect that such accounts can only be stable and permanent 'insofar as it is appropriate for accounts to achieve irrefutability and incontrovertibility and not to fall short of this standard'. Timaeus is talking about the stable nature of λόγοι rather than simply about the fact that they describe something with a stable nature. Equally, the label 'εἰκώς' implies something far more fundamental than just that an account is about an εἰκών.

Clearly, the text requires a stronger reading, for all that this opens it up to criticism. Timaeus is claiming that an 'account borrows its character from the nature of its subject matter'.[32] In fact, he states that accounts are 'kin' (συγγενεῖς) of their subject-matter. It will prove worthwhile briefly to consider the Platonic background for the link between an account and that which the account describes.

The most obvious parallel for the idea that λόγοι derive their status from their subject-matter is found in the *Cratylus*. At 430b1–e1, Socrates declares that, as 'imitations' (μιμήματα), names are (or should be) like (ὅμοιον) the things that they name. At 439a1–3, he exclaims:

'They also speak greatly of the great and warmly of the hot?' to which Ctesippus replies 'I know that they speak frigidly of the cold, and call their way of arguing frigid'(τοὺς γοῦν ψυχροὺς ψυχρῶς λέγουσί τε καὶ φασὶν διαλέγεσθαι).

[31] See 117 above. [32] Carone (2005) 25–6.

Ἔχε δὴ πρὸς Διός· τὰ δὲ ὀνόματα οὐ πολλάκις μέντοι ὡμολογήσαμεν τὰ καλῶς κείμενα ἐοικότα εἶναι ἐκείνοις ὧν ὀνόματα κεῖται, καὶ εἶναι εἰκόνας τῶν πραγμάτων;

Stop for Heaven's sake! Haven't we agreed more than once that names which are rightly given are like (ἐοικότα) the things named and are images (εἰκόνας) of them?

Clearly, the idea that linguistic expressions somehow share in or mimic the status of their subject-matter is not restricted to the *Timaeus*. Names (ὀνόματα) are likenesses (μιμήματα or εἰκόνες) of what they describe. Indeed, *Critias* 107b5–e3 tells us that λόγοι too are likenesses of their subject-matter:

μίμησιν μὲν γὰρ δὴ καὶ ἀπεικασίαν τὰ παρὰ πάντων ἡμῶν ῥηθέντα χρεὼν που γενέσθαι· [. . .] ἐκ δὴ τοῦ παραχρῆμα νῦν λεγόμενα, τὸ πρέπον ἂν μὴ δυνώμεθα πάντως ἀποδιδόναι, συγγιγνώσκειν χρεών· οὐ γὰρ ὡς ῥᾴδια τὰ θνητὰ ἀλλ' ὡς χαλεπὰ πρὸς δόξαν ὄντα ἀπεικάζειν δεῖ διανοεῖσθαι.

I suppose that all the accounts we give must be likenesses and representations (μίμησιν . . . καὶ ἀπεικασίαν) . . . The account I give, presented as it is off the cuff, should be forgiven if it fails to offer a wholly proper representation; for it is essential to bear in mind that mortal objects are far from easy, in fact, they are difficult to represent (ἀπεικάζειν) in a fashion in line with opinion.

It is worth noting that, in both the *Critias* and, in particular, the *Cratylus*, the connection between names and accounts and the objects of their naming or description is explicitly one of resemblance or likeness. λόγοι share the status of what they describe by being, in some sense, a likeness of that thing.[33] Indeed, the *Cratylus* suggests that it is a criterion of a word's success that it is like that to which it refers. Consequently, it would seem that an account should only be considered to describe something (accurately) if it shares that thing's nature.

Clearly, the relationship between the nature of λόγοι and that of their subject-matter is more than a passing fancy of the *Timaeus*.[34] The *Cratylus* hints that such a relationship is necessary for names and, by extension, λόγοι, if they are to describe their subjects

[33] Halliwell (2002) 47–8 describes the '"primary" representation existing in the fabric of human language and thought' which incorporates artistic *mimesis* as a kind of 'secondary' representation.

[34] Ashbaugh (1988) 141n11 asserts, without elaboration, that the link between an account and its subject-matter dates back to Homer.

successfully.[35] It thus supports the reading of the συγγενεῖς-claim that I have set out above as a necessary condition of a successful account. Bearing this necessity in mind, it is almost time to consider the explanations that have previously been given of Timaeus' claim to likelihood. At this point, however, it is worth making one further, very important observation about the connection that Timaeus draws between likely account and likeness. A typical approach to 29b5–c3 seems to be as follows:

(i) Timaeus ascribes stability, certainty and (29c3) truth to accounts of stable originals.
(ii) Timaeus ascribes likelihood to accounts of likenesses.
(iii) Timaeus asserts that likely accounts are ἀνὰ λόγον to stable accounts, elaborating this point with the proportion: 'Being is to Coming-to-be as truth is to convincingness' (29c3).
(iv) Likenesses are deficient in comparison with their originals and, analogously, likely accounts are deficient in comparison to stable accounts.
(v) Conclusion: therefore, likely accounts must lack one or all of the qualities of stable accounts, i.e. they are unstable, uncertain, untrue, or all of these.

Clearly, (i) and (ii) are justified by the text. I will go on to argue below that (iv) is mistaken in emphasizing the negative, rather than the positive, implications of the notion of likeness. For now, however, it is worth considering how well (iii) really represents what Timaeus says:

So, accounts of what is permanent and stable and evident with the help of reason are stable and permanent, insofar as it is appropriate for accounts to achieve irrefutability and incontrovertibility and not to fall short of this standard, but accounts of that which is created to be like that [which is stable and unchanging], being of a likeness, are likely and stand in proportion to those others.

Timaeus' assertion is not the general claim that 'accounts of likenesses are likely and stand in proportion to stable accounts.' His claim is much more specific. He says that (successful) accounts of what has been likened to (i.e. created as a likeness of) *the stable original*, being of a likeness, will (a) be likely and (b) stand in

[35] Socrates applies the descriptive requirement to statements as well as names and verbs at *Cratylus* 431a7–c2.

proportion to stable accounts of the stable original. One must be exceptionally careful not to conflate (a) and (b) for the following reason: (a) is applicable to *all* accounts of likenesses (or accounts of all likenesses). Meanwhile, (b) is applicable only to accounts of something *likened to a stable original*.[36] In order for (b) to be generally applicable it would have to make the less specific assertion that 'accounts of likenesses, being of likenesses, will stand in proportion to accounts of their originals'.

Interpretations of Timaeus' εἰκώς

In discussing rhetorical, primarily forensic, means of persuasion, Christopher Carey makes the following observation:

> Common to all speakers is the basic need to secure the goodwill of the hearer. The speaker will often use the *proemium* to lay claim to qualities which the audience will respect, or stress the disadvantages of his situation as a claim to sympathy.[37]

Of course, Timaeus is offering cosmology rather than apology.[38] Nevertheless, it is worth considering whether his *proemium* represents an appeal for pity in difficult circumstances or an attempt to impress upon his audience the authority of his account.[39] Is Timaeus pleading for his audience to show leniency in their judgements because, through circumstances beyond his control, he is limited to *mere* likelihood? Or is he championing his account as possessing the *merit* of being 'likely'?[40]

36 29c3 will be likewise limited in scope. I postpone discussion of what it means for these accounts to stand in proportion to accounts of the original until Ch. 4.

37 Carey (1994) 27.

38 Although, as Johansen (2004) 52 notes, Timaeus' appeal to his audience as κριταί at 29d1 may be an invitation to the reader to think of the εἰκώς arguments employed in the law courts. Note that Timaeus' reference to κριταί here may be a reference to Critias' promise at 27a6–b6 to introduce the subjects of his account into 'our courtroom and make them citizens' (εἰσαγαγόντα αὐτοὺς ὡς εἰς δικαστὰς ἡμᾶς ποιῆσαι πολίτας). See 165–6.

39 See Capra (2010) 205–6 for the suggestion that Timaeus' *proemium* is intended to echo the form and vocabulary of epic.

40 Or, as Zeyl (2000) xxxiii suggests, both: 'The use of the word "likely" thus reflects both the limitations (it is no more than likely) and the validity (it is no less than likely) of the account.'

Most readers of the *Timaeus* have understood the claim to likelihood as an admission of some kind of deficiency in the cosmology. This negative tendency is hardly surprising when one considers what Plato has to say about τὸ εἰκός in dialogues other than the *Timaeus*. At *Phaedrus* 267a6–7, Socrates notes that Tisias and Gorgias 'saw that likelihoods are more to be honoured than truths' (πρὸ τῶν ἀληθῶν τὰ εἰκότα εἶδον ὡς τιμητέα μᾶλλον), with the implication that rhetoric tends to sacrifice truth in order to maximize persuasiveness. *Theaetetus* 162e2–163a1 draws a more explicitly critical contrast between proof and likelihood:

καὶ ἃ οἱ πολλοὶ ἂν ἀποδέχοιντο ἀκούοντες, λέγετε ταῦτα, ὡς δεινὸν εἰ μηδὲν διοίσει εἰς σοφίαν ἕκαστος τῶν ἀνθρώπων βοσκήματος ὁτουοῦν· ἀπόδειξιν δὲ καὶ ἀνάγκην οὐδ' ἡντινοῦν λέγετε ἀλλὰ τῷ εἰκότι χρῆσθε, ᾧ εἰ ἐθέλοι Θεόδωρος ἢ ἄλλος τις τῶν γεωμετρῶν χρώμενος γεωμετρεῖν, ἄξιος οὐδ' ἑνὸς μόνου ἂν εἴη. σκοπεῖτε οὖν σύ τε καὶ Θεόδωρος εἰ ἀποδέξεσθε πιθανολογίᾳ τε καὶ εἰκόσι περὶ τηλικούτων λεγομένους λόγους.

And whatever the crowds want to hear, you give it to them, telling them that it would be strange if there was no one who was wiser than any old cow; and keep your lips sealed about proof and necessity and rely instead on likelihood. Mind you, if Theodorus or some other geometer were to employ likelihood in his calculations, he'd be pretty shoddy. So you and Theodorus should give some thought to whether, in such important matters, you are prepared to accept arguments which are persuasive and plausible.

In the light of this apparent Platonic hostility towards likelihood, it is perhaps understandable that interpreters have succumbed to the temptation to interpret Timaeus' τὸ εἰκός in a similarly negative fashion. It seems that the most popular method for explicating the nature of the 'likelihood' ascribed to the λόγοι of likenesses is by drawing a contrast with the stable accounts to which they are said to stand ἀνὰ λόγον. Perhaps accounts of likenesses are likely because they lack one (or more) of the qualities possessed by stable and irrefutable λόγοι. We know from 27d5–28a4 that the stable λόγοι are about Being and that they are the content of understanding:

Ἔστιν οὖν δὴ κατ' ἐμὴν δόξαν πρῶτον διαιρετέον τάδε· τί τὸ ὂν ἀεί, γένεσιν δὲ οὐκ ἔχον, καὶ τί τὸ γιγνόμενον μὲν ἀεί, ὂν δὲ οὐδέποτε; τὸ μὲν δὴ νοήσει μετὰ λόγου περιληπτόν, ἀεὶ κατὰ ταὐτὰ ὄν, τὸ δ' αὖ δόξῃ μετ' αἰσθήσεως ἀλόγου δοξαστόν, γιγνόμενον καὶ ἀπολλύμενον, ὄντως δὲ οὐδέποτε ὄν.

In my opinion we should start with this distinction: what is that which always is but has no Coming-to-be, and then what is that which is always coming-to-be but never really is? The former is grasped by understanding with the aid of reason and is always the same. The latter, meanwhile, is perceived by unreasoning sense-perception, always coming-to-be and passing-away, but never really being.

We also know (from 29b3) that these λόγοι are about originals (παραδείγματα) rather than copies and (29b5–7) that they are, of course, stable (μονίμους) and irrefutable (ἀμεταπτώτους). In addition, 29c3 appears to attribute ἀλήθεια to these accounts. In what way(s), if any, do λόγοι of likenesses fall short of these standards and why should this limit them (if it is a limitation) to 'likelihood'?

Likelihood as a lack of certainty

I have argued that an essential lack of certainty lies at the heart of Xenophanes' claim to offer an account ἐοικότα τοῖς ἐτύμοισι. Indeed, it seems quite natural to cash out τό εἰκός in terms of a lack of, or in opposition to, certainty. After all, we tend to depend on likelihood only in the absence of certainty. When making judgements for ourselves, if we don't *know*, we can satisfy ourselves with a calculation of what seems most likely.[41] Equally, when seeking to deceive others, we might employ likelihood (as opposed to the truth) in order to capitalize on their lack of certainty.[42] Successful lies need to be plausible. The 'certainty' of λόγοι about paradigms seems to be connected to their stability and their role as

41 Thus Johansen (2004) 52 introduces the analogy of the law court: 'It is clearly assumed by the procedures of the law court that there is some truth of the matter as to who killed Mrs Jones. However, if there is no conclusive evidence the difficulty is that the jurors cannot have certainty about who killed her. Any verdict they reach will be based on mere conviction rather than knowledge. The jury's belief as to who committed the crime may of course happen to be true, but in the absence of firm evidence the belief will be merely likely [. . .] The term "likely" then highlights the degree of uncertainty with which we make our claims; it does not cast doubt on whether the claims can be true or false.' See *Theaetetus* 201b3ff.

42 See *Critias* 107b7–108a4, where Critias notes that we will be more content with likelihood in cases where we have less experience of the thing being represented by an image.

the content of knowledge. Since εἰκώς accounts lack these qualities we may be justified in locating the source of their 'lesser' status in a deficiency of certainty.[43] On this reading εἰκώς is understood to mean 'likely to be true' as opposed to 'like the truth'.[44]

Why should we think that accounts of likenesses lack certainty? After all, as I noted above, it seems obvious that one can speak with great certainty about many likenesses. Perhaps the most obvious answer, and one which has proved popular with scholars, is that the likeness described by an εἰκώς λόγος is created in the realm of Coming-to-be.[45] As such, it is in a state of constant change and eternally devoid of stability. *Timaeus* 29b4–5 declares that an account shares the status of its subject-matter (τοὺς λόγους, ὧνπέρ εἰσιν ἐξηγηταί, τούτων αὐτῶν καὶ συγγενεῖς ὄντας). So, the thinking goes, an account of an unstable subject-matter, such as the realm of Coming-to-be, will itself be unstable. The instability of an account is, in turn, sufficient to render it uncertain; therefore an account of an unstable subject-matter will, as a direct consequence of its instability, be uncertain. At first, this looks like a satisfyingly simple explanation of the 'likely' status of accounts of likenesses. However, closer scrutiny throws up a potential objection. For, whilst it incorporates the notion that the status of an account and that of its subject-matter are connected, it fails to address the explicit link that Timaeus draws between the status of the account as εἰκώς and the fact that its subject-matter is an εἰκών. On this reading, the account is εἰκώς because it is of Coming-to-be, rather than because it is of an εἰκών.[46]

43 *Timaeus* 72d4–8 might be adduced in support of this reading. There Timaeus claims that his account may be true, but that to know that it is so would be impossible without divine confirmation. As humans, we are denied certainty about the truth-status of our accounts. For a more detailed discussion of this passage and its possible connection with Xenophanes B35, see Ch. 4.

44 Of course, one might think that an account that is like what is already established as the truth is therefore likely to be true. Burnyeat (2005) 146 asserts that 'it was certainly a well-established meaning by Plato's time that something can be called εἰκώς if it is like what is (already known or believed to be) true'. Berti (1997) 120 argues that cosmology is εἰκώς insofar as it is similar to knowledge (as opposed to similar to truth).

45 See, for example, Vlastos (1965a) 382–3, Carone (2005) 26 and Cornford (1937) 29: 'In Plato's view there can be no exact science or knowledge of natural things because they are always changing.'

46 I accept that all likenesses, since they are created, will occur in the realm of Coming-to-be. See Johansen (2004) 55. However, I resist the suggestion that it is their status as Coming-to-be rather than as likeness which influences the likely accounts.

Can Timaeus' likelihood be opposed to certainty whilst maintaining the influence of the subject-matter's status as likeness? One possibility is that the source of the accounts' uncertainty and likelihood is in the likeness-relation that holds between image and model. A reading along these lines would be attractive insofar as it would be applicable to all cases of created likenesses.[47]

One such interpretation is that offered by Rowe, who argues that the uncertainty of accounts of likenesses derives from the accounts' deficient relationship to the original. Rowe asserts that 'the account of the *eikôn* is lacking just because it's an account of the *eikôn* rather than of the thing that *eikôn* represents – and therefore fails to give more than a "likely" representation *of that original thing*.'[48] This interpretation is applicable to accounts of all kinds of likenesses and avoids locating the source of likelihood in the unstable nature of the sensible realm. However, rather than explaining why an account of a likeness will be likely, it only explains why and how an account of a likeness will be a likely account *of the original*. This may be an attractively neat solution, but it is unjustified by the text. Indeed the close association drawn between the status of the account and its individual subject-matter militates against it. Timaeus is explicitly talking about the likelihood of an account of the image, not of the original.[49]

Sedley recognizes and emphasizes that cosmology is an attempt 'to find out about the likeness – that is, the world – in its own

[47] By 'created likenesses' I mean those likenesses intentionally created *as such*, i.e. artefacts. Cornford (1937) 28 is mistaken in separating Timaeus' talk of likenesses from his discussion of creation by the Demiurge when he claims that 'Not all images are made by artists. Among likenesses, Plato often instances reflections on water or in a mirror. For these all that is required is the thing reflected, the reflection, and the medium which holds it.' That Plato discusses such 'accidental' images is beyond dispute. However, it is clear that, in this passage of the *Timaeus*, he is describing images created to be like their original, as the use of ἀπεικασθέντος at 29c2 demonstrates. This is in contrast to the similes in the central books of the *Republic*, where εἰκόνες refers most often to reflections.

[48] Rowe (2003) 29.

[49] Rowe (2007) 255–65 offers a revised version of this interpretation. Rowe argues that a 'likely' account is merely likely because, in giving an account of surface appearances, one is 'substituting a necessarily less true account for a truer one – the one substituted [i.e. cosmology] being still, in a way, an account *of* the model, only of the model realized in the "image"'. In this case too, however, the problem seems to be that such an interpretation reads the likely account as being an account of the model (or 'of the model realized in the "image"'), rather than, as Timaeus emphasizes, of the likeness.

right'.[50] Like Rowe, he argues that the uncertainty, i.e. the likelihood, of cosmology derives from the relationship between original and likeness. The purpose of cosmology is to reconstruct 'the creative reasoning by which the Demiurge worked out how best to make a likeness of his model in matter'. We must replicate the reasoning of the Demiurge by first considering the model itself and consequently which of the various possible likenesses would best represent that original.[51] However, no matter how good our reasoning, 'we can never be sure of rediscovering the creator's choices among competing alternative likenesses, and the reasoning that underlay them. That is why discourse about a mere likeness will never result in more than likelihood.'[52]

It is, I think, a real advantage of this reading that it is generally applicable to all kinds of created likenesses. If I were to consider how any painter might seek to represent me, in terms not just of my appearance but also my personality, on canvas, I would first reflect upon my own nature and then consider what a good representation might be and how best to create that representation. Not being the painter, however, I could not be certain that my reasoning, no matter how good it might be or how well I might claim to know myself, would coincide with his expert opinion and actual practical choices.

There is, however, a disadvantage to this interpretation. Although the uncertainty of the account is derived in part from the paradigm–likeness relationship, it is not a necessary consequence of this relationship. Sedley states that '[d]eciding which likeness is, all things considered, the best, and was therefore the one chosen by the Demiurge, cannot for a human observer be an exact science, there being so many competing considerations at stake, many of them inscrutable to us'.[53] Now, although our human nature, as

[50] Sedley (2007) 110.

[51] Cosmology must, on this reading, be an essentially *a priori* exercise. Hankinson (1998) 108–9 seems to be offering a similar explanation when he asserts that 'We may deduce that the Artisan acted for the best – but we cannot determine fully how that intention was carried through.' It is not clear whether Hankinson is actually attributing uncertainty to the account as a description of the sensible world or of the intelligible realm. His description of the likely account as an 'account *of reality*' would seem to suggest the latter, in which case he would be subject to the same objection as Rowe.

[52] Sedley (2007) 113. [53] Sedley (2007) 111.

29c4–d3 suggests, may prevent us from achieving certainty about the relationship, this is not to say that there is no certain account to be achieved. A successful cosmologist could feasibly produce an account that accurately reproduces both the nature of the likeness and the reasoning that underlies its creation, but they could never know for certain that it was true.[54] If, however, the Demiurge were to give an account of the likeness, he, since the reasoning is his own, would not be subject to such limitations. Theoretically, any account of the likeness given by the Demiurge would therefore not be likely – it would be certain. It would not, therefore, be true to say that all accounts of likenesses are limited to uncertainty and likelihood.[55]

The suggestion that an account of a likeness could be certain seems at odds with the text which, as Johansen notes, implies that 'accounts of likenesses can *in principle* only be likely. In other words, likelihood is *in principle* the best we can hope for when dealing with a likeness. No knowledge of the paradigm can change the fact that the likeness of a paradigm is a likeness. So it would seem to apply to everyone, man and god, that a likely account is the best we can hope for when dealing with a likeness.'[56] It is not, therefore, sufficient to explain likelihood as depending in part on our nature as mortals and not exclusively on the nature of the likeness.

Likelihood opposed to truth

One alternative to explaining 'likelihood' as a lack of certainty is to read it as expressing a lack of truth. *Timaeus* 29c3 explains the proportion that holds between stable accounts of originals and likely accounts of likenesses by asserting that 'as Being is to

[54] Thus Sedley's interpretation of Timaeus' εἰκώς is reminiscent of the reading of Xenophanes B35 (and B34) offered in Ch. 1.

[55] Sedley (2007) 111n42 claims that 'Timaeus is pointedly evasive' on the question of whether the Demiurge would possess a stable account of the creation but concludes that 'the dichotomous analysis of accounts at 29b3–c3 is restricted to human ones'. In Ch. 4, I will argue that 29d1–3 establishes that human nature is limited not to likelihood in general, but to giving likely μῦθοι as opposed to the likely λόγοι that a god might produce.

[56] Johansen (2004) 56.

Coming-to-be, so truth is to πίστις'. This is often taken to mean that the relationship between the εἰκώς account, i.e. πίστις, and the stable account, i.e. truth, is parallel to that between Coming-to-be and Being.[57] At 27d5, Timaeus sets out the fundamental topic of his cosmology: 'what is that which always is but has no Coming-to-be, and then what is that which is always Coming-to-be but never really is?' The mutual exclusivity of Being and Coming-to-be is clearly emphasized here. The implication of 29c3 is taken to be that truth and πίστις should also be mutually exclusive; an account that is εἰκώς will be opposed to or, at least, devoid of truth.

Timaeus 29c3, then, is read by some as implying that truth is present in the stable accounts of stable subject-matters but absent from 'likely' accounts of likenesses. Perhaps Timaeus' claim to likelihood implies a lack of truth, rather than of certainty. If this were the case, Plato's cosmology would evoke the tradition for Περὶ φύσεως works to commence with a truth-claim.[58] Timaeus would be saying that his account is 'like the truth (but not actually true)'.[59]

As we have seen, Timaeus presents the realm of Coming-to-be as a likeness (εἰκών) and asserts that, as such, it will be described by a likely (εἰκώς) account. At 28a1–4, meanwhile, he declares that belief (δόξα) is the cognitive state set over the realm of Coming-to-be. Consequently, the likely account describing Coming-to-be will express, or be expressed in terms of, belief. Now, since this likely account excludes truth, it seems that truth must also be excluded from the beliefs about Coming-to-be that it describes or of which it is composed. On this reading, Timaeus appears to be implying the impossibility of true belief, since truth, according to 29c3, belongs to the realm of Being and understanding (νοήσις) but not to the realm of Coming-to-be and belief (δόξα). Can Plato really be having Timaeus deny the possibility of true belief?

At 37b3–8, in discussing the motions of the World Soul which is composed of circles of the Same and Different, Timaeus says:

57 For a more detailed discussion of the meaning of πίστις at 29c3, see Ch. 4.

58 Runia (1997) discusses the degree to which Plato 'has very deliberately placed Timaeus' λόγος in the tradition of Presocratic Περὶ φύσεως literature'. See Ch. 4.

59 Ashbaugh (1988) offers a reading along these lines.

λόγος δὲ ὁ κατὰ ταὐτὸν ἀληθὴς γιγνόμενος περί τε θάτερον ὂν καὶ περὶ τὸ ταὐτόν, ἐν τῷ κινουμένῳ ὑφ' αὑτοῦ φερόμενος ἄνευ φθόγγου καὶ ἠχῆς, ὅταν μὲν περὶ τὸ αἰσθητὸν γίγνηται καὶ ὁ τοῦ θατέρου κύκλος ὀρθὸς ἰὼν εἰς πᾶσαν αὐτοῦ τὴν ψυχὴν διαγγείλῃ, δόξαι καὶ πίστεις γίγνονται βέβαιοι καὶ ἀληθεῖς, ὅταν δὲ αὖ περὶ τὸ λογιστικὸν ᾖ καὶ ὁ τοῦ ταὐτοῦ κύκλος εὔτροχος ὢν αὐτὰ μηνύσῃ, νοῦς ἐπιστήμη τε ἐξ ἀνάγκης ἀποτελεῖται·

But an account comes-to-be, whether true with regard to the Different or to the Same, without speech or sound within the self-moving thing. When it comes-to-be about what is perceptible and the circle of the Different travels straight and declares it to the whole of its soul, then stable and true beliefs and convictions (δόξαι καὶ πίστεις) come about. But when it is about the something rational and the circle of the Same travels smoothly and pronounces it, by necessity it produces understanding and knowledge.

This passage clearly talks of 'true beliefs'. It even goes so far as to suggest that these beliefs might be stable (βέβαιοι), a quality attributed to the subject-matter of unchanging accounts (of Being) at 29b6.[60] It seems Timaeus is, on the one hand, setting up belief and truth as mutually exclusive, and, on the other hand, offering a discussion of how these supposedly impossible true beliefs actually come about.[61]

Can this apparent inconsistency be dissolved? One possible solution would attribute a kind of truth to belief and likely accounts different from that possessed by knowledge and stable accounts.[62] Cornford, for example, allows that the likely account can relate to truth without actually being true, asserting that 'no account of the material world can ever amount to an exact and self-consistent statement of unchangeable truth'.[63] According to Cornford, the ever-changing nature of the perceptible subject-matter prevents it from being described by stable and consistent truth. This need not imply, however, that it is completely unrelated to truth. He argues

60 See Johansen (2004) 50–1.

61 Note also that these true beliefs are described as *coming-to-be* (γίγνονται).

62 Thus Johansen (2004) 51 suggests that it might be possible for Timaeus to hold the view that 'beliefs and convictions about perceptible matters can have some degree of truth and certainty, whilst still contrasting the status of such beliefs with the optimal, unqualified truth and certainty that we can only have when thinking about being. It would therefore be possible for Timaeus to contrast conviction with truth *simpliciter* at 29c3 not because he holds that convictions cannot be true, but because he thinks they can only be true in some qualified way.'

63 Cornford (1937) 28–32.

that Plato presents a myth that is ultimately false, i.e. not literally true, but representative of the truth (that the world exhibits design rather than randomness). The likely account cannot be true in itself, but it can and should, Cornford argues, express a metaphorical truth.[64] The likely account excludes literal, certain and stable truth, but can express fictional or metaphorical truth.[65] He emphasizes that there is in Timaeus' account 'an irreducible element of poetry which refuses to be translated into the language of scientific prose'.

There are two readily identifiable problems with Cornford's approach. The first has been set out by Johansen:

> One indication that Timaeus' description of the account of the cosmos as *eikōs* is not supposed to mark the distinction between the metaphorical and the literal is that Timaeus is usually careful to mark off images *within* his account. So at 48b5–c2 when criticizing those who take fire and other simple bodies to be the elements or letters (*stoicheia*) of the universe, he says that they would not even be plausibly (*eikotōs*) likened (*apeikasthēnai*) to syllables by an intelligent person [...] On Cornford's reading we lose the contrast between such cases, where Timaeus explicitly says he is using an *eikōn*, and the rest of the account.

Even if Plato did not signpost his similes within the dialogue, there remains a further, more fundamental problem with this interpretation. Cornford derives the likely status of the account from the fact that its subject-matter is Coming-to-be rather than from its status as a likeness.[66] Now, if accounts are the kin of their subject-matter,

64 Cornford (1937) 29 correctly criticizes Taylor (1928) 59–61 for his suggestion that Plato's likely account is 'the nearest approximation which can "provisionally" be made to exact truth' due to the continuous variation in its subject-matter. Taylor's reading is at fault insofar as it assumes that there is some overall and literal truth (indeed, he dismisses the kind of 'fictional truth' reading that Cornford offers) to which we can approximate our accounts. For Taylor, the difference between the truth of knowledge and that of belief is merely one of degree. The most unfortunate implication of Taylor's interpretation is that we would have to conceive of Becoming as changing towards a state of total and stable being, which cannot be the case, as 27d6–7 indicates.

65 Carone (2005) 15 summarizes this attitude: 'whereas Plato is far from endorsing the literal truth of every, or indeed of any myth, he does seem to create myths and self-consciously use them for his own philosophical purposes, so that they too can convey truth'. Rowe (2003) 25 notes that Cornford seems to assimilate μῦθος to εἰκώς.

66 Cornford (1937) 29. See also, Osborne (1996) 186: 'words that interpret the realm of becoming, as Timaeus' words are to do, will have a degree of likelihood; they will be subject to revision like the subject matter to which they are correlated'. Rowe (2003) 25–6 criticizes Cornford for depending too fully on the label μῦθος as expressing the non-literal status of the likely account. As Rowe rightly points out, the term λόγος is

as 29b5 asserts, one would expect that λόγοι describing what is unstable and in a state of constant change would themselves be unstable and subject to constant revision. However, this is not the connection that Timaeus makes. The kinship he describes is that between likely accounts and likenesses. The εἰκώς nature of the account is introduced, and should be understood, independently of any considerations about the changeability of Coming-to-be.

Likelihood as reasonableness

Burnyeat's interpretation of Timaeus' εἰκώς emphatically rejects the idea that it derives from the changeability of Coming-to-be.[67] He argues that, rather than expressing a limitation imposed upon accounts of the cosmos, εἰκώς is a standard towards which such accounts should aim.[68]

For Burnyeat, the key to the meaning of Timaeus' εἰκώς lies in recognizing its use as a term of approbation, which can be variously translated 'fitting', 'appropriate', or his preferred term 'reasonable'.[69] Thus, he argues, 'something is εἰκώς not only if it is like what is true, but also if it is like what *ought* to be, or it is like what you or the situation need and require'.[70] A 'reasonable' account will succeed in expressing that its subject-matter, in this case the cosmos, has been created as it should have been.[71] It will describe the cosmos 'as like what reason says *ought* to be as the materials allow'.[72] Burnyeat offers a helpful craft analogy:

Consider some of the ways in which we disclose the reasonableness and appropriateness of an architect's or a carpenter's creation. The table legs are made thus

applied to the account far more frequently than μῦθος, as well as in conjunction with εἰκώς.

67 Burnyeat (2005) 143–4. 68 See 119–22 above.

69 See also Ashbaugh (1988) 62. See 68–70 on the translation of Parmenides' ἐοικώς as 'fitting'.

70 Burnyeat (2005) 146.

71 Burnyeat notes that a 'reasonable' account may also be 'probable' insofar as 'the most reasonable account of the cosmos, the one that explains how reasonable its construction really is, is simultaneously and thereby the most probable'. Morgan (2000) 273 also notes that 'in many instances the language of probability is coupled with that of fitness and necessity'. For Morgan, I take it, the point is not that a fitting account will prove to be probable, but that a probable account is a fitting description of the cosmos.

72 Burnyeat (2005) 158.

> and so because that is a good way to combine stability with grace. The ceilings are raised high to give people using the building a sense of space and freedom, which is an excellent thing in a building if you can afford it. The 'because' or 'to give this result' in such sentences refers the good features of the table or the building to the choices made by the craftsmen and the teleological reasons they had for making them that way. [. . .] But the *Divine* Craftsman does not just have teleological reasons for his choices. His overall goal simply *is* to impose reason on necessity, to introduce rational order into disorderly chaos. In his case, the product he aims for is precisely that, rational order. For us, therefore, to become connoisseurs of the cosmos is to appreciate the rationality of its order. And to do that is to come to appreciate something of the reasons for which it was created as it was. To the extent that Timaeus succeeds in disclosing the reasons the Divine Intellect has for making the cosmos thus and so, to that extent he will be retracing the reason*ing* that lies behind the act of creation.[73]

Accounts of the cosmos will achieve 'reasonableness' when they properly express the 'reasonableness' of their subject-matter. The 'reasonableness' of the cosmos is the degree to which it demonstrates the rational order that the Demiurge aims to create. A cosmological account must aim to reveal the practical reasoning that leads to the cosmos having been created with the features that it possesses.[74]

I have already proclaimed my support for Burnyeat's contention that Timaeus' εἰκώς is a standard at which accounts should aim rather than a description of the limitations inherent in any attempt to describe a likeness. Burnyeat's positive spin on εἰκώς is attractive insofar as it avoids the assumptions, discussed below, that 'likelihood' should be understood as a negative quality.[75] I agree that an account of the cosmos should aim to express the fact that it has been created by the Demiurge in such a way as to display reason. I do not, however, think that this is what Timaeus means when he claims that accounts of likenesses in general should be 'likely'.[76] The likelihood of a *description of the cosmos* will, in

73 Burnyeat (2005) 156–7.

74 Burnyeat emphasizes that the reasoning captured by a 'reasonable' account is practical and creative rather than theoretical. There is some similarity between this interpretation and that of Sedley (discussed above 131–3), although the latter stresses the uncertainty involved in attempting to demonstrate the creative reasoning of the Demiurge.

75 See also Martijn (2006) 157.

76 Burnyeat (2005) 151–2 is correct in his assertion that 'the subject of [29c1–2] is not any old statement about a likeness, still less any old statement about the sensible world, but

fact, be cashed out in terms of 'reason'. This is because it is a likeness *of a model that displays reason*. The point is that, just as the cosmos is a 'reasonable' species of εἰκών, so the description of the cosmos is a 'reasonable' species of an εἰκώς account. Burnyeat's interpretation does not go far enough in taking account of the link that Timaeus draws between εἰκών and εἰκώς.[77] The reasoning that Burnyeat describes is primarily creative reasoning rather than the more specific reasoning involved in the creation *of a likeness*.[78]

I want to develop a reading that is in sympathy with Burnyeat's account, but which recognizes and emphasizes the influence of the cosmic subject-matter as an εἰκών. In order to pursue this line, it will be necessary to reconsider the Platonic conception of likenesses and the widespread supposition that the notion of 'likeness' implies some kind of essential deficiency.

Likeness as a positive relation

There is an assumption underlying those interpretations which read εἰκώς as expressing a lack either of truth or of certainty that an εἰκών is a deficient version of its model.[79] Certainly, as Plato emphasizes in the *Cratylus*, a likeness cannot be a complete replication of its original:

> ... ἀλλὰ τὸ ἐναντίον οὐδὲ τὸ παράπαν δέῃ πάντα ἀποδοῦναι οἷόν ἐστιν ᾧ εἰκάζει, εἰ μέλλει εἰκὼν εἶναι. σκόπει δὲ εἰ τὶ λέγω. ἆρ' ἂν δύο πράγματα εἴη τοιάδε, οἷον Κρατύλος καὶ Κρατύλου εἰκών, εἴ τις θεῶν μὴ μόνον τὸ σὸν χρῶμα

accounts exegetic of a certain type of likeness, namely, one fashioned after an eternal unchanging model'. However, the claims Timaeus makes about statements about this particular kind of likeness are, I take it, founded on the basic claim that *all* accounts of likenesses will be likely, not just those about likenesses fashioned after an eternal unchanging model. See Betegh (2010) 215.

77 See Burnyeat (2005) 164, where he renders 'reasonable' as εὔλογος, thereby liberating 'likelihood' of its link to 'likeness'.

78 Note that, in describing the 'architect's or carpenter's creation', Burnyeat focuses on the best qualities of the creations without explicitly relating them to any model. Of course, a Platonic architect or carpenter does create by likening, but Burnyeat fails to make clear that the goodness at which creators should aim is both that of the model, as the suitable paradigm, and that of the likeness, as the best possible likeness of the good paradigm.

79 Cornford (1937) 28 asserts that 'the visible world being *only* a likeness of the real, no account of it can be more than a likely story'. Rowe (2003) 28–9: 'but if one is dealing with what is *merely* modelled on that first thing [something stable and lasting], and is an *eikôn*, [...] then our *logoi* "will be (just) *eikotes* [...]"' (my emphases).

καὶ σχῆμα ἀπεικάσειεν ὥσπερ οἱ ζωγράφοι, ἀλλὰ καὶ τὰ ἐντὸς πάντα τοιαῦτα ποιήσειεν οἷάπερ τὰ σά, καὶ μαλακότητας καὶ θερμότητας τὰς αὐτὰς ἀποδοίη, καὶ κίνησιν καὶ ψυχὴν καὶ φρόνησιν οἵαπερ ἡ παρὰ σοὶ ἐνθείη αὐτοῖς, καὶ ἑνὶ λόγῳ πάντα ἅπερ σὺ ἔχεις, τοιαῦτα ἕτερα καταστήσειεν πλησίον σου; πότερον Κρατύλος ἂν καὶ εἰκὼν Κρατύλου τότ' εἴη τὸ τοιοῦτον, ἢ δύο Κρατύλοι;

ΚΡ. Δύο ἔμοιγε δοκοῦσιν, ὦ Σώκρατες, Κρατύλοι.[80]

On the contrary, it absolutely must not completely replicate that of which it is an image, if it is to be a likeness. Think on this. Would there be two things, Cratylus and the likeness of Cratylus, if some god represented, as a painter would, not only your complexion and shape, but also made everything within like your innards and reproduced the same softness and warmth and endowed them with the same motion and soul and intelligence as are in you and, basically, replicated every quality that you have and plonked the replica down next to you? Would there be Cratylus and a likeness of Cratylus, or two Cratyluses?

Cr: I think there would be two Cratyluses, Socrates.

If there were no difference between a model and its likeness, they would be the same as, rather than simply like, each other. The gap between original and likeness is also introduced at *Sophist* 240a7–b2:

ΘΕΑΙ. Τί δῆτα, ὦ ξένε, εἴδωλον ἂν φαῖμεν εἶναι πλήν γε τὸ πρὸς τἀληθινὸν ἀφωμοιωμένον ἕτερον τοιοῦτον;
ΞΕ. Ἕτερον δὲ λέγεις τοιοῦτον ἀληθινόν, ἢ ἐπὶ τίνι τὸ τοιοῦτον εἶπες;
ΘΕΑΙ. Οὐδαμῶς ἀληθινόν γε, ἀλλ' ἐοικὸς μέν.

Th: What, Stranger, could we say an image is other than another such thing that has been likened to the true one?
ES: Do you mean another that is true? Or what do you mean by 'such'?
Th: Not at all true [itself], but merely like [the true thing].

Both passages have been read as describing the 'inescapable difference between images and their objects'.[81] The *Timaeus* has been treated as reiterating this difference in such a way as to emphasize the gap between the cosmic model (the Forms) and deficient likeness (the perceptible world).[82] It is assumed that, analogously, the likely account of the perceptible world is deficiently related to the

80 *Cratylus* 432b2–c6. 81 Halliwell (2002) 47.
82 Thus Carone (2005) 47 claims that 'The *Timaeus* emphasizes, perhaps more than any other dialogue, the ontological gap between Forms and sensibles.'

stable truth which describes the Forms and this deficiency is, as we have seen, commonly cashed out in terms of truth or certainty.

In emphasizing the difference between models and likenesses, however, such interpretations of the *Timaeus* have overlooked another fundamental aspect of the likeness-relation. For, although it is necessarily different from its model, a likeness is also always *like* its model.[83] Indeed, a likeness is necessarily of something else and can only be properly conceived of, *qua* image, if this relation is acknowledged.[84] Now, whilst some might want to point to this dependence as evidence of the essential deficiency of a likeness, I think it can be viewed in a more positive light. Insofar as a likeness is necessarily related to its paradigm, one can say that it is also necessarily influenced by that paradigm. A likeness will only be a (successful) likeness if it is like its original, i.e. if it succeeds in representing its original. The notion of 'representation' seems to me adequately to capture both the essential difference and the necessary similarity between likeness and original. *x* 'represents' *y* by being different from *y* whilst expressing (in a qualified fashion) the nature of *y*.

Perhaps the best way to clarify the positive nature of the likeness-relation is via a consideration of the creative activities and intentions of the Demiurge. When one sets out to create a likeness, clearly one aims at similarity rather than difference. This is reflected in Timaeus' descriptions of the Demiurge's creation of the cosmic likeness. It should be noted that, even in the *proemium*, Timaeus describes the cosmos as having been 'likened to' (ἀπεικασθέντος) rather than merely 'like' the intelligible

[83] Ashbaugh (1988) 10 rightly notes that 'The paradigm–image distinction is also a relation.' Even Carone (2005) 63, although she argues elsewhere (213n87) that Timaeus' talk of 'paradigms', 'copies' and 'imitation' is 'something that tends to stress, in principle, the ontological distance rather than "communication" or "participation" between both [the perceptible and intelligible] domains', admits that 'to grant that [images] are inaccurate is very different from claiming that there is no likeness whatsoever between them and the original'.

[84] Cherniss (1965) 376 points out that an image has meaning 'only in reference to something else apart from it' (although he does use this point to emphasize the inferiority of the image as 'a transitory adumbration'). Patterson (1985) 26 (also 38–44) notes that 'it is the being of a certain sort of object that "makes" an image be the sort of thing it is'. See also Cook Wilson (1889) 109–10.

model.[85] The idea of 'likening' expresses a positive intention in a way that the notion of 'likeness' need not. The Demiurge, in creating the perceptible realm, intends to produce something that resembles the intelligible model:

τῷ γὰρ τῶν νοουμένων καλλίστῳ καὶ κατὰ πάντα τελέῳ μάλιστα αὐτὸν ὁ θεὸς ὁμοιῶσαι βουληθεὶς ζῷον ἓν ὁρατόν, πάνθ' ὅσα αὐτοῦ κατὰ φύσιν συγγενῆ ζῷα ἐντὸς ἔχον ἑαυτοῦ, συνέστησε.[86]

Because the god wanted more than anything to make it like the best of the intelligible things and complete in every way he created it as a single visible animal, which contains in itself all the animals that are its natural kin.

The Demiurge's motivation is positive. He sets out to create a cosmos that is a successful likeness of the Forms. True enough, a successful likeness could not be a replica, for then it would no longer be a likeness, but would be another set of Forms. Nevertheless, it is deliberately and positively modelled on those Forms. In making the world good, the Demiurge wants to make it as like himself as possible (29e1–2).[87] His intention is not to create a world that is deficiently good, but one that is as close to a perfect paradigm as is possible. Admittedly, the necessity of creating the copy in matter determines, in part, that it will fall short of this perfection, but it seems inappropriate to suggest that the Demiurge deliberately aims to produce something deficient.[88]

It would, I think, be a mistake to suppose that the Demiurge, setting out to make a likeness, aimed at replication but was thwarted by the limits of his matter and so ended up settling for an imperfect copy. At this point, it is worth reconsidering our understanding of likeness as a necessarily deficient copy of an original. Only if one assumes that the most complete likeness is a replica is it necessary to class anything that falls short of replication as 'deficient'.[89] If, however, one understands the gap between original and copy as

85 See also 39e4, where Timaeus stresses the similarity between the cosmic likeness and the model to which it is likened (ἀπεικάζετο) by the Demiurge.

86 *Timaeus* 30d1–31a1.

87 τούτου δ' ἐκτὸς ὢν πάντα ὅτι μάλιστα ἐβουλήθη γενέσθαι παραπλήσια ἑαυτῷ.

88 Note that to fall short of perfection is not simply equivalent to failing to be a replica of the model.

89 Johansen (2004) 53 claims 'it is implied in the concept of "likeness" that there are certain limitations to the properties shared by the likeness and its models'. These 'limitations' are, I suggest, better understood as necessary differences.

one of necessary difference rather than deficiency, replication will no longer be the ultimate goal. In fact, replication is incompatible with the creation of a likeness and, consequently, a likeness that fails to replicate is not a deficient likeness, merely a deficient replica.[90] A portrait is not deficient because it fails to replicate its sitter, for, if it succeeded, it would no longer be a portrait.[91] The cosmic εἰκών is like a very good portrait, insofar as it can represent its model, but is never intended as an exact reproduction.

Those who read the cosmic εἰκών's failure to replicate the intelligible forms as a deficiency are, I suggest, labouring under a misapprehension. They are further mistaken in importing this notion of deficiency into the idea of likelihood expressed by εἰκώς. Likeness can, as I have suggested, be understood as a positive relation. For a portrait to be like its sitter is not for it to fall short, but rather to represent them whilst being different from them. The words considered by Socrates in the *Cratylus* are likenesses which are created to mimic or represent the nature of what they name.[92] The success of these representations certainly does not derive from their replicating what they name, but from representing their objects in the medium of language.[93] Likewise, the success of the cosmic likeness is not dependent on its replicating the Forms, but rather on its ability to represent them in the medium of matter.[94]

I am not denying that some likenesses will be better than others. After all, the Demiurge is setting out to produce the best likeness possible. Rather, I am suggesting that the success of competing likenesses should not be judged in terms of their simple correspondence with the model, but rather in how well they represent the nature of that model whilst being different from it.[95] A portrait

90 Patterson (1985) 38 cites *Cratylus* 432b2–c6 as a 'concise rebuttal of the common sense opinion that the criterion of truth or correctness for an image is simply similarity to its model'.

91 Both *Critias* 107d2–5 and *Phaedo* 74a5–8 suggest that perfect 'likeness' between image and model is conceptually possible. I take it that this is not equivalent to complete replication. See Sedley (2006) 311–12.

92 See, for example, *Cratylus* 426c1–427d1, where Socrates argues that the letter 'rho' is useful for imitating (ἀφομοιοῦν, μιμεῖται, ἀπεικάζει) motion.

93 See *Cratylus* 430a6–8.

94 For a discussion of how this 'success' should be cashed out in ethical terms, see 186–90.

95 Admittedly, *Sophist* 235d6–256c7 contrasts εἰκαστική and φανταστική, with the former being superior to the latter in accurately replicating the dimensions and colouring of the

aims to represent its three-dimensional model in two dimensions. Music might be composed with the aim of representing moods and movement. Words, as we know from the *Cratylus*, are sounds and signs created to represent the things that they name. Note that, insofar as all likenesses, in order to be successful, must represent their originals, it will also be true to say that these images are necessarily informed by the nature of their models. This notion of representation is a positive one and should be incorporated into our understanding of Platonic likenesses, at least in the *Timaeus*. Consequently, as I will argue below, the notion of likelihood should also be understood as informed by this positive relation.

Likelihood as a positive quality

A successful likeness is one that represents its original. A successful likely account is, I suggest, one that expresses the status of its subject-matter as a likeness, i.e. as related to and influenced by the original.[96] The Demiurge is concerned to create a likeness that represents the original as completely as possible. Our accounts of that likeness must not overlook its nature as representative of its original. In fact, it is precisely this relation that they should aim to express. A likely account is likely in this sense because it describes a likeness *qua* likeness. A likeness is positively related to its original by being modelled on it, so that it is a positive representation of the paradigm. Accordingly, an account of a likeness will be likely if it succeeds in describing that relation to the original and, most importantly, how this relation is fundamental in dictating the nature of the likeness.[97] Thus, a comprehensively εἰκώς account

model rather than, as with φανταστική, sacrificing truth in favour of apparent beauty. The suggestion here does seem to be that the worth of likenesses can be measured in terms of their correspondence to the original. However, the contrast can also be understood as one between likenesses that are created to represent their originals (in this case through accurate dimensions) and those that are created purely to please their audience, paying no attention to the model, thus demonstrating the essentially positive motivation of (proper) likeness-making.

96 See Betegh (2010) 218 for a similar suggestion. Turnbull (1998) 145 hints at this kind of reading with his assertion that a translation of εἰκώς as '"likely" will do only if it is understood as "of a likeness"'.

97 Osborne (1996) 186–9 argues for a reading of εἰκώς as 'likely' 'in a rather special sense, in which the term conveys the degree to which it [the account] is likened to, or

will not only have to describe the nature of its subject-matter (the likeness), but also demonstrate some understanding of the nature of the original. For whenever we talk about a likeness *qua* likeness, a consideration of the original is implicit in what we say.[98] Indeed, our notion of a likeness will be incomplete if we fail to consider of what it is a likeness. Likenesses cannot be properly understood or described in isolation from their originals. If we do attempt to describe them without acknowledging their status as likenesses, we are simply characterizing something in its own right, rather than *qua* likeness. We can talk about the portrait of Simmias as a painting, noting its colouring and dimensions, or we can talk about it as a portrait, i.e. as a likeness, describing these things as implicitly (or explicitly) relating to the model for the portrait, Simmias himself. Only the latter kind of account, which acknowledges the representative nature of the portrait, will be deemed εἰκώς and will thus incorporate some consideration of the original, in this case, Simmias. We can give descriptions of the cosmos that ignore the fact that it is created as a likeness of the eternal paradigm. A likely account of the cosmos, however, will describe it as a representation of the stable paradigm and will, in some sense, consider the nature of the model as well as that of its likeness. Ashbaugh notes that 'physical objects [. . .] are always becoming and never truly are; thus they can only be explained in terms of the intelligible things that they resemble.'[99] I think that we can do away with the talk about Being and state that all likenesses *qua* likeness derive their nature from being likened to their originals. As such they can only be fully understood and explained by accounts which recognize this relation, i.e. likely accounts.

exemplifies, the original rather than the probability regarding whether it might be true or false'. For Osborne, it is the manner in which the account itself represents the original rather than its success in describing the representation that is the cosmos, which renders its 'likely'. The account is thus not so much a description of a likeness as a likeness in its own right.

98 Note that this approach is different from that of Rowe (see 131 above). The point is not that an account is merely likely because it only succeeds in describing the likeness rather than the original. Rather it is likely because it succeeds in describing the likeness *as essentially related to the original.*

99 Ashbaugh (1988) 9.

A likely cosmology

In general, then, any successful account of a likeness will be likely insofar as it successfully describes a subject-matter *as a likeness of its model*. This is true of all likely accounts of all likenesses. Consequently, a likely account of the likeness that is the cosmos should aim to explain how it is representative of the stable model to which it has been likened. It should demonstrate how the cosmos relates to the model. Of course, the cosmos is essentially different from its model, just as all likenesses must be different from their originals. For whilst the model is Being, the likeness is Coming-to-be and, as Timaeus tells us, there is no Being in Coming-to-be and no Coming-to-be in Being (27d6–28a1). This difference has been emphasized by some readers of the *Timaeus* at the expense of the fact that there is a strong connection between Being and Coming-to-be, insofar as the latter has been likened to the former.[100] There may be no Being in Coming-to-be, but this is not to say that Being has no influence over Coming-to-be.[101] After all, a portrait, for all that it is a painting rather than a person, is importantly, even essentially, influenced by the nature of the person that is its subject. Indeed, the nature of Coming-to-be is to a great extent dictated by that of Being. The cosmos is, for example, created as a single living thing in order that it should resemble the intelligible Living Thing (30c2–31c1). As I have proposed, the best way to describe this relation of likeness between two different things is as a kind of 'representation'. The perceptible cosmos, which has come to be, is absolutely different from Being, but, insofar as it is likened to Being, it represents the nature of Being. Most obviously, the cosmos is imbued with order and beauty as a result of being modelled on the intelligible realm.

As an εἰκών of the intelligible realm, the cosmos represents the nature of Being, although created in the realm of Coming-to-be. It

100 At 52b6–c5, Timaeus notes that a likeness, since it depends on its model for its nature, will 'cling to being'.

101 As Lloyd (1991) 349 puts it 'Becoming is not to be confused with Being, but what comes to be comes to be what it becomes by virtue of participating in or imitating Being.' The influence is noted by Carone (2005) 29, although, on her reading, the important factor is the Demiurge as a 'mediator between the immutable Forms [. . .] and our sensible and changing realm'.

demonstrates the reason and design and teleological aims imposed on it as part of the process of likening it to its model. My suggestion is that an account of the cosmos will only succeed in being εἰκώς if it recognizes that these qualities are present in the world *because* the world is a representation of the intelligible model.[102] An account that describes the cosmos as anything other than a Coming-to-be representation of Being will fall short of being εἰκώς. Any account that sets out to describe the cosmos independently of the fact that it is as it is because it is modelled on Being, will, since it does not relate the status of the cosmos as representation, fail to be a likely account.

It is high time to return to the *proemium* and apply the interpretation I have been developing to the text. As I understand it, Timaeus' εἰκώς-claim can be summarized as follows:

(i) A necessary condition of a successful account is that it shares the nature of its subject-matter (29b3–5).
(ii) A successful account of what is stable and permanent will be stable and permanent (29b5–c1).
(iii) A successful account of a likeness will be likely, i.e. will take account of the relation between likeness and original (29c2).
(iv) A successful account of the likeness that is the cosmos will take account of the relation between the stable original and the cosmos (29c1–2).

It is worth noting that this reading is quite compatible with Burnyeat's concern to emphasize the approbative nuances of the term εἰκώς. An account that describes a likeness *qua* likeness can clearly be considered appropriate, capturing as it does the nature of the *descriptum* and its vital relation to its model.[103]

[102] Johansen (2004) 56–60 argues that Timaeus' account is 'likely' because 'it is of a likeness that occurs in a different ontological mode, coming-into-being, from that of its model, being. Given the different ontological modes what is required to establish a likeness between likeness and original is a certain kind of reasoning whereby features that belong to the likeness are shown to be analogous to features that belong to the model.' I take it that the likelihood-claim is intended to be applicable to all likenesses, whether they are created in a different ontological mode to their model or not.

[103] Burnyeat (2005) 146 adduces *Sophist* 225a8–10 as evidence in favour of his interpretation. The Eleatic Stranger casts around for a suitable name for a particular kind of fighting and suggests that βιαστικόν would be an εἰκὸς καὶ πρέπον ὄνομα. Perhaps this could be read as 'representative and appropriate' just as well as 'fitting and appropriate', especially when one bears the *Cratylus* in mind.

Representative passages

I now turn to some of the other passages in which Timaeus alludes to the εἰκώς nature of his account with the aim of demonstrating that the 'likely' interpretation offered above is, at the very least, compatible with them.[104] It will prove beneficial to reconsider these passages in the light of my interpretation of the *proemium*'s εἰκώς. I should reiterate that I have no desire to insist that every instance of εἰκώς and its cognates in the *Timaeus* has to be read as expressing precisely and only this notion. When Timaeus expresses his desire to offer a 'likely account', we can read εἰκώς as meaning, at least in part, that he regards his cosmology as 'plausible'.[105] However, I do want to argue that, in several instances, Timaeus uses the label to remind his audience, not that his account is uncertain or untrue, but that he is describing the cosmos as a likeness of the intelligible. Often, when Timaeus refers to his εἰκώς account, he appears to be emphasizing that the nature of the cosmos can and should be explained as a result of its having been crafted to represent the nature of its model.

I begin by considering the various occurrences in the *Timaeus* of the adverb εἰκότως, a word that generally carries the sense 'reasonably' or 'suitably'.[106] It appears with this meaning at 48b5–c2:

νῦν γὰρ οὐδείς πω γένεσιν αὐτῶν μεμήνυκεν, ἀλλ' ὡς εἰδόσιν πῦρ ὅτι ποτέ ἐστιν καὶ ἕκαστον αὐτῶν λέγομεν ἀρχὰς αὐτὰ τιθέμενοι στοιχεῖα τοῦ παντός,

[104] Timaeus reminds us that he is aiming for or offering an εἰκώς account at 30b7, 44d1, 48d2–e1, 49b6, 53d5, 55d5, 56a1, b4, d1, 57d6, 59c6, 67d1, 68b7, 68d2, 72d7 and 90e8. I postpone discussion of some of these passages (59c6, 68b7, 68d2 and 72d7) until Ch. 4, where I treat them in the context of a discussion of εἰκὼς μῦθος.

[105] I do, however, want to resist the suggestion that this 'plausibility' is intended to contrast with truth in the manner of its use in, for example, *Theaetetus* 162e2–163a1. An instance of εἰκώς most easily read as 'plausible' is found at 40e1, where Timaeus asserts that we must accept the stories of those who claim to be the offspring of the gods 'even if they speak without likely or necessary proofs' (καίπερ ἄνευ τε εἰκότων καὶ ἀναγκαίων ἀποδείξεων λέγουσιν). Although, I do think we could also read this as an implicit criticism of the failure of such story-tellers to consider the nature of the cosmos as a likeness. At *Phaedo* 92c9–d5, Simmias dismisses such 'plausible proofs' (i.e. arguments based on plausibility or probability) as 'pretentious'. *Timaeus* 40d6–e4 is discussed below at 185.

[106] LSJ 485. Burnyeat (2005) 147 is perhaps influenced by this in offering his 'reasonable' interpretation.

προσῆκον αὐτοῖς οὐδ' ἂν ὡς ἐν συλλαβῆς εἴδεσιν μόνον εἰκότως ὑπὸ τοῦ καὶ βραχὺ φρονοῦντος ἀπεικασθῆναι.

Up to now, no one has ever talked about the genesis of these things, but, as if speaking to people who know what fire and each of the others is, we say that they are the 'principles' of the universe, positing them as its 'letters'. However, there is no way appropriate to them in which they could reasonably (εἰκότως) be likened even to mere 'syllables', not even by a fellow endowed with scanty intelligence.

This passage is not about the connection between the cosmic likeness and its model.[107] It is simply about how suitable it is to compare fire and the other bodies to 'syllables'. There is no reason to think that εἰκότως describes anything more significant than the appropriateness of the simile. Likewise, at 62a4, Timaeus notes that fire affects body in such a way as to give it the property (and name) which we 'reasonably' call 'hot'.[108] This is a comment on the appropriate nature of language rather than on the link between the cosmic copy and model. Even in these cases, however, I think there is a hint of the connection that Timaeus establishes in the *proemium* between what is εἰκώς and what is an εἰκών. As we saw from the *Cratylus*, a word is appropriate if it is like what it names. Similarly, Timaeus would presumably consider a comparison or simile to have been reasonably made only if the objects of comparison are actually like one another.[109] Fire and the other bodies are not like 'syllables' and thus the comparison is not 'reasonably' made.

107 It is, as Johansen (2004) 51–2 notes, one of those occasions where Timaeus takes care to mark off a simile within his account. See 136.

108 *Timaeus* 61e2–62a5: 'The fineness of sides and the sharpness of angles and the smallness of parts and the swiftness of speed, by all of which it is energetic and slicing and always sharply cuts what it encounters, must be considered by those recalling the Coming-to-be of its shape and that it is this substance in particular and no other that divides our bodies and cuts them up into small pieces and provides the affection and name which we now reasonably call "hot".' (τὴν δὲ λεπτότητα τῶν πλευρῶν καὶ γωνιῶν ὀξύτητα τῶν τε μορίων σμικρότητα καὶ τῆς φορᾶς τὸ τάχος, οἷς πᾶσι σφοδρὸν ὂν καὶ τομὸν ὀξέως τὸ προστυχὸν ἀεὶ τέμνει, λογιστέον ἀναμιμνῃσκομένοις τὴν τοῦ σχήματος αὐτοῦ γένεσιν, ὅτι μάλιστα ἐκείνη καὶ οὐκ ἄλλη φύσις διακρίνουσα ἡμῶν κατὰ σμικρά τε τὰ σώματα κερματίζουσα τοῦτο ὃ νῦν θερμὸν λέγομεν εἰκότως τὸ πάθημα καὶ τοὔνομα παρέσχεν).

109 Bury (1929) 111 translates 'they do not so much as deserve to be likened with any likelihood'.

The case for reading Timaeus' use of εἰκότως as influenced by the etymological connection with εἰκών is clearest in the two instances where the adverb qualifies the verb διαπορέω. At 49b2–7, Timaeus prefaces his discussion of the Receptacle:

εἴρηται μὲν οὖν τἀληθές, δεῖ δὲ ἐναργέστερον εἰπεῖν περὶ αὐτοῦ, χαλεπὸν δὲ ἄλλως τε καὶ διότι προαπορηθῆναι περὶ πυρὸς καὶ τῶν μετὰ πυρὸς ἀναγκαῖον τούτου χάριν· τούτων γὰρ εἰπεῖν ἕκαστον ὁποῖον ὄντως ὕδωρ χρὴ λέγειν μᾶλλον ἢ πῦρ, καὶ ὁποῖον ὁτιοῦν μᾶλλον ἢ καὶ ἅπαντα καθ' ἕκαστόν τε, οὕτως ὥστε τινὶ πιστῷ καὶ βεβαίῳ χρήσασθαι λόγῳ, χαλεπόν. πῶς οὖν δὴ τοῦτ' αὐτὸ καὶ πῇ καὶ τί περὶ αὐτῶν εἰκότως διαπορηθέντες ἂν λέγοιμεν;

What has just been said [that there is a Receptacle] may be true, but we have to talk about it more clearly. Although this is difficult, particularly because it necessitates that we first face a previous difficulty about fire and the others. For to say of each one that it is of such a kind that we should call it water rather than fire, and such that we should call it one thing rather than everything or each thing, in such a way as to employ a trustworthy and stable account, is difficult.[110] So how should we reasonably puzzle about this matter and what should we say about such things?

When Timaeus wonders how he can 'reasonably' (εἰκότως) work through the problems posed by fire and the other bodies, he is hinting at the kind of account he wants to offer, one that explains how the nature of physical world is a likeness of the intelligible realm.[111] It will turn out that this account involves positing a Receptacle in which likenesses (μιμήματα) of the Forms of fire etc. come to be in some qualified and unstable fashion. I will consider the 'likelihood' of Timaeus' physical theory in more detail below. For the time being, it will suffice to note that, from the outset, Timaeus hints at the need to engage in 'likely' reasoning about even the microcosmic nature of the cosmos.

Before turning to the microcosmic details of the likely account, one last instance of εἰκότως remains to be considered. This final

110 I take it that the elusive 'trustworthy and stable account' is that which describes the Form of fire etc. Timaeus is suggesting that, rather than attempting dialectic about the Forms, we should concentrate on describing the cosmic likeness.

111 Timaeus' admission of the difficulty of talking about fire and water 'in such a way as to employ a trustworthy and stable account' refers to the instability of the perceptible instances of these kinds (as he goes on to make clear at 49b7–50a4). The instability of the likely cosmology results from the fact that it is about a likeness that is unstable rather than from the fact that it is about a likeness *per se*.

example makes clear the connection between puzzling 'reasonably' about the cosmos and explaining its nature as a likeness. At 55c7–d4, at the conclusion of his discussion of the five solid structures, Timaeus notes that one question might remain:

ἃ δή τις εἰ πάντα λογιζόμενος ἐμμελῶς ἀποροῖ πότερον ἀπείρους χρὴ κόσμους εἶναι λέγειν ἢ πέρας ἔχοντας, τὸ μὲν ἀπείρους ἡγήσαιτ' ἂν ὄντως ἀπείρου τινὸς εἶναι δόγμα ὧν ἔμπειρον χρεὼν εἶναι, πότερον δὲ ἕνα ἢ πέντε αὐτοὺς ἀληθείᾳ πεφυκότας λέγειν ποτὲ προσήκει, μᾶλλον ἂν ταύτῃ στὰς εἰκότως διαπορήσαι.

Someone who was considering the whole matter harmoniously might be confused as to whether they should say there are infinite or finite worlds. To answer 'infinite' would be to hold the view of someone unfinished in matters about which they should be finished. But whether one ought to say that there is really one world or five worlds, this is more the kind of thing one might pause and reasonably puzzle over.

To puzzle 'reasonably' about the matter of whether there are five worlds or one is to think about which answer would best explain the world as representation of the intelligible realm. In fact, Timaeus goes on to emphasize that his answer, that there is one world, is 'in accordance with the likely account' (55d4–6):

τὸ μὲν οὖν δὴ παρ' ἡμῶν ἕνα αὐτὸν κατὰ τὸν εἰκότα λόγον πεφυκότα μηνύει θεόν, ἄλλος δὲ εἰς ἄλλα πῃ βλέψας ἕτερα δοξάσει.

Our opinion, in accordance with the likely account, indicates that the universe is one god, whilst someone else, looking to other considerations, might think differently.

I take it that this answer is 'in accordance with the likely account' precisely because it describes the world as related to its model.[112] At 31a2–4, Timaeus has argued that the world must be one, rather than infinite, 'if it is crafted in accordance with its model'.[113]

At 30b4–c1, Timaeus tells us that the Demiurge, guided by his desire to create the best possible cosmos, concluded that an intelligent thing would be better than something unintelligent and that intelligence belongs to the soul:

112 See Taylor (1928) 379.

113 πότερον οὖν ὀρθῶς ἕνα οὐρανὸν προσειρήκαμεν, ἢ πολλοὺς καὶ ἀπείρους λέγειν ἦν ὀρθότερον; ἕνα, εἴπερ κατὰ τὸ παράδειγμα δεδημιουργημένος ἔσται.

διὰ δὴ τὸν λογισμὸν τόνδε νοῦν μὲν ἐν ψυχῇ, ψυχὴν δ' ἐν σώματι συνιστὰς τὸ πᾶν συνετεκταίνετο, ὅπως ὅτι κάλλιστον εἴη κατὰ φύσιν ἄριστόν τε ἔργον ἀπειργασμένος. οὕτως οὖν δὴ κατὰ λόγον τὸν εἰκότα δεῖ λέγειν τόνδε τὸν κόσμον ζῷον ἔμψυχον ἔννουν τε τῇ ἀληθείᾳ διὰ τὴν τοῦ θεοῦ γενέσθαι πρόνοιαν.

Because of this reasoning he put intelligence in soul and then soul in body and thus created the universe, so as to create a work that would be the most beautiful and best that its nature would allow. Thus it is necessary to say, in keeping with the likely account, that this cosmos came, through the god's providence, to be, in truth, an ensouled, intelligent living thing.

In referring to the εἰκώς status of his account at this particular point, Timaeus is emphasizing that the nature of his subject-matter, the cosmos, is dictated by the Demiurge's desire to create a likeness as much like himself, i.e. as good, as possible. The εἰκώς account to which Timaeus aspires is one that describes the creation of the cosmos in a way that expresses its relation to the model.[114] Thus, to explain that the cosmos has a certain nature as a result of being likened by god to the good paradigm is to speak in a way that is 'in keeping with the likely account' (κατὰ λόγον τὸν εἰκότα). On my interpretation of εἰκώς, this passage acts as a timely and significant reminder of the fact that a cosmology should aim to express the nature of its subject-matter as a likeness.[115]

So far, the influence of the model on the cosmic εἰκών described by the εἰκώς account has been at the macrocosmic level. Yet Timaeus also seeks to trace the influence of the model on the microcosmic details of the world. The next instance of εἰκώς is at

[114] Admittedly, this passage describes a period before the Demiurge has selected the appropriate model. I take it that, since he wants ultimately to create something as much like himself as possible in terms of goodness, he goes on to select the Form of Living Thing as the model best suited to achieving this aim.

[115] Note that Timaeus recommends calling the cosmos an ensouled and intelligent living thing τῇ ἀληθείᾳ. The fact that we can, at one and the same time, speak both κατὰ λόγον τὸν εἰκότα and τῇ ἀληθείᾳ militates against reading εἰκώς as expressing a lack of truth. In fact, the way that Timaeus connects the nature of the likeness to that of its model supports the suggestion, developed below, that the truth of an εἰκώς account is a qualified truth derived from and related to the unqualified stable truth which describes the intelligible realm. Cornford (1937) 34n1, although he argues for reading the likelihood of the cosmology as indicating its metaphorical nature, reads τῇ ἀληθείᾳ as indicating that 'it is literally true (not merely "probable") that the world is an intelligent living creature'. See 133–7 above and Ch. 4.

44c4–d2, where Timaeus turns from briefly describing the potential intellectual and physical improvement or failure of mortals, to introduce his account of the creation of bodies:

περὶ δὲ τῶν νῦν προτεθέντων δεῖ διελθεῖν ἀκριβέστερον, τὰ δὲ πρὸ τούτων, περὶ σωμάτων κατὰ μέρη τῆς γενέσεως καὶ περὶ ψυχῆς, δι' ἅς τε αἰτίας καὶ προνοίας γέγονε θεῶν, τοῦ μάλιστα εἰκότος ἀντεχομένοις, οὕτω καὶ κατὰ ταῦτα πορευομένοις διεξιτέον.

But the present topic must be treated in more detail, and first things first, regarding how the bodies came to be, part by part, and regarding the soul, through what reasons and forethought of the gods it came to be, maintaining what is most likely, that, and on that basis, is how we must proceed in giving our account.

Timaeus reminds his audience of the need to pursue not just a likely account, but the *most* likely account, when discussing the creation of bodies and souls. A traditional reading of this passage would, I suppose, take Timaeus to be offering a *caveat* that, although we must talk about such matters in detail, we must aim for the best of the merely plausible, i.e. untrue or uncertain, accounts available to us.[116] On the reading that I have been recommending, however, the mention of εἰκώς is, as at 30b4–c1, intended to remind us that any account we offer should aim to express the fact that its subject-matter is as it is because it is a likeness. The 'reasons and fore-thought' (αἰτίας καὶ προνοίας) of the gods should be understood as the creative reasoning and forethought involved in producing, in a deficient medium, the likeness of what is unqualifiedly good and intelligent. In encouraging us to aim for the most εἰκώς account, Timaeus is exhorting us to attempt to produce an account that most completely and comprehensively describes the influence of Being on the likeness formed in the realm of Coming-to-be.

The desire to offer an εἰκὼς account that emphasizes the status of the cosmos as εἰκών is further demonstrated by Timaeus' discussion of the role of Necessity from 47e onwards. Of course, the details of Timaeus' physical theory and, in particular, the Receptacle are notoriously controversial.[117] I happily admit that my treatment is less concerned with explaining the abstruse details of

[116] Taylor (1928) 274 reads this passage, as with those others that mention εἰκώς, as implying that our hypotheses about the physical world are, at best, provisional.

[117] On the difficulty of the Receptacle, see Zeyl (2000) liv–lxiv.

the theory than with highlighting the fact that it is presented as part of an εἰκώς account.

Above, I discussed the occurrence of εἰκότως at 48b5–c2. That section is followed by a methodological digression (48c2–e1):

νῦν δὲ οὖν τό γε παρ' ἡμῶν ὧδε ἐχέτω· τὴν μὲν περὶ ἁπάντων εἴτε ἀρχὴν εἴτε ἀρχὰς εἴτε ὅπῃ δοκεῖ τούτων πέρι τὸ νῦν οὐ ῥητέον, δι' ἄλλο μὲν οὐδέν, διὰ δὲ τὸ χαλεπὸν εἶναι κατὰ τὸν παρόντα τρόπον τῆς διεξόδου δηλῶσαι τὰ δοκοῦντα, μήτ' οὖν ὑμεῖς οἴεσθε δεῖν ἐμὲ λέγειν, οὔτ' αὐτὸς αὖ πείθειν ἐμαυτὸν εἴην ἂν δυνατὸς ὡς ὀρθῶς ἐγχειροῖμ' ἂν τοσοῦτον ἐπιβαλλόμενος ἔργον· τὸ δὲ κατ' ἀρχὰς ῥηθὲν διαφυλάττων, τὴν τῶν εἰκότων λόγων δύναμιν, πειράσομαι μηδενὸς ἧττον εἰκότα, μᾶλλον δέ, καὶ ἔμπροσθεν ἀπ' ἀρχῆς περὶ ἑκάστων καὶ συμπάντων λέγειν. θεὸν δὴ καὶ νῦν ἐπ' ἀρχῇ τῶν λεγομένων σωτῆρα ἐξ ἀτόπου καὶ ἀήθους διηγήσεως πρὸς τὸ τῶν εἰκότων δόγμα διασῴζειν ἡμᾶς ἐπικαλεσάμενοι πάλιν ἀρχώμεθα λέγειν.

But now allow me to continue thus: I should not just now state the 'principle' or 'principles' of everything, or even what I think about them, for no other reason than that it is difficult, on the present mode of exposition, to show what one thinks. So don't expect me to say this for I couldn't even persuade myself that I'm up to the job of correctly attempting to deal with such a task. But I'll stick by what I spoke of at the start, the strength of likely accounts, and I'll aim for something no less likely, but rather more likely than another's.[118] I'll aim, as before, to speak about things, both individually and collectively, from the beginning. And so now, at the beginning of this account let us call on the god to be our saviour and to preserve us throughout a strange and unfamiliar exposition and point us towards a belief in things that are likely. So let us begin from the beginning once more.

Some might be tempted to take this passage as evidence in favour of understanding Timaeus' εἰκώς-claim as an admission that his cosmology is somehow deficient. After all, he acknowledges the difficulty of showing his opinions clearly 'on the present mode of exposition'. Cornford, for example, suggests that 'this warning [. . .] may mean that no one can ever really know the ultimate constitution of the body, because there can be no such thing as physical science, but only a "probable" account'.[119]

Predictably, I want to resist this deficiency reading. Note that Timaeus is yet again talking about εἰκώς accounts not as being that for which we should settle in the absence of something better, but

[118] See n9 above. [119] Cornford (1937) 162. See also Taylor (1928) 309–10.

rather a standard at which we should aim.[120] When Timaeus asserts that he will stick with the 'strength' (δύναμις) of εἰκώς accounts, this is a reminder not that his account is inevitably untrue or uncertain (it would, I think, be rather odd for either of these to be classed as a δύναμις) but rather that a successful account of a likeness will possess persuasive force.[121] This force will result from the fact that the account successfully describes the representative relation that holds between likeness and original. His desire to give an account no less likely but more so than what he has said up to now indicates that he intends to go beyond merely tracing the correspondence between the model and its representation and to offer a description of the mechanics of representation. Rather than simply settling for the conclusion that the cosmos is a living creature because it is modelled on the Form of Living Thing, Timaeus wants to investigate the details of how and where the representation is created. This more detailed treatment, starting from a new beginning, will be more εἰκώς simply because it is more comprehensive.[122]

What, then, are we to make of Timaeus' admission that it is difficult for him to show his thoughts clearly 'on the present mode of exposition'? Well, I do not think this has to be read as an admission of the deficiency of the likely account. Rather, it is an indication that such fundamental questions are simply not within the remit of cosmology. Timaeus is not lamenting that his likely account is too uncertain to talk clearly about such 'principles', he is pointing out that cosmology, since it is about the cosmos rather than

[120] Note further that, at 59c5–d3, Timaeus claims that to consider likely accounts about the cosmos is to engage in an activity that provides a 'temperate and sensible pastime'. See Ch. 4.

[121] On my reading, the likely account possesses persuasive force in addition to, or as a result of its being 'likely', rather than 'likelihood' being equivalent to persuasiveness.

[122] The need to give the most comprehensive εἰκώς account is re-emphasized at 57c7–d6. There, Timaeus recommends that someone wanting to use a likely account to talk about nature must pay attention to the infinite variety of bodies which results from the original varieties of the elementary triangles: 'On account of which, when mixed with themselves and with one another, they are infinitely varied. This is something which those intending to use a likely account about nature should bear in mind.' (διὸ δὴ συμμειγνύμενα αὐτά τε πρὸς αὑτα καὶ πρὸς ἄλληλα τὴν ποικιλίαν ἐστὶν ἄπειρα· ἧς δὴ δεῖ θεωροὺς γίγνεσθαι τοὺς μέλλοντας περὶ φύσεως εἰκότι λόγῳ χρήσεσθαι.) Presumably, the most likely account will be that which describes how each different body is, in its way, a representation of the Forms. See also 67d1–2.

what predates or pre-exists the cosmos, is not suited to discussing such things. In Chapter 4, I will argue that the certainty of Timaeus' cosmology is limited, but that it is the status of the account as a μῦθος rather than as εἰκώς which indicates this limitation. Timaeus is not admitting that his account cannot express his views with clarity because it is merely likely. In fact, as he goes on to make clear, he is aiming for a likely account because this is the kind of exposition that best explains the nature of the subject-matter as a likeness.

Before offering a conclusion, I want to look at three final instances in which Timaeus refers to his account as εἰκώς. At 55d8–56a3, having established the nature of each of the solid figures, Timaeus argues that the most stable should be assigned to earth:

γῇ μὲν δὴ τὸ κυβικὸν εἶδος δῶμεν· ἀκινητοτάτη γὰρ τῶν τεττάρων γενῶν γῆ καὶ τῶν σωμάτων πλαστικωτάτη, μάλιστα δὲ ἀνάγκη γεγονέναι τοιοῦτον τὸ τὰς βάσεις ἀσφαλεστάτας ἔχον· βάσις δὲ ἥ τε τῶν κατ' ἀρχὰς τριγώνων ὑποτεθέντων ἀσφαλεστέρα κατὰ φύσιν ἡ τῶν ἴσων πλευρῶν τῆς τῶν ἀνίσων, τό τε ἐξ ἑκατέρου συντεθὲν ἐπίπεδον ἰσόπλευρον ἰσοπλεύρου τετράγωνον τριγώνου κατά τε μέρη καὶ καθ' ὅλον στασιμωτέρως ἐξ ἀνάγκης βέβηκεν. διὸ γῇ μὲν τοῦτο ἀπονέμοντες τὸν εἰκότα λόγον διασῴζομεν, ὕδατι δ' αὖ τῶν λοιπῶν τὸ δυσκινητότατον εἶδος, τὸ δ'εὐκινητότατον πυρί, τὸ δὲ μέσον ἀέρι.

Let's assign the cube to earth. Since earth is the most immobile and most plastic of the four kinds of bodies, and the solid which has the most stable faces will necessarily be most like this. Of the triangles we posited at the start, the face of those which have equal sides is naturally more stable than that of those with unequal sides, and of the equilateral planes, each of which is composed of equilateral triangles, the square is, both in its parts and as a whole, necessarily more stable. Thus, if we assign this shape to earth, we will preserve our likely account. And, of the remaining shapes, we will assign the least mobile to water, the most mobile to fire and the one in between to air.

By attributing the most stable shape to the most stable body, Timaeus is offering an explanation which 'preserves' his aim of producing a likely account. He is describing the microcosmic composition of his cosmos in such a way as to express its relation to the nature of its model. The physical elements are described as representing the natures of the Forms that are their models. At 56b3–5, Timaeus notes once more that his account is likely:

ἔστω δὴ κατὰ τὸν ὀρθὸν λόγον καὶ κατὰ τὸν εἰκότα τὸ μὲν τῆς πυραμίδος στερεὸν γεγονὸς εἶδος πυρὸς στοιχεῖον καὶ σπέρμα·

Let it be our account, in accordance both with what is correct and with what is likely, that of the shapes we have constructed, the pyramid is the element and seed of fire.

Timaeus thinks his assignment of shapes to elements is *both* correct *and* likely. He may be remarking on the fact that his account is both true and, at least in this case, plausible. After all, truth and plausibility do not always coincide, so that we should perhaps be pleasantly surprised when they do. I think that we can also read the passage along the lines that I have been recommending. Timaeus is noting that his account is both correct, insofar as it accurately describes the solids and bodies and likely, insofar as it explains that there is a connection between the physical nature of the bodies and the Forms to which they are likened.[123]

Finally, at 56c8–d1, Timaeus once again emphasizes the likelihood of his account: 'from everything we have said about the kinds, this is what would be most in accordance with what is likely' (ἐκ δὴ πάντων ὧνπερ τὰ γένη προειρήκαμεν ὧδ' ἂν κατὰ τὸ εἰκὸς μάλιστ' ἂν ἔχοι). Timaeus can be understood as claiming that what will follow will be the 'most plausible' account, or the 'most fitting', or he may be reminding us once more that his account will be that which 'best (i.e. most comprehensively) describes the nature of the subject-matter as a likeness'. I don't think that there is any pressing need to choose between these different readings. In fact, I think we can read εἰκώς as expressing all of these senses simultaneously. I do, however, think that it is important to note the connection between the likelihood of Timaeus' cosmology and the fact that it describes a likeness.[124]

[123] On this passage, see Gregory (2000) 250–1.

[124] Although I cannot provide a compelling reason to link the reference to the εἰκώς nature of the account at 90e6–91a1 to the status of its subject-matter as a likeness, it does not seem to be obviously incompatible with my reading. Timaeus states that 'κατὰ λόγον τὸν εἰκότα' cowardly men are reborn as women. One possibility is that Timaeus is reminding us that the cosmos, including humans, is created as a likeness of a good image and that ignoring the influence of the good will result in becoming less like that perfect paradigm. On the need to become like god, see Ch. 4.

Conclusion

I have argued that Timaeus' εἰκώς-claim is, in part, intended to emphasize the need to describe a likeness *as a likeness*. It is possible to give an account of a likeness that is not εἰκώς, but such an account will fail to express the nature of its *descriptum* as an εἰκών. Non-εἰκώς descriptions of likenesses will not be συγγενεῖς of their subject-matter. It is a particular advantage of this explanation of εἰκώς that it is applicable to all kinds of created likenesses. A portrait can be described by a non-εἰκώς account, in which case it will be considered as a painting in its own right, independent of its connection to its model. Or it can be the subject-matter of an εἰκὼς λόγος, in which case it will be treated as significantly related to and influenced by the nature of its model. Timaeus is aspiring to give the latter kind of account of the cosmos. He could describe it without acknowledging that it is a likeness, but this status is fundamental to his teleological cosmology. The cosmos has been created as a likeness of the intelligible realm and, as such, it can only properly be described by an account that acknowledges the influence of Being as a model on the likeness that is Coming-to-be.

I am well aware that some will find this positive spin of εἰκώς hard to swallow. Some may feel that I am attributing to Timaeus too radical a redefinition of the term. They may object that the negative implications of εἰκώς as it occurs in other Platonic dialogues cannot be so easily discounted. In the face of such objections, I must confess that I am relatively unapologetic. I think Timaeus is using εἰκώς as a piece of technical, more or less metaphysical, jargon. Certainly, such a usage would be unthinkable in the mouth of Socrates, but it seems to me perfectly in keeping with Timaeus' characterization by Critias as someone who 'has made it his particular business to know about the nature of the universe'. The fact that it is Timaeus, and not Socrates, who introduces the notion of the εἰκώς account of an εἰκών also encourages me in my belief that the negative implications of εἰκώς in the other dialogues need not count against my reading.[125] In fact, I think the burden of proof

[125] Of course, at 29d4–6, Socrates does interrupt to express his general approval of Timaeus' *proemium* and of the claim that we should look for no more than an εἰκὼς

is on those who want to read εἰκώς as 'merely' likely. Why should we think that Timaeus shares Socrates' critical preoccupation with the vacuous appeal of rhetoric? I do not want to deny that part of the sense of Timaeus' εἰκώς may be 'plausible'. It would, I think, be perverse to insist that this sense is absent. My suggestion is simply that the primary, explicitly intended meaning of Timaeus' εἰκώς is 'likely' in the sense of 'successfully descriptive of a likeness'. So, whilst I think Timaeus' εἰκώς is principally intended to express this kind of technical likelihood, I do think the more familiar rhetorical sense of 'likely', i.e. 'plausible', can perfectly well be incorporated here. It is the further step of introducing 'mere' plausibility which seems to me to be unjustified.

One of the reasons that I have tried to resist those readings which emphasize the negative aspects of 'likelihood', explaining it as a deficiency of truth or certainty, is that such interpretations run the risk of overemphasizing the gap between Coming-to-be and Being. I do not deny that there is a necessary difference between a model and its likeness, but I do think that many readers of the *Timaeus* have been distracted by this apparent 'deficiency' and have consequently failed to recognize the importance of the positive relationship between a model and its likeness. Although, as we are told at 27d5–28a4, Being and Coming-to-be are mutually exclusive, Coming-to-be is created as a representation of Being. The nature of Coming-to-be, despite being unstable and transient, is fundamentally informed by the stable and perfect nature of its model. Coming-to-be is a likeness of Being (as opposed to a 'mere' likeness).

There are, I think, significant epistemological ramifications of this ontological connection. We must recognize that the object of our belief and perceptions, for all that it is unstable and imperfect, is also a representation of something that is stable and perfect. Our understanding of the perceptible world, however limited it may be, should include an awareness of its relation to the intelligible realm. Perceptibles should not be dismissed as totally unworthy of our attention. Rather, they should be recognized as deriving a

μῦθος in particular (on which, see Ch. 4). This is not, I think, evidence that Timaeus is speaking with a Socratic voice.

real epistemological value from their relation to the intelligible. I am not arguing that we should not, given the chance, prefer to contemplate the Forms rather than the perceptible cosmos. However, I do think that, in the *Timaeus*, Plato is recommending the study of the cosmos as of epistemological and even ethical value, insofar as it is a likeness of what is real and good. The perceptible realm is not truly real in the way that the intelligible realm is truly real but, vitally, nor is it wholly unreal or unrelated to what is truly real. This, albeit qualifiedly, positive attitude towards the cosmos as an object of consideration is significantly different from the Parmenidean dismissal of Coming-to-be as utterly disconnected from Being. In the next chapter, I will argue that Plato intends Timaeus' *proemium* to be a correction of Parmenides' epistemology and that the possibility of recognizing the influence of Being provides us with a route beyond the mortal epistemic limitations identified by Xenophanes.

CHAPTER 4

IMITATION AND LIMITATION IN TIMAEUS' *PROEMIUM*

Introduction

In the previous chapter, I offered an interpretation of Timaeus' εἰκώς-claim as expressing the necessary requirement for a successful account of a likeness to describe that likeness's relation to its model. My suggestion is that Timaeus is using εἰκώς in a technical sense whereby the semantic connection to εἰκών significantly informs its meaning. Timaeus' account is 'likely' insofar as it successfully describes a likeness *as a likeness*. This sense is, I think, fully compatible with εἰκώς in the *Timaeus* also carrying the standard meaning of 'plausible'. I take it that an account that describes the cosmos as a likeness will, for Timaeus, be a more plausible and persuasive cosmological account than one that does not. In arguing for this reading, I have sought to resist the kind of interpretation that takes Timaeus' εἰκώς to indicate that the account is *merely* likely, i.e. that it expresses a deficiency of either truth or certainty. In this chapter, I want to consider two further claims made by Timaeus. Both have been taken as evidence in favour of reading Timaeus' εἰκώς-claim as expressing some kind of limitation. The first is his assertion, providing the immediate context of the εἰκώς-claim, that those accounts which describe something created as a likeness of what is stable will stand in proportion to the stable accounts which properly describe the stable original (29b5–c3):

τοῦ μὲν οὖν μονίμου καὶ βεβαίου καὶ μετὰ νοῦ καταφανοῦς μονίμους καὶ ἀμεταπτώτους, καθ' ὅσον τε καὶ ἀνελέγκτοις προσήκει λόγοις εἶναι καὶ ἀνικήτοις, τούτου δὲ μηδὲν ἐλλείπειν· τοὺς δὲ τοῦ πρὸς μὲν ἐκεῖνο ἀπεικασθέντος, ὄντος δὲ εἰκόνος εἰκότας ἀνὰ λόγον τε ἐκείνων ὄντας· ὅτιπερ πρὸς γένεσιν οὐσία, τοῦτο πρὸς πίστιν ἀλήθεια.

So, accounts of what is permanent and stable and evident with the help of reason are stable and permanent, insofar as it is appropriate for accounts to achieve irrefutability and incontrovertibility and not to fall short of this standard, but accounts of that which is created to be like that [which is stable and unchanging], being of a likeness, are likely and stand in proportion to those others. As Being is to Coming-to-be, so truth is to convincingness.

The second claim, with which Timaeus concludes his methodological *proemium*, is that we should not be surprised if we find ourselves unable to produce an entirely consistent and accurate account. Rather, we should be content with an account no less εἰκώς than that offered by anyone else.[1] Indeed, being possessed of a human nature, we should expect nothing more than an εἰκὼς μῦθος (29c4–d3):

ἐὰν οὖν, ὦ Σώκρατες, πολλὰ πολλῶν πέρι, θεῶν καὶ τῆς τοῦ παντὸς γενέσεως, μὴ δυνατοὶ γιγνώμεθα πάντῃ πάντως αὐτοὺς ἑαυτοῖς ὁμολογουμένους λόγους καὶ ἀπηκριβωμένους ἀποδοῦναι, μὴ θαυμάσῃς· ἀλλ' ἐὰν ἄρα μηδενὸς ἧττον παρεχώμεθα εἰκότας, ἀγαπᾶν χρή, μεμνημένους ὡς ὁ λέγων ἐγὼ ὑμεῖς τε οἱ κριταὶ φύσιν ἀνθρωπίνην ἔχομεν, ὥστε περὶ τούτων τὸν εἰκότα μῦθον ἀποδεχομένους πρέπει τούτου μηδὲν ἔτι πέρα ζητεῖν.

So if, Socrates, we turn out frequently to be unable to produce accounts on a variety of topics, namely the gods and the coming-to-be of the universe, which are entirely mutually consistent and accurate in every way, don't be surprised. But if we supply accounts no less likely than any other's we should be content, bearing in mind that I as a speaker and you, sitting in judgement, possess a human nature, so that it is fitting that we should accept the likely story about these matters and search for nothing more.

In what follows, I will offer an interpretation of these passages which is in keeping with my reading of the εἰκώς-claim as primarily positive. The traditional reading of Timaeus' 'proportion' justifiably links 29c3 to the epistemology of the *Republic*. I will propose a further allusive target: Parmenides. πίστις at 29c3 is usually taken to refer to a cognitive state, equivalent to the *Republic*'s δόξα. In fact, there is good reason to read πίστις not as a cognitive state, but, as I have argued is the case for Parmenides, as a quality possessed by an account. Indeed, Timaeus' use of πίστις at 29c3 can usefully be read as a direct allusion to Parmenides' use of the term. By alluding to Parmenides, Plato is, I suggest, seeking to counter his predecessor's denigration of mortal cosmologies.

[1] See Ch. 3 n9 on Burnyeat's proposal that μηδενὸς at 29c7 should be read as masculine.

The standard reading of 29c4–d3 takes it to express the view that mortals are limited to 'mere likelihood'. I will argue that Timaeus is not, in fact, claiming that mortals are limited to an εἰκώς account. Rather, he is asserting that we are limited to a particular kind of εἰκώς account, an εἰκὼς μῦθος. This restriction derives in large part from mortals' inability to confirm their account. As we will see, Timaeus explicitly contrasts this inability with the divine capability to achieve confirmation. Finally, I will suggest that, by emphasizing the possibility of overcoming our mortal limitations, Timaeus is offering an answer to the kind of epistemological pessimism identifiable in the fragments of Xenophanes.

Before turning to the allusive resonances of these particular passages, it is worth taking the time briefly to consider to what degree and in what fashion the *Timaeus* should be understood as engaging with the thought of Plato's predecessors.

The allusive nature of the *Timaeus*

It is generally accepted that Plato intended the *Timaeus* to be read against the background of the *Peri Phuseōs* tradition.[2] It contains, however, no explicit criticism or discussion of the theories of earlier natural philosophers.[3] Rather, as Netz notes, 'the natural form of critique would be to suggest the target by allusion and then, by the difference from the target, to suggest the critique'.[4] Sometimes the criticism is more obvious, but even in these cases, it is rarely explicit. Thus, Timaeus' criticism of the tendency of some to posit 'principles' as basic material constituents at 48b3–c2 is clearly aimed at Empedocles, although Timaeus does not state this outright.[5]

2 On this relationship, see Naddaf (1997), Runia (1997) and Netz (2002), who (261) suggests Plato is offering a 'prophylactic' against the erroneous natural philosophy of the Presocratics.

3 Unlike Socrates' explicit criticism of Anaxagoras at *Phaedo* 97b8–99d2. In fact, the *Timaeus* can be read as providing the kind of account for which Socrates longs in the *Phaedo*. See Sedley (1989).

4 Netz (2002) 262n3.

5 Zeyl (2000) 37n51. Netz (2002) 262n3 suggests a further allusive criticism of Empedocles: 'Plato's use of ratios governing the four elements is as good as a direct reference to Empedocles, while Plato's seriously mathematical ratios are an implied critique: how

In addition to this general relationship to the Presocratics, many have noted a significant and specific connection to the poetry of Parmenides. Thus, in his discussion of Timaeus' *proemium*, Runia suggests that, 'if we should seek a model among these [Presocratic] predecessors, then we might suggest Parmenides. [...] It is not too extravagant to suggest that Plato has as it were coalesced Parmenides' *proemium* and his way of truth together into his own *proemium*, while the rest of Timaeus' *logos* takes over the task of Parmenides' way of seeming.'[6]

Happily for me, one of the most striking similarities between the cosmologies of Plato and Parmenides is their proclaimed status as εἰκώς/ἐοικώς. Now, although this similarity has been noted, it appears rarely to have been considered significant.[7] My contention is that this Parmenidean echo is deliberate and momentous, insofar as Plato wishes, in part, to present (the status of) the cosmology of the *Timaeus* as a correction of Parmenidean ontology and epistemology. In fact, the possibility of a Parmenidean influence on the *Timaeus* was acknowledged as early as Theophrastus.[8]

Another obvious point of resemblance between the *Timaeus* and Parmenides' poem is their shared distinction between Being as the object of νόησις and Coming-to-be as the object of δόξα.[9] The presence of this distinction in the *Timaeus* is often cited as indicating a connection with the ontology and epistemology of the *Republic* and it would, I think, be foolish to deny such a relation. But the fact that Timaeus may be alluding to the *Republic* does not rule out the possibility that he is simultaneously engaging with

poor Empedocles appears in comparison!' See Hershbell (1974) on the Empedoclean influences on the *Timaeus*.

6 Runia (1997) 111.

7 Palmer (1999) 26 suggests that Plato may have recognized Parmenides as qualifying his cosmology in a similar fashion to that of Xenophanes. See also Wilamowitz (1899) 204–5, Cornford (1937) 30, Meyer-Abich (1973) 20–1 and Popper (1998) 28.

8 Sedley (2002a) 42–5 argues that 'Theophrastus' recorded interpretation of Parmenides' physics is so close [to his treatment of the *Timaeus*] as to guarantee that he saw Plato in direct line of descent from Parmenides.' He goes on to suggest that Theophrastus may have traced this line of descent through Parmenides to Xenophanes.

9 Popper (1998) 28, in discussing *Timaeus* 27e–30c, calls this 'the Parmenidean distinction'. Gregory (2000) 252 asserts that Parmenides shares Timaeus' concern with producing accounts that are '*sungenes* with their explananda'.

the ontology and epistemology of Parmenides.[10] This possibility deserves closer scrutiny than it has generally been afforded.[11]

Elsewhere, some have seen a similarity in the way that both Parmenides' goddess (B8.60–61) and Timaeus (29c7–8) consider the relation of their cosmologies to rival accounts.[12] Timaeus urges his audience to be content with an account no less likely than that offered by anyone else; the goddess asserts that she is offering her διάκοσμος ἐοικώς 'so that no opinion (γνώμη) of mortals shall ever outstrip you'.[13] Just as both authors present their account as εἰκώς/ἐοικώς, so they appear to share a significant concern with the status of their cosmologies as capable of seeing off the challenge of any rivals.

One other similarity is perhaps worth acknowledging, if somewhat tentatively. In discussing Parmenides' poem, I argued for the importance of recognizing the forensic background of several of his key terms.[14] Some have identified a similar forensic

10 One might think, bearing in mind the Parmenidean feel of the arguments at the end of *Republic* 5, that an engagement with the epistemology of the *Republic* is to some extent an engagement with Parmenides. On the Parmenidean background to *Republic* 5, see Palmer (1999) 31–87.

11 Ballew (1974) is one of the few who treat the connection between the *Timaeus* and Parmenides in any significant fashion. She notes the similarity in the way both treat cosmology and epistemology schematically and their shared use of the 'like knows like' principle. Her conclusion (209) remains tentative: 'Whether Plato actually borrowed from Parmenides is still open to question, but two facts remain: one that Plato was familiar with Parmenides' thought, and two, that whatever differences there may be in the metaphysical systems of the two works, the *Timaeus*' epistemological system of straight and circular thought is also developed from Parmenides' poem.' Meyer-Abich (1973) 20–1 makes the intriguing suggestion that Plato intended the relationship between his *Parmenides* and *Timaeus* to be analogous to that between the two parts of Parmenides' poem.

12 See Cornford (1939) 46n2, Burnyeat (2005) 148n13 and 153 and Mourelatos (2010) 238–41.

13 Burnyeat (2005) 148n13 sees particularly strong evidence for a connection in the fact that Timaeus goes on to describe the limitations of human nature (ἐγὼ ὑμεῖς τε οἱ κριταὶ φύσιν ἀνθρωπίνην ἔχομεν), which he sees as echoing the goddess's concern with the opinions of mortals (βροτῶν). I will argue that Timaeus' concern with the limits imposed by human nature is more profitably compared to the epistemology of Xenophanes. For whilst Xenophanes regards such restriction as unavoidable, Parmenides' goddess is describing a mortal tendency to settle for opinion and specious plausibility rather than an inevitability. See Ch. 2 n147 for the suggestion that Parmenides' use of βροτῶν may allude to Xenophanes B14.

14 See 80–93.

undertone in Timaeus' reference to his audience as 'judges' (κριταί) at 29d1.[15] Now, as I have noted, although I interpret Timaeus' εἰκώς-claim as primarily informed by the semantic connection with εἰκών, I take this to be perfectly compatible with the rhetorical use of the term as indicating plausibility. Certainly, it is worth noting that several of those terms I identified as carrying forensic connotations in Parmenides (εἰκώς, πίστις and κρίσις) occur in Timaeus' *proemium*. Below, I will argue that 29c3 in particular alludes to Parmenides. Before doing so, however, it will be useful to consider the traditional reading of Timaeus' proportion as echoing the epistemology of the *Republic*.

Parallel (divided) lines

The proportion of 29c3, 'as Being is to Coming-to-be, so truth is to convincingness' (ὅτιπερ πρὸς γένεσιν οὐσία, τοῦτο πρὸς πίστιν ἀλήθεια) is offered as an elaboration of the claim that accounts of what is created to be like what is stable will stand in proportion (ἀνὰ λόγον) to stable accounts about the stable original.[16] Timaeus asserts that the relationship between the model (in this case, Being) and the likeness (Coming-to-be) is analogous to that between accounts of the model and accounts of the likeness.[17] What aspect of the relationship between Being and Coming-to-be is Timaeus adducing? Is it the way that Coming-to-be falls short of Being, so that we should understand accounts of the likeness as falling short of the truth (ἀλήθεια)? Or is it that, as Being is the

[15] Johansen (2004) 52 plausibly suggests that Timaeus may be inviting us to think of the εἰκώς of the law courts by referring to his audience as κριταί. See Ch. 3 n38.

[16] It is hard to see how Taylor (1928) 74 can be correct in his assertion that 29c3 is a 'mere "epexegesis", resuming the sense of an enunciation but adding nothing to it'. Clearly, Timaeus is adding something to what he has already said, if only because he is introducing new terms (ἀλήθεια and πίστις) to his explanation.

[17] Johansen (2004) 50 explains the proportion as follows: 'We now have four terms: (a) what is stable, (b) an account of what is stable, (c) what has come into being as a likeness, and (d) an account of a likeness. [. . .] an account is in a determinate relationship to its subject matter because it is an interpreter of its subject matter. We can therefore express the relationship between the terms as: as (a) stands to (b), so (c) stands to (d). The terms of this analogy can in turn be converted as follows: as (a) stands to (c) so (b) stands to (d). Or as Timaeus puts it: as being stands to becoming so truth (*aletheia*) stands to conviction (*pistis*).' Ashbaugh (1988) 24–5 schematizes the proportion.

model for Coming-to-be, so truth should be the model for accounts of Coming-to-be? Or is it, perhaps, both of these?

The most popular approach to interpreting Timaeus' proportion is to draw a parallel with one of the epistemological proportions set out in the *Republic*. Thus, Taylor claims that 29c3's πίστις 'must be equivalent to δόξα of [the proportion set out at] *Republic* 510a9'.[18] At *Republic* 509d6ff., Socrates identifies two realms, the visible (τὸ ὁρώμενον) and the intelligible (τὸ νοούμενον), corresponding to the two main unequal sections of a line. He goes on to subdivide the 'visible' section of the line 'in terms of relative clarity and opacity' (σαφηνείᾳ και ἀσαφείᾳ) between less clear images (εἰκόνες) and slightly clearer and less opaque originals of those images. It is not, however, this talk of images which excites Taylor's interest, but the fact that, at 510a8–10, Socrates segues from his division of the visible section to that of the intelligible by posing the following question:

Ἦ καὶ ἐθέλοις ἂν αὐτὸ φάναι, ἦν δ' ἐγώ, διῃρῆσθαι ἀληθείᾳ τε καὶ μή, ὡς τὸ δοξαστὸν πρὸς τὸ γνωστόν, οὕτω τὸ ὁμοιωθὲν πρὸς τὸ ᾧ ὡμοιώθη;

Now, looking at our division in terms of truth and its opposite, would you be prepared to say that the relation between the likeness and the thing it is a likeness of is equivalent to the relation between the object of opinion[19] and the object of understanding?

On Taylor's reading, 'the relation between the likeness and the thing it is a likeness of' is equivalent to that between Coming-to-be (which is created as a likeness) and Being (the model of which Coming-to-be is a likeness) in the *Timaeus*. Consequently, 'the object of opinion' should be equivalent to 29c3's πίστις, and 'the object of understanding' to ἀλήθεια.[20] Here, however, there seems to be a difficulty, for it is striking that, whilst ἀλήθεια at *Republic*

[18] Taylor (1928) 74. See also Cornford (1935) 29, Owen (1965) 337, Osborne (1996) 187, Brisson (2001) 230 and Mourelatos (2010) 232. Note, however, that Santa Cruz (1997) 133–6 rejects the equivalence of εἰκὼς λόγος with the *Republic*'s δόξα, arguing that it more properly corresponds to διάνοια.

[19] At this point, Socrates alters his terminology from τὸ ὁρωμένον to τὸ δοξαστόν.

[20] Note that Taylor actually states that 29c3's πίστις must be equivalent to δόξα rather than το δοξαστόν. On this reading, ἀλήθεια will refer not to the object of understanding (τὸ γνωστόν), but to understanding (νόησις) itself.

510a8–10 is a quality which characterizes the objects being compared, in the *Timaeus*, it has become a term in the proportion.[21] This difference is remarked upon by Burnyeat, who notes 'The proportion [of 29c3] makes everyone think of the *Republic*, rightly I am sure. Yet you will not find quite *this* proportion [. . .] in any of the places where proportions are set out in the *Republic*.'[22] Burnyeat goes on to suggest that 'the closest is *Republic* 534a[2–8], which does say, among other things, that being is to becoming as ἐπιστήμη (not ἀλήθεια) is to πίστις (and διάνοια to εἰκασία)':

καὶ δόξαν μὲν περὶ γένεσιν, νόησιν δὲ περὶ οὐσίαν· καὶ ὅτι οὐσία πρὸς γένεσιν, νόησιν πρὸς δόξαν, καὶ ὅτι νόησις πρὸς δόξαν, ἐπιστήμην πρὸς πίστιν καὶ διάνοιαν πρὸς εἰκασίαν· τὴν δ' ἐφ' οἷς ταῦτα ἀναλογίαν καὶ διαίρεσιν διχῇ ἑκατέρου, δοξαστοῦ τε καὶ νοητοῦ, ἐῶμεν, ὦ Γλαύκων, ἵνα μὴ ἡμᾶς πολλαπλασίων λόγων ἐμπλήσῃ ἢ ὅσων οἱ παρεληλυθότες.

Opinion is concerned with Coming-to-be, intellection with Being. And as Being is to Coming-to-be, so intellect is to opinion, and as intellection is to opinion, so knowledge is to belief and thought to imaging. But as for the ratios between the things these are set over and the division of either the opinable or the intelligible section into two, let's pass these by, Glaucon, lest they involve us in arguments many times longer than the ones we've already gone through.

What are we to make of the fact that, in this passage, ἐπιστήμη replaces *Timaeus* 29c3's ἀλήθεια? Can we really read the two as equivalent? After all, whilst truth is obviously necessary for understanding, one would tend to regard it neither as equivalent to nor sufficient for understanding. Burnyeat, however, argues that this equivalence is unproblematic, stating that, at *Timaeus* 29c3, '[ἀλήθεια] stands where ἐπιστήμη stood in *Republic* 534a, on the side of mind rather than the objects of mind. It therefore has to refer to a cognitive state rather than a cognised state.'[23]

As I have noted, that there is some connection between the epistemologies of the *Timaeus* and *Republic* seems plausible and significant. There are, of course, clear and deliberate allusions to

[21] This problem is equally applicable to Archer-Hind's (1888) 89 claim that 29c3 expresses 'precisely' the analogy of *Republic* 511e.

[22] Burnyeat (2005) 152.

[23] Burnyeat (2005) 152 cites the argument of Szaif (1996) 61–7 who draws a parallel with the Stoic use of ἀλήθεια as a term to describe the systematic knowledge of τὸ ἀληθές. Note that Szaif's reading of *Timaeus* 29c3 is based on the assumption that it is an allusion to the *Republic*. See also Rowe (2003) 29.

the *Republic* from the outset of the *Timaeus*, most obviously in Socrates' paraphrase of the political discussions of the previous day (17c1–19a9) and his request that his companions present the figures from his story in action (19b2–20c3).[24] I do, however, have a concern about the dissolution of the difference between the two proportions achieved by reading ἀλήθεια as a cognitive state. Burnyeat reformulates the proportion of *Timaeus* 29c3 as follows:

As being is to becoming, so is ἀλήθεια to πίστις *and* so are (successful) type (i) [i.e. stable] accounts to successful type (ii) [i.e. likely] accounts.

Burnyeat thus reads the connection between ἀλήθεια and πίστις as *supplementary* to that between the two kinds of account.[25] But the text presents the relation between ἀλήθεια and πίστις as that between the *two kinds of account*, rather than between the cognitive states set over those accounts.[26] In what follows I will offer an interpretation of 29c3 that seems more in keeping with this aspect of the text. Central to my reading is the contention that, in addition to its connection with the *Republic*, 29c3 should be read as alluding to Parmenides' epistemology.

A Parmenidean allusion

Beyond the *Republic*, Burnyeat suggests another possible parallel for 29c3:

[Plato] is both echoing and subverting Parmenides' distinction between 'the unshaken heart of well-rounded ἀλήθεια, on the one hand, and on the other, the opinions of mortals, in which there is no true πίστις' (fr. 1, 29–30).[27]

Parmenides' goddess labels the cosmology she presents ἐοικώς, whilst Timaeus aims for an εἰκώς account. The goddess cites πίστις ἀληθής as the quality possessed by truth but lacking from

[24] On the connection between the *Republic* and *Timaeus* see Carone (2005) 24–5 and Johansen (2004) 7–23.

[25] Burnyeat (2005) 154: 'in the proportion [of 29c3] πίστις, like ἀλήθεια, is a cognitive state, not the εἰκότες λόγοι that give rise to it'.

[26] Howald (1922) 67 reads πίστις as synonymous with εἰκώς. Runia (1989) 441n18 calls the distinction at 29b–c a '"logological" division'.

[27] Burnyeat (2005) 153.

deceptive, ἐοικώς representation of mortal beliefs; Timaeus cites the relation between πίστις and ἀλήθεια as a gloss on the status of his cosmology as εἰκώς. The similarities are striking enough to indicate that Plato is deliberately echoing his predecessor. The differences suggest that the allusion is intended as a correction of Parmenides.[28]

Recognizing this allusion will, I think, be helpful in two important ways. First, it helps us with what I have suggested is an unsatisfactory reading of πίστις and, in particular, ἀλήθεια as cognitive states. In Chapter 2, I argued that Parmenides' πίστις is not a cognitive state, but rather a quality attributed to accounts.[29] It refers to the persuasive force of an account rather than the persuasion that an account induces. Thus, at B1.29–30, the goddess tells Parmenides that he will learn the beliefs (δόξας) of mortals, 'in which there is no true cogency (πίστις ἀληθής)'. At B8.26–28, the goddess tells of how the force of 'true cogency' (πίστις ἀληθής) has driven out Coming-to-be and Passing-away. For Parmenides, πίστις ἀληθής is a quality possessed by a true account which describes the intelligible realm of Being, but lacking from the subjectively persuasive, specious cosmological accounts of Coming-to-be that mortals tend to fabricate.

Bearing this Parmenidean parallel in mind, I suggest that we should read πίστις at *Timaeus* 29c3 in a similar fashion, as a quality possessed by an account, rather than as a cognitive state. Doing so enables us to read ἀλήθεια similarly and thus avoid taking it to be equivalent to ἐπιστήμη. Rather than interpreting 'ἀλήθεια is to πίστις' as expressing a relationship between knowledge and belief, we can render the proportion as 'As Being is to Coming-to-be, so truth is to convincingness.'[30]

The Parmenidean background is also significant for our understanding of the purpose of the proportion at 29c3. What is

28 I am further encouraged by the fact that Proclus *In Timaeum* 1.345 cites Parmenides B1.29–30 (and B2) in his explanation of *Timaeus* 29c3. See Martijn (2006).

29 See 90–3.

30 In Ch. 2, I translated Parmenides' πίστις as 'cogency' (see 92), because this seemed to me to go some way to expressing the sense of compulsion implicit in his use of the term. For its occurrence at *Timaeus* 29c3, I have followed Zeyl (2000) in opting for the translation 'convincingness' insofar as this renders the term as one describing a quality of an account without implying that any kind of Parmenidean necessity is at work.

significant here is the way Plato 'subverts' Parmenides' formula of πίστις ἀληθής. At the end of B1, Parmenides' goddess denies that accounts of Coming-to-be possess πίστις ἀληθής:

> . . . χρεὼ δέ σε πάντα πυθέσθαι
> ἠμὲν Ἀληθείης εὐπειθέος ἀτρεμὲς ἦτορ
> ἠδὲ βροτῶν δόξας, ταῖς οὐκ ἔνι πίστις ἀληθής.
>
> . . . And it is right that you should learn all things,
> Both the unmoving heart of persuasive truth,
> And the beliefs of mortals, in which there is no true cogency.

I have argued that Parmenides opposes the ἐοικώς nature of mortal beliefs about Coming-to-be to the πίστις ἀληθής of the goddess's description of Being.[31] I suggested that Parmenides' use of ἐοικώς at B8.60 indicates in part that, for all that it may bear some similarity to the truly cogent arguments of the *Aletheia*, the *Doxa* is itself no more than specious. Such accounts do not justify the faith that mortals hold in them, for they possess only subjective appeal. For Parmenides, truth can only be achieved by descriptions of Being and there is neither truth nor genuine cogency in accounts of Coming-to-be.

Whilst Parmenides' goddess condemns the beliefs of mortals about Coming-to-be as lacking in πίστις ἀληθής, Timaeus' proportion attributes πίστις to accounts about the cosmic εἰκών, i.e. about Coming-to-be. Admittedly, this is not πίστις ἀληθής, but πίστις *simpliciter*. What the proportion tells us, however, is that this πίστις is somehow related to truth, or rather that it is related to truth in the same way that Coming-to-be is related to Being.

What is the relation between Coming-to-be and Being? Those wanting to read the proportion as evidence in favour of a denigration of the cosmological εἰκώς account may point to *Timaeus* 27d5–28a4:

> Ἔστιν οὖν δὴ κατ' ἐμὴν δόξαν πρῶτον διαιρετέον τάδε· τί τὸ ὂν ἀεί, γένεσιν δὲ οὐκ ἔχον, καὶ τί τὸ γιγνόμενον μὲν ἀεί, ὂν δὲ οὐδέποτε; τὸ μὲν δὴ νοήσει μετὰ λόγου περιληπτόν, ἀεὶ κατὰ ταὐτὰ ὄν, τὸ δ' αὖ δόξῃ μετ' αἰσθήσεως ἀλόγου δοξαστόν, γιγνόμενον καὶ ἀπολλύμενον, ὄντως δὲ οὐδέποτε ὄν.

[31] See Ch. 2 107–8.

In my opinion we should start with this distinction: what is that which always is but has no Coming-to-be, and then what is that which is always coming-to-be but never really is? The former is grasped by understanding with the aid of reason and is always the same. The latter, meanwhile, is perceived by unreasoning sense-perception, always coming-to-be and passing away, but never really being.

One possibility is that 29c3 makes a point quite similar to the view I have attributed to Parmenides. On this reading, the implication of Timaeus' proportion would be that, just as Being and Coming-to-be are mutually exclusive, so the truth of stable accounts and the persuasiveness of Timaeus' εἰκώς account are mutually exclusive. On this reading, Timaeus' cosmology, like that offered by Parmenides' goddess, is no more than specious.

It will surprise no one that I want to resist this kind of deflationary reading of 29c3. Indeed, I think the text justifies such resistance. For Timaeus' proportion is not offered in the context of this discussion of the essential difference between Being and Coming-to-be; it is offered as explanatory of the claim that an account 'of what is likened to the stable original, being of a likeness, will be likely'. So, rather than explicating the *difference* between accounts of Coming-to-be and Being, it is presented as a gloss on the way an account of an image *relates to* its original. The message of 29c3 is that a successful account of the cosmos (which possesses πίστις) should relate to a successful account of its model (which possesses truth) in the same way that the image itself (Coming-to-be) relates to the model (Being). I take the salient aspect of this relation to be that which Timaeus has mentioned immediately before introducing the proportion: that of one thing being likened to another. Coming-to-be is as it is because it has been created as a likeness of Being. Likewise, a persuasive description of Coming-to-be should be similarly informed by the truths of a description of Being.[32] On my reading, the proportion glosses the εἰκώς claim thus: a successful account of a likeness will be likely, i.e. will represent the relation between likeness and original. For as the model (Being) influences the image (Coming-to-be), so the truth (of an account

[32] Thus Gill (1993) 58 reads 29c3's πίστις as expressing how an εἰκώς account merits 'trust' or 'credibility'. Wright (2000a) 7 suggests that 'conviction (*pistis*) belongs with opinion and is acceptable for day-to-day activities if the opinion on which it is based is right opinion'.

about Being) should influence the convincingness (of an account about Coming-to-be).

Whilst, as 27d5–28a4 tells us, there is no Being in Coming-to-be, Coming-to-be is modelled on Being and is thus a representation of Being. As I have been arguing, an account of a likeness will be 'likely' insofar as it describes the likeness *as a likeness*. What 29c3 tells us is that, in the case of the particular likeness that is the cosmos, to describe it as a likeness will be to give an account which is somehow influenced by or representative of the truth about Being. This is not to say that the account should aim to be an account of Being, for that would entail its no longer being a description of the likeness. Rather, the likely account should be an account of the likeness that, in describing it as a likeness of Being, is informed by the truth about Being.

In Chapter 3, I argued against those who read Timaeus' εἰκώς-claim as indicating a lack of truth, citing 37b3–8 as evidence that it is indeed possible to achieve true beliefs about Coming-to-be.[33] At this point, some may be wondering how this can be reconciled with 29c3. For if truth stands to πίστις (i.e. the quality possessed by the εἰκώς account of the cosmos) as Being stands to Coming-to-be and there is no Being in Coming-to-be (27d5–28a1), then it seems there should be no truth in πίστις (or no πίστις ἀληθής). Does this mean that there is no truth in the likely cosmology after all? In fact, I do think we are intended to read ἀλήθεια and πίστις as analogous to Being and Coming-to-be in being mutually exclusive. But this seems to be compatible with the possibility of achieving truth about Coming-to-be as long as we understand there to be a difference in the kinds of truth achievable about Being and Coming-to-be. I suggest that the truth of successful accounts of Being, i.e. ἀλήθεια at 29c3, is *unqualified* truth. For, as is often recognized, Coming-to-be is a fickle and unstable object and, as such, it cannot be described by unqualified truth. However, it can and should be described with qualified truths. Indeed, we can think of the relationship between πίστις and ἀλήθεια as a relationship between qualified and unqualified truth. An account of Coming-to-be should possess πίστις insofar as it expresses contingent

[33] See 133–7.

and qualified truths about the cosmos informed by and in some sense representative of the unqualified ἀλήθεια which describes its model.[34] This relationship between qualified and unqualified truth is analogous to that between Coming-to-be and Being. Most importantly, it reflects the influence of Being on the nature of Coming-to-be. Coming-to-be is utterly separate from Being, but has been created as a likeness of Being. Similarly, the πίστις account of Coming-to-be does not possess, but rather is informed by, the unqualified ἀλήθεια of an account of Being.

Parmenides' goddess offers two alternatives: the πίστις ἀληθής of a true account of Being or the specious appeal of a merely ἐοικώς account of Coming-to-be. For Plato, it seems, there is a brand of πίστις that can be possessed by an εἰκώς account. Although it is not Parmenides' πίστις ἀληθής, it is πίστις significantly informed by ἀλήθεια. The convincingness of Timaeus' cosmology derives not from its (unqualified) truth, but from its describing something created as a likeness of Being. By altering Parmenides' formula of πίστις ἀληθής, to create a kind of πίστις that is not itself ἀληθής but is informed by ἀλήθεια, Timaeus points to a third way between Parmenides' two paths. In doing so, he is, I suggest, seeking to rehabilitate the status of talk about the perceptible world. For Parmenides, such talk is utterly devoid of truth. However, in alluding to this strict division between truth and cosmology, Plato implicitly criticizes it by reminding us that, since Coming-to-be is modelled on Being, it is fundamentally influenced by the nature of Being. As a result, accounts of Coming-to-be will not be devoid of any kind of truth whatever.[35] For, whilst they can never possess unqualified ἀλήθεια, they can achieve 'convincingness' insofar as they will, by describing a likeness of Being, be informed by the truth which describes the model.[36] For Plato, cosmology is of

[34] Finally, then, we see that 29c3 does resemble the proportions of *Republic* 510a8–10 and 511e, since it too illustrates degrees of truth. Thus Osborne (1996) 187 notes that Timaeus' 'ontological hierarchy is matched by an epistemological hierarchy of truth'.

[35] See Ballew (1974) 208 who notes that Parmenides regards opinions and sensations as worthless and detrimental to the pursuit of knowledge because appearances 'are not'; in the *Timaeus*, however, resemblances, *qua* resemblances of the real, can be helpful to the pursuit of knowledge.

[36] Thus Lloyd (1991) 350 argues that, for Plato, the fact that the perceptible world has certain qualities in a qualified way saves the perceptibles from the incoherence which

value because to talk about the cosmos is to talk about a likeness of intelligible reality.[37]

Timaeus 29c4–d3

I return, finally, to the conclusion of Timaeus' *proemium*:

ἐὰν οὖν, ὦ Σώκρατες, πολλὰ πολλῶν πέρι, θεῶν καὶ τῆς τοῦ παντὸς γενέσεως, μὴ δυνατοὶ γιγνώμεθα πάντῃ πάντως αὐτοὺς ἑαυτοῖς ὁμολογουμένους λόγους καὶ ἀπηκριβωμένους ἀποδοῦναι, μὴ θαυμάσῃς· ἀλλ' ἐὰν ἄρα μηδενὸς ἧττον παρεχώμεθα εἰκότας, ἀγαπᾶν χρή, μεμνημένους ὡς ὁ λέγων ἐγὼ ὑμεῖς τε οἱ κριταὶ φύσιν ἀνθρωπίνην ἔχομεν, ὥστε περὶ τούτων τὸν εἰκότα μῦθον ἀποδεχομένους πρέπει τούτου μηδὲν ἔτι πέρα ζητεῖν.

So if, Socrates, we turn out frequently to be unable to produce accounts on a variety of topics, namely the gods and the coming-to-be of the universe, which are entirely mutually consistent and accurate in every way, don't be surprised. But if we supply accounts no less likely than any other's we should be content, bearing in mind that I as a speaker and you, sitting in judgement, possess a human nature, so that it is fitting that we should accept the likely story about these matters and search for nothing more.

In Chapter 3, I argued that a successful account of a likeness will necessarily be likely, insofar as it will describe its subject-matter as a likeness. In addition, I suggested that likelihood is a quality to be aspired to, rather than one for which we should settle. Towards the end of his introduction, however, Timaeus does seem to suggest, not only that one 'should be content' (ἀγαπᾶν χρή) with an account that is no less likely than that offered by anyone else, but also that, being possessed of a human nature, one should 'search for nothing more' (μηδὲν ἔτι πέρα ζητεῖν) than a 'likely story' (τὸν εἰκότα μῦθον). Some have taken this as evidence that Timaeus is claiming that humans are limited to mere likelihood in describing the cosmos.[38] Unsurprisingly, I do not think that

threatens Parmenides' *Doxa*. See also Johansen (2004) 162 who criticizes Cornford for collapsing Timaeus' position into a Parmenidean-style dismissal of the physical world as unintelligible.

37 Vlastos (1965b) 9 suggests a difference between Plato, for whom the sensible world is the object of δόξα, and Parmenides, for whom it is the creature of δόξα.

38 Sedley (2007) 111 suggests that Timaeus' 'appeal to human cognitive inadequacy' is connected to our inability to give anything more than a likely account about the creation of the cosmos.

Timaeus is limiting mortals to likelihood. Rather, he is noting that we are restricted to giving a particular kind of likely account: an εἰκὼς μῦθος. The limitation is signalled not by εἰκώς, but by the introduction of the term μῦθος. We should, Timaeus tells us, aspire to give a likely account, but we should be content if we can do no more than produce a likely μῦθος.

Timaeus begins by warning Socrates not to be surprised if 'we turn out frequently to be unable to produce accounts on a variety of topics, namely the gods and the coming-to-be of the universe, which are entirely mutually consistent and accurate in every way'.[39] Note that Timaeus is not claiming that such consistent and accurate accounts about Coming-to-be are impossible but, rather, he is acknowledging that they are difficult to achieve.[40] This may well be a result of the fickle nature of the subject-matter that is Coming-to-be, but it is not, I suggest, a direct result of its being a likeness.[41]

Timaeus goes on to claim that we should be content 'if we are able to supply accounts no less likely than any other's'. One must be careful not to read this claim as setting likelihood in opposition to consistency and accuracy. Timaeus is not saying 'we cannot have accurate accounts about Coming-to-be (or likenesses) so we should settle for merely likely ones'. Rather, he is establishing the priorities one should recognize in trying to talk about the cosmos. Whether or not one can achieve accuracy and consistency, one should always aim to produce a likely account, i.e. one should always aim to discuss the cosmos *qua* likeness. Further, one can be satisfied so long as the account of the cosmos that results is no

39 I follow Burnyeat (2005) 155 in reading this inconsistency as between multiple λόγοι rather than as the internal inconsistency of a single account.

40 Thus Burnyeat (2005) 154 translates 'If therefore, Socrates, in many respects concerning many things [i.e. *not* in all respects or all things], regarding the gods and the generation of the universe, we find ourselves unable to furnish accounts which are in every way in agreement with each other and made completely precise, do not be surprised.' The gloss (and emphasis) 'i.e. *not* in all respects or all things' is Burnyeat's. It is also noteworthy that Timaeus comments on the difficulty of producing *complete*, as opposed to *any*, consistency and accuracy. Nor is Timaeus, as Cornford (1935) 28 claims, asserting that 'since the world is only a likeness of the real [. . .] there can be no exact, or even self-consistent, science of Nature'. It is also noteworthy that Timaeus comments on the difficulty of producing *complete*, as opposed to *any*, consistency and accuracy.

41 It may also, as Morgan (2000) 271–2 suggests, be due to the limitations of language as essentially provisional. Timaeus may be hinting at this at 29b7–c1.

less likely, i.e. no less descriptive of its status as a likeness, than that offered by anyone else.[42]

What, finally, are we to make of Timaeus' reference to human nature? Again, one needs to be careful not to read the passage as stating that 'we should be content with likelihood since we are only human'. Timaeus is making two separate points: (a) we should be content with accounts no less likely than those offered by anyone else,[43] and (b) as humans, we should accept an εἰκὼς μῦθος, and look for nothing more. The emphasis here is, I think, on μῦθος rather than εἰκώς. The point is not that, as humans, we can hope for nothing more than an εἰκώς account but that, as humans, we can hope for nothing more than a μῦθος (which should aspire to be εἰκώς).[44] On this reading, an account of the cosmos given by god would, just like those of humans, aim to be εἰκώς, i.e. representative. But, whereas humans are limited to an εἰκὼς μῦθος, god can aim for something better. μῦθος in this regard expresses the kind of limitation that others have read into εἰκώς. Humans are limited to an εἰκὼς μῦθος not because they are restricted to accounts which are merely εἰκώς, but because they can hope for nothing better than a μῦθος. What is the nature of this restriction to μῦθος?

Mythic limitations

My suggestion is that 29c4–d3 does indeed express a certain kind of qualification as to the kind of cosmological accounts that humans can provide. But rather than reading εἰκώς as expressing this qualification, it is the term μῦθος that is significant here. Now, Plato's use of and attitude towards μῦθος is a notoriously complex

[42] Which is, of course, compatible with its being 'no less plausible than any other's'.

[43] Timaeus seems to assume that there are degrees of likelihood. On my reading, the degree of likelihood reflects the extent to which an account succeeds in describing a likeness as related to its model. Timaeus is not, as Taylor (1928) 75 suggests, exhorting us to achieve 'the nearest approximation [to truth] that we can get'.

[44] Gill (1993) 59 notes that our ability to produce an account is 'limited by the extent to which we, as human beings, can understand the supra-human, or "divine" scale of what is involved; thus the resulting account is characterized as a "likely story" (*eikos muthos*), rather than a "likely account" (*eikos logos*)'.

issue.[45] I make no claims to give a comprehensive treatment of this question here, either in general or with regard to the *Timaeus* in particular. I think it highly likely that Timaeus' reference to his account as a μῦθος is intended to signal far more than a limitation. So, for example, it seems to allude to the kind of 'mythic' cosmology provided by Hesiod.[46] Equally, it can be read as pointing to the narrative form of Timaeus' account.[47] My focus, however, is on what I take to be the deficiency expressed by Timaeus' use of the term μῦθος. This may be only one aspect of the term, but it is significant for my purposes insofar as it seems to overlap with the kind of deficiency that others have read into his use of εἰκώς.

As we have seen, at 29c7–d3, Timaeus suggests a connection between human nature and the production of an εἰκὼς μῦθος. Something similar is to be found at 68c7–d7:[48]

τὰ δὲ ἄλλα ἀπὸ τούτων σχεδὸν δῆλα αἷς ἂν ἀφομοιούμενα μείξεσιν διασῴζοι τὸν εἰκότα μῦθον. εἰ δέ τις τούτων ἔργῳ σκοπούμενος βάσανον λαμβάνοι, τὸ τῆς ἀνθρωπίνης καὶ θείας φύσεως ἠγνοηκὼς ἂν εἴη διάφορον, ὅτι θεὸς μὲν τὰ πολλὰ εἰς ἓν συγκεραννύναι καὶ πάλιν ἐξ ἑνὸς εἰς πολλὰ διαλύειν ἱκανῶς ἐπιστάμενος ἅμα καὶ δυνατός, ἀνθρώπων δὲ οὐδεὶς οὐδέτερα τούτων ἱκανὸς οὔτε ἔστι νῦν οὔτε εἰς αὖθίς ποτε ἔσται.

With regard to the other colours, it should be fairly clear from the examples given by what mixtures they would be created as a likeness in such a way as to preserve the likely story. But if someone investigating these things in practice were to test them out, he would show himself to be ignorant of the difference between the human and the divine natures, since while god sufficiently possesses the knowledge and power to mix many things into one and to dissolve one into many, there is no human being who is up to such a task, either now or in the future.

45 On the complexities of Plato's use of myth, see Partenie (2009).
46 On this connection see Pender (2010) and Sedley (2010).
47 As suggested by Betegh (2010) 222–4. Burnyeat (2005) 144–5 notes that the εἰκὼς μῦθος is a theogony, describing the birth of the cosmos which is a god. He presents a compelling case for translating μῦθος as 'myth' rather than 'some anodyne substitute such as "story", "tale", "account".' I have nevertheless chosen to render μῦθος as 'story', a word which I feel captures the essence of μῦθος as an unverified account. Sedley (2007) 93 remarks that 'the speech's outward form is largely that of a creation myth, although the register of its discourse switches repeatedly between myth, fable, prayer, scientific analysis, and philosophical argument'.
48 As noted by Johansen (2004) 62–3.

Timaeus claims that it is easy enough to produce a 'likely story' about colour-mixture.[49] Further, just as at 29c7–d3, he goes on to warn that such a likely story should be the limit of our ambitions. In this case, he specifies that what is beyond us is the practical verification of these mixtures. In this context, Timaeus draws an explicit contrast between human and divine natures. However, the implication is not that god could, through his superior understanding and power, achieve an account of colour-mixture that is more than εἰκώς. Just like any budding mortal cosmologist, god should aim to give an εἰκώς, i.e. representative, account of the creation of the likenesses (ἀφομοιούμενα) of colours (perhaps by explaining how perceptible colours are the best possible representations of the Forms). Where he would aim to surpass humans is in providing an account that is better than a μῦθος.

Timaeus seems to think it would be a relatively straightforward endeavour to produce an εἰκὼς μῦθος about colour-mixture. This should be contrasted with his assertion, made only lines before (68b6–8), that, in discussing the proportions of such mixtures, it would be impossible to give an εἰκὼς λόγος:

> τὸ δὲ ὅσον μέτρον ὅσοις, οὐδ' εἴ τις εἰδείη, νοῦν ἔχει τὸ λέγειν, ὧν μήτε τινὰ ἀνάγκην μήτε τὸν εἰκότα λόγον καὶ μετρίως ἄν τις εἰπεῖν εἴη δυνατός.
>
> But, it wouldn't be sensible to state the proportions [of these mixtures], even if one could know them. It would be impossible, even approximately, to give either a proof or a likely account of these matters.

So, whilst it is impossible to give an εἰκὼς λόγος of the precise proportions involved in colour-mixture, it is easy to achieve an εἰκὼς μῦθος of the general mixtures which produce various colours. Presumably, attempting a practical verification of colour-mixture would involve knowing the precise proportions involved. So, it seems, insofar as we lack the εἰκὼς λόγος about those proportions, we are limited to an εἰκὼς μῦθος.

What then, in this context, is the difference between a λόγος and a μῦθος? Johansen suggests that it is one of degrees of likelihood:

[49] Likewise, at 59c5–d3, we are told that: 'the rest of such things are no more longer tricky to explain, aiming at the form of a likely story' (τἆλλα δὲ τῶν τοιούτων οὐδὲν ποικίλον ἔτι διαλογίσασθαι τὴν τῶν εἰκότων μύθων μεταδιώκοντα ἰδέαν).

> [Timaeus' use of] *muthos* reminds us that the most likely account that is available to us as human beings may not be the account (*logos*) that is the most likely *tout court*. The *muthos/logos* distinction thus survives as a distinction within the general category of likely accounts (*logoi*). Amongst likely accounts (*logoi*) some accounts (referred to as *logoi*) are likelier than others (referred to as *muthoi*). *Logos* here is used both for the genus 'account' and for a particular species of account which has greater rationality than the other species of account referred to as *muthos*. We have then a distinction within the genus of accounts (*logoi*) between the species *logoi* and the species *muthoi*.[50]

Johansen's classification of a (genus) εἰκὼς λόγος and its two species, (species) εἰκὼς λόγος and (species) εἰκὼς μῦθος, is particularly useful.[51] However, I want to resist the suggestion that the salient difference between the two species is one of degrees of likelihood. Johansen glosses 'degree of likelihood' as the extent to which accounts 'present the cosmos as more or less like its paradigm'.[52] On this reading, it seems that the relationship of similarity between copies and paradigm is somehow determined by the author of the account. On my reading, the 'degree of likelihood' that one should aim to maximize is simply the extent to which an account describes a likeness as a likeness. One could thus give an equally likely account of two copies, even in a case where one is, in whatever way, more like its paradigm. This is because, whether the likeness bears a close resemblance or not, it is created as a likeness and it is in explaining this that an account becomes εἰκώς.

I suggest that one significant difference between a (species) εἰκὼς λόγος and an εἰκὼς μῦθος is that of the degree to which they can be verified. I noted above that the limitation to μῦθος is explicitly linked to our human nature and that, consequently, god is free from such constrictions. Timaeus returns to the difference between human and divine at 72d4–7:

[50] Johansen (2004) 63. Burnyeat (2005) 145 argues that Timaeus' μῦθος 'is a λόγος as well as a myth. Timaeus' myth, unlike Hesiod's, is as well reasoned as any of the PreSocratic cosmogonies in the περὶ φύσεως tradition.'

[51] Thus, when, at 67d1–2, Timaeus asserts 'so, with reference to colours, it would be most likely and suitable for a reasoned account to give this explanation' (τῇδ' οὖν τῶν χρωμάτων πέρι μάλιστα εἰκὸς πρέποι τ' ἂν ἐπιεικεῖ λόγῳ διεξελθεῖν) he must be referring to the (genus) εἰκὼς λόγος.

[52] Johansen (2004) 61.

Τὰ μὲν οὖν περὶ ψυχῆς, ὅσον θνητὸν ἔχει καὶ ὅσον θεῖον, καὶ ὅπῃ καὶ μεθ' ὧν καὶ δι' ἃ χωρὶς ᾠκίσθη, τὸ μὲν ἀληθὲς ὡς εἴρηται, θεοῦ συμφήσαντος τότ' ἂν οὕτως μόνως διισχυριζοίμεθα.

So, in matters concerning the soul, how much of it is mortal and how much divine, where these parts are and connected to what and why they are situated separately, that the truth has been told is something we could affirm only via divine confirmation.

Although Timaeus can give an account of the nature of soul, he is unable to affirm its truth. Only god, he says, could offer the confirmation necessary for certainty.[53] He immediately goes on to assert:

τό γε μὴν εἰκὸς ἡμῖν εἰρῆσθαι, καὶ νῦν καὶ ἔτι μᾶλλον ἀνασκοποῦσι διακινδυνευτέον τὸ φάναι καὶ πεφάσθω.

But that what has been said is, at least, likely is something we should be bold enough to state, both now and more so as we continue in our investigations, so let this be our claim.

The point is not that we should settle for likelihood instead of confirmed truth, but that, even if we cannot produce an εἰκὼς λόγος, i.e. a verifiable representative account, we can comfort ourselves with the fact that we have at least achieved some kind of representative account, albeit unverifiable. There is a clear similarity between this passage and 68c7–d7, where we saw that the ease of providing an εἰκὼς μῦθος was contrasted with the human inability to verify this account. At 68b6–8 the impossibility of offering an εἰκὼς λόγος is explicitly an alternative to the impossibility of offering a demonstration (ἀνάγκην). Presumably, such a demonstration would provide confirmation of our account and thus achieve the impossible feat of converting our εἰκὼς μῦθος into an εἰκὼς λόγος. An account which is not or cannot be verified is a μῦθος.

One final instance of εἰκὼς μῦθος remains to be considered. At 59c5–d3, Timaeus reflects on the possibility and suitability of producing likely accounts:

τἆλλα δὲ τῶν τοιούτων οὐδὲν ποικίλον ἔτι διαλογίσασθαι τὴν τῶν εἰκότων μύθων μεταδιώκοντα ἰδέαν· ἣν ὅταν τις ἀναπαύσεως ἕνεκα τοὺς περὶ τῶν ὄντων ἀεὶ καταθέμενος λόγους, τοὺς γενέσεως πέρι διαθεώμενος εἰκότας ἀμεταμέλητον

53 See also the contrast between human and divine knowledge at 53d4–7.

ἡδονὴν κτᾶται, μέτριον ἂν ἐν τῷ βίῳ παιδιὰν καὶ φρόνιμον ποιοῖτο. ταύτῃ δὴ καὶ τὰ νῦν ἐφέντες τὸ μετὰ τοῦτο τῶν αὐτῶν πέρι τὰ ἑξῆς εἰκότα δίιμεν τῇδε.

There would be nothing complicated about going on to produce an explanation of other such things on the template of the likely stories we have been pursuing. Whenever anyone, for the sake of relaxation, sets aside accounts about things that always are, enjoying the carefree pleasure of going over the likely accounts about Coming-to-be, he would be endowing his life with a temperate and sensible pastime. So now we'll cut loose and press on with what is likely about what comes next.

Now, this passage does not overtly link the εἰκὼς μῦθος to human nature. However, as Johansen notes, Timaeus is 'assuming a human point of view' in recommending the relaxing pursuit of likely μῦθοι, for the divine mind would never require a break from thinking about the Forms.[54]

In the *Republic*, Socrates defines μῦθοι as the kind of account employed when confirmation is impossible to achieve. At *Republic* 382c10–d3, Socrates states that, since the distant past is beyond our experience, we must settle for a less rigorous kind of account than we might otherwise prefer:

καὶ ἐν αἷς νυνδὴ ἐλέγομεν ταῖς μυθολογίαις, διὰ τὸ μὴ εἰδέναι ὅπῃ τἀληθὲς ἔχει περὶ τῶν παλαιῶν, ἀφομοιοῦντες τῷ ἀληθεῖ τὸ ψεῦδος ὅτι μάλιστα, οὕτω χρήσιμον ποιοῦμεν;

Isn't it [falsehood] in the case of those stories (ταῖς μυθολογίαις) we were just talking about, those that we tell because we aren't able to know the truth about events in the distant past, making fiction as like the truth as we can, so as to make the lie useful?

μῦθοι are, in this respect, what we turn to when confirmation is beyond our grasp.[55] Penelope Murray goes so far as to declare that 'human beings, not being gods, can never know the truth, hence myth-making is an *essential* human activity'.[56] In the case

54 Johansen (2004) 64.

55 See Gill (1993) 56: 'It is characteristic of what we call Plato's "myths" that they present, usually in narrative or descriptive form, accounts of subjects of which we do not, and indeed cannot, know the truth (not, at least, in the form in which this is presented in the myths).' Morgan (2000) 278 states that Timaeus' description of his account as μῦθος is specifically designed to block any attempt to look for unattainable precision about such matters. See also Murray (1999) 254 and Wright (1979) 368.

56 Murray (1999) 260 (my emphasis). Johansen (2004) 65 notes a connection between the *Timaeus* and the *Republic* insofar as, in both dialogues, 'it is the contrast between what

of cosmology and, perhaps more obviously, cosmogony, it is clear that we are indeed working in terms of uncertainty in building our account. The *Republic* passage resorts to μῦθοι because events are so far in the past that they are beyond our experience. Of course, the origin of the cosmos is excluded from human experience because anthropogony is a part of that process. Equally, the details of physics, on the level of both the microcosmic and the macrocosmic, are beyond the reach of our perception and experience. No matter how convincing and reasonable our accounts may be, we are unable to verify them against direct experience and they must, therefore, remain unproven, i.e. μῦθοι.[57] This issue of uncertainty lies at the heart of Critias' complaint at *Critias* 107a7–e3, although he appears to think that the impossibility of verification is to be envied, if only because it will stop people contradicting you:

περὶ θεῶν γάρ, ὦ Τίμαιε, λέγοντά τι πρὸς ἀνθρώπους δοκεῖν ἱκανῶς λέγειν ῥᾷον ἢ περὶ θνητῶν πρὸς ἡμᾶς. ἡ γὰρ ἀπειρία καὶ σφόδρα ἄγνοια τῶν ἀκουόντων περὶ ὧν ἂν οὕτως ἔχωσιν πολλὴν εὐπορίαν παρέχεσθον τῷ μέλλοντι λέγειν τι περὶ αὐτῶν· περὶ δὲ δὴ θεῶν ἴσμεν ὡς ἔχομεν . . . ὅτι τὰ μὲν οὐράνια καὶ θεῖα ἀγαπῶμεν καὶ σμικρῶς εἰκότα λεγόμενα, τὰ δὲ θνητὰ καὶ ἀνθρώπινα ἀκριβῶς ἐξετάζομεν. ἐκ δὴ τοῦ παραχρῆμα νῦν λεγόμενα, τὸ πρέπον ἂν μὴ δυνώμεθα πάντως ἀποδιδόναι, συγγιγνώσκειν χρεών· οὐ γὰρ ὡς ῥᾴδια τὰ θνητὰ ἀλλ' ὡς χαλεπὰ πρὸς δόξαν ὄντα ἀπεικάζειν δεῖ διανοεῖσθαι.

But, Timaeus, it's easier to give the appearance of speaking adequately when talking about the gods to men, than when discussing mortals amongst ourselves. For when one's audience is inexperienced and completely ignorant about the subject-matter it is greatly advantageous to someone who is going to talk about it, and we are well aware how ignorant we are about the gods . . . when we talk about the celestial and divine we will put up with only a faint likelihood,[58] but mortal and divine matters we examine minutely. The account I give, presented as it is off the cuff, should be forgiven if it fails to offer a wholly proper representation; for it is essential to bear in mind that mortal objects are far from easy, in fact they are difficult to represent in a fashion in line with opinion.

we can know and what god can know that makes *muthologia*, or "falsehood-telling" (*pseudos legein*), appropriate to us, but not to god'.

57 Gill (1993) 56–60 discusses the unverifiability of other Platonic myths: the story of Atlantis and the *Statesman* myth 'belong to the distant past, from which we are separated by various kinds of cultural and natural discontinuity'; the myths of the *Gorgias* and *Phaedo* describe human life after death and thus go beyond general experience. Gill is mistaken in attributing the unverifiable nature of *Timaeus*' μῦθος to the fact that it is merely 'likely' or 'credible'.

58 Critias, notwithstanding Timaeus' invention, uses 'likelihood' in the traditional (and, I have suggested, compatible) sense of 'plausibility'.

A Xenophanean influence?

I have proposed that Timaeus' account is a μῦθος because it is unverifiable. In Chapter 1, I argued that Xenophanes qualifies his account as ἐοικότα τοις ἐτύμοισι because, whilst he hopes that they may be true, he believes that their truth can never be known with certainty. The impossibility of verification is stated explicitly in B34:

καὶ τὸ μὲν οὖν σαφὲς οὔτις ἀνὴρ ἴδεν[59] οὐδέ τις ἔσται
εἰδὼς ἀμφὶ θεῶν τε καὶ ἅσσα λέγω περὶ πάντων·
εἰ γὰρ καὶ τὰ μάλιστα τύχοι τετελεσμένον εἰπών,
αὐτὸς ὅμως οὐκ οἶδε· δόκος δ' ἐπὶ πᾶσι τέτυκται.

And there has never been any man who has achieved certainty
Nor will there be anyone who knows about the gods and what I say about everything.
For even if anyone really managed to enunciate how things are
He would still not himself have knowledge. Rather, opinion is allotted to all.

Even if an investigation into 'the gods and what I say about everything' were to hit upon the truth, it could never be recognized as such. Whereas, for Homer, the privileged figure of seer, poet or divine favourite may share the knowledge and certainty of the gods, Xenophanes places an absolute and impassable barrier between the epistemic potential of man and that of god: god is 'not at all the same as mortals in body or in thought' (B23).

Xenophanes' denial of revelation and inspiration (B18) is shared by Timaeus.[60] For, although Timaeus prefaces his account with a prayer (27c1–d4), it is strikingly different from the kind of appeal to the Muses that we find, for example, at *Iliad* 2.484–487.[61] Whilst the Homeric example is very much an appeal for information, Timaeus merely voices the hope that the gods (and his audience) will approve of what he has to say:

59 Following Fränkel (1974) 122ff. in preferring the ἴδεν of Sextus and Diogenes Laertius to the γένετο of Plutarch. See also Ioli (2003) esp. 201–5.

60 As noted by Johansen (2004) 61.

61 Timaeus adds two more prayers to that in his introduction. One at his new beginning at 48d4–e1 and another at the conclusion of his speech at *Critias* 106a1–b7.

Ἀλλ', ὦ Σώκρατες, τοῦτό γε δὴ πάντες ὅσοι καὶ κατὰ βραχὺ σωφροσύνης μετέχουσιν, ἐπὶ παντὸς ὁρμῇ καὶ σμικροῦ καὶ μεγάλου πράγματος θεὸν ἀεί που καλοῦσιν· ἡμᾶς δὲ τοὺς περὶ τοῦ παντὸς λόγους ποιεῖσθαί πῃ μέλλοντας, ᾗ γέγονεν ἢ καὶ ἀγενές ἐστιν, εἰ μὴ παντάπασι παραλλάττομεν, ἀνάγκη θεούς τε καὶ θεὰς ἐπικαλουμένους εὔχεσθαι πάντα κατὰ νοῦν ἐκείνοις μὲν μάλιστα, ἑπομένως δὲ ἡμῖν εἰπεῖν. καὶ τὰ μὲν περὶ θεῶν ταύτῃ παρακεκλήσθω· τὸ δ' ἡμέτερον παρακλητέον, ᾗ ῥᾷστ' ἂν ὑμεῖς μὲν μάθοιτε, ἐγὼ δὲ ᾗ διανοοῦμαι μάλιστ' ἂν περὶ τῶν προκειμένων ἐνδειξαίμην.

Well, Socrates, surely anyone with even a modicum of sense will always call upon the god at the outset of every venture, whether small or great. And we are about to produce accounts about the universe, regarding how it has an origin or is without one, and, lest we wander completely off course, it is essential, calling on the gods and goddesses, to pray that everything we say is acceptable to them above all and consequently to us. Let this be our appeal to the gods. As for our own interests, we must appeal for them to be satisfied in a manner in which you would find the learning easiest and I would set out the present subject-matter in a manner which best displays my intent.

Timaeus hopes for the approbation of the gods, but there is no guarantee either that he will get it or that he would be aware of it. Timaeus' attitude towards the interaction of gods and men is further demonstrated at 40d6–e4:

Περὶ δὲ τῶν ἄλλων δαιμόνων εἰπεῖν καὶ γνῶναι τὴν γένεσιν μεῖζον ἢ καθ' ἡμᾶς, πειστέον δὲ τοῖς εἰρηκόσιν ἔμπροσθεν, ἐκγόνοις μὲν θεῶν οὖσιν, ὡς ἔφασαν, σαφῶς δέ που τούς γε αὑτῶν προγόνους εἰδόσιν· ἀδύνατον οὖν θεῶν παισὶν ἀπιστεῖν, καίπερ ἄνευ τε εἰκότων καὶ ἀναγκαίων ἀποδείξεων λέγουσιν, ἀλλ' ὡς οἰκεῖα φασκόντων ἀπαγγέλλειν ἑπομένους τῷ νόμῳ πιστευτέον. οὕτως οὖν κατ' ἐκείνους ἡμῖν ἡ γένεσις περὶ τούτων τῶν θεῶν ἐχέτω καὶ λεγέσθω.

With regard to the other deities, it is beyond us to know or to speak of their origin, but we should believe the pronouncements of our predecessors, who are, so they say, the offspring of the gods. Clearly they are in a position to know about their own ancestors. So it is impossible to disbelieve the children of the gods, even if they speak without likely or necessary proofs. But as they are pronouncing on matters close to home, we should follow custom and believe them. Thus we should accept their account and say what it is.

Most read this passage as ironic.[62] Whether or not Timaeus is being sincere in urging us to accept the accounts of those who claim to

[62] Thus Taylor (1928) 245: 'this passage is purely, though politely ironical'. See also Burnyeat (2005) 151 and Cornford (1935) 138–9. Sedley (2002b) 42n9 suggests that we should follow the example of the ancient commentators and avoid attributing irony to Timaeus (as opposed to Socrates).

be descended from the gods, it is striking that he notes that 'they speak without likely or necessary proofs'. Even those who claim to be the kin of the gods are unable to provide a verification of their accounts. Any belief we might adopt with regard to their stories is dependent on accepting, in the absence of confirmation, that they know what they are talking about. We have to trust them and, in much the same manner as that exhorted by Xenophanes, accept their stories as necessarily uncertain candidates for truth.

Timaeus seems to harbour a similar opinion of the epistemological potential of mortals to that of Xenophanes. Although it would be difficult to argue with any confidence that Plato is deliberately alluding to his predecessor, it is, I think, useful to note this similarity.[63] Timaeus agrees with Xenophanes that *qua* human, we simply cannot achieve confirmation of the truth of any account of the cosmos.[64] Xenophanes is led to conclude that we should accept our limitations and concentrate on attempting to improve our particular mortal kind of understanding. We should be content with accounts that are ἐοικότα τοις ἐτύμοισι. The response of Timaeus is rather different. Despite his assertion that we should search for nothing more than the εἰκὼς μῦθος (i.e. a representative but unverified account) about the cosmos, it will become clear that, in fact, we can and should aim for something better. For, as it turns out, whilst we are subject to the limitations of human nature, we also have a share in the divine.

A share in the divine

At 72d4–7, quoted above, Timaeus notes that it is impossible to confirm the truth about the nature of the soul and 'how much of it is mortal and how much divine' (ὅσον θνητὸν ἔχει καὶ ὅσον θεῖον). In describing the origin of man, Timaeus recounts how the Demiurge ensured our mortality by delegating our creation to the

63 There may be some justification for reading Timaeus' words at 29c4–5 (θεῶν καὶ τῆς τοῦ παντὸς γενέσεως) as a direct allusion to Xenophanes B34 (θεῶν τε καὶ ἅσσα λέγω περὶ πάντων). See Mourelatos (2010) 239.

64 See Mourelatos (2010) 245–7, although he sees Timaeus' use of εἰκώς as expressing the limitation.

lesser, created gods.[65] He does not hand the process over, however, until he has himself 'sown the seed' of a share in the immortal, which he then passes on to the lesser gods (41c6–d3):

καὶ καθ' ὅσον μὲν αὐτῶν ἀθανάτοις ὁμώνυμον εἶναι προσήκει, θεῖον λεγόμενον ἡγεμονοῦν τε ἐν αὐτοῖς τῶν ἀεὶ δίκῃ καὶ ὑμῖν ἐθελόντων ἕπεσθαι, σπείρας καὶ ὑπαρξάμενος ἐγὼ παραδώσω· τὸ δὲ λοιπὸν ὑμεῖς, ἀθανάτῳ θνητὸν προσυφαίνοντες, ἀπεργάζεσθε ζῷα καὶ γεννᾶτε τροφήν τε διδόντες αὐξάνετε καὶ φθίνοντα πάλιν δέχεσθε.

And, to the degree that it is fitting for them to possess something that shares the name 'immortal', which is called 'divine' and rules those of them who are willing always to follow justice and your guidance, I shall begin by sowing the seed. The rest is up to you: by combining what is mortal with the immortal, create and generate living things, nourish them and help them grow, and when they die, welcome them back again.

Humans are, in their ability to achieve certainty, essentially different from god. However, as now becomes clear, they also possess a share of the divine and thus, perhaps, a share in the epistemic potential of god. *Qua* human, we are limited to never being sure that our account is correct. *Qua* divine, we may well be able to surpass, to some extent, these epistemological restrictions.[66]

The route beyond μῦθος is twofold. For, in addition to the capacity to achieve verification, we need access to the data that will provide this confirmation. Of course, since the world has been created as a likeness of the intelligible realm, it possesses an order and rationality that appeals to our (divine) reason. An εἰκώς account will describe the perceptible realm as a likeness of the intelligible. A *certain* εἰκώς account (i.e. a (species) εἰκὼς λόγος) will identify evidence of the influence of the intelligible in the perceptible realm. The classic example of such evidence is astronomy.[67] We

[65] According to the words put into the mouth of the Demiurge, the delegation is necessary because, if he were to create the animals, they would 'rival the gods' in possessing immortality (41c2–6).

[66] At 34c2–4, Timaeus notes that the tendency of language to be random may reflect the randomness of the world in which we have a share. I read this as, on the one hand, a comment about the instability of language, as at 29b7–c1, and, on the other, a reminder that we are a part of the cosmos we seek to describe. The term 'random' (εἰκῇ) obviously alludes to the nature of the cosmos as an εἰκών.

[67] Sedley (1989) 377: 'astronomy becomes *par excellence* the discipline which can bridge the gulf between sensible and intelligible worlds and enable man to transcend his own mortal existence'.

witness the regularity of the rotations of the heavens. We can then employ our reason, i.e. our share in the divine, to recognize this regularity. In turn, this recognition will nourish our divine reason (90b1–d7):

τῷ μὲν οὖν περὶ τὰς ἐπιθυμίας ἢ περὶ φιλονικίας τετευτακότι καὶ ταῦτα διαπονοῦντι σφόδρα πάντα τὰ δόγματα ἀνάγκη θνητὰ ἐγγεγονέναι, καὶ παντάπασιν καθ' ὅσον μάλιστα δυνατὸν θνητῷ γίγνεσθαι, τούτου μηδὲ σμικρὸν ἐλλείπειν, ἅτε τὸ τοιοῦτον ηὔξηκότι· τῷ δὲ περὶ φιλομαθίαν καὶ περὶ τὰς ἀληθεῖς φρονήσεις ἐσπουδακότι καὶ ταῦτα μάλιστα τῶν αὑτοῦ γεγυμνασμένῳ φρονεῖν μὲν ἀθάνατα καὶ θεῖα, ἄνπερ ἀληθείας ἐφάπτηται, πᾶσα ἀνάγκη που, καθ' ὅσον δ' αὖ μετασχεῖν ἀνθρωπίνῃ φύσει ἀθανασίας ἐνδέχεται, τούτου μηδὲν μέρος ἀπολείπειν, ἅτε δὲ ἀεὶ θεραπεύοντα τὸ θεῖον ἔχοντά τε αὐτὸν εὖ κεκοσμημένον τὸν δαίμονα σύνοικον ἑαυτῷ, διαφερόντως εὐδαίμονα εἶναι. θεραπεία δὲ δὴ παντὶ παντὸς μία, τὰς οἰκείας ἑκάστῳ τροφὰς καὶ κινήσεις ἀποδιδόναι. τῷ δ' ἐν ἡμῖν θείῳ συγγενεῖς εἰσιν κινήσεις αἱ τοῦ παντὸς διανοήσεις καὶ περιφοραί· ταύταις δὴ συνεπόμενον ἕκαστον δεῖ, τὰς περὶ τὴν γένεσιν ἐν τῇ κεφαλῇ διεφθαρμένας ἡμῶν περιόδους ἐξορθοῦντα διὰ τὸ καταμανθάνειν τὰς τοῦ παντὸς ἁρμονίας τε καὶ περιφοράς, τῷ κατανοουμένῳ τὸ κατανοοῦν ἐξομοιῶσαι κατὰ τὴν ἀρχαίαν φύσιν, ὁμοιώσαντα δὲ τέλος ἔχειν τοῦ προτεθέντος ἀνθρώποις ὑπὸ θεῶν ἀρίστου βίου πρός τε τὸν παρόντα καὶ τὸν ἔπειτα χρόνον.

So, whoever has devoted himself to appetites and rivalries and has really exerted himself in these matters, all his thoughts are bound to become mortal and, so far as it is really possible to become utterly mortal, he will lack nothing in this regard, having cultivated his mortality. But whoever has been zealous in his pursuit of the love of learning and true wisdom and has exercised these parts of himself above all, his thoughts are bound, if he touches on truth, to be immortal and divine. And so far as it is possible for human nature to have a share in the immortal, he will in no way fall short but, seeing as he is always caring for the divine part and looking after the well-ordered spirit that lives within him in good order, he will be supremely happy. There is one way of caring for absolutely everything, which is to provide the appropriate nourishment and motions. The motions which are akin to our divine part are the thoughts and revolutions of the universe; each of us should follow these, correcting the revolutions in our heads, which were corrupted at birth, by learning the harmonies and revolutions of the universe so as to liken our understanding to its object, in accordance with its original nature. Having achieved this likeness we will reach the goal of the good life offered to mankind by the gods for the present and the future.

Not only are we capable of surpassing our human limitations, it is an ethical requirement that we try to do so.[68] For, in recognizing

[68] Netz (2002) 261 suggests that we are prompted to consider the unfamiliarity of the universe and thus are 'moved to think of it *in abstraction from everyday human experience*' (my emphasis).

the manner in which the cosmos represents its paradigm, we liken ourselves to god.[69] Timaeus begins his cosmology by proclaiming that accounts are συγγενεῖς of their subject-matter. It is striking that, towards the end of his account (90c7–8) he mentions another kind of relation, that between man and god ('The motions which are akin to our divine part are the thoughts and revolutions of the universe'). The motions of the heavens are 'akin to' the divine part within us. In fact, by engaging in astronomy and habituating our minds to thinking about such regular and representative celestial motions (as opposed to the erratic and base concerns closer to earth) we can encourage our own minds to represent the thought of god.[70] In fact, the cosmic likeness becomes the paradigm for our thoughts. By likening our thoughts to something modelled on the intelligible realm (and, importantly, recognizing that it is likeness of the intelligible realm) we come closer to the mind that performed the original act of likening.[71]

As humans, it is appropriate for us to be content with a μῦθος about the cosmos. However, just as we should recognize the likeness of the cosmos to its perfect paradigm and thus aim to give an εἰκὼς μῦθος, so we should come to realize the need to liken ourselves to our divine paradigm.[72] It becomes clear that there is a strong ethical impetus, insofar as we have a share of divine reason,

[69] Osborne (1996) 108 notes the alternative possibility: 'The closer to earth mankind gets, the further he gets from divinity and intelligence and the more importance he gives to the material explanations of things.'

[70] As Sedley (2000) 798 states: 'the divine world-soul and our own souls, akin in their very origins, are structured in such a way as to enable us, via the study of astronomy and mathematics, to share god's own thoughts'. Brisson and Meyerstein (1995) 29 extend the relevance of this possibility with their claim that 'in a universe governed by a mathematically structured soul, all change is necessarily governed, as far as possible, by mathematical precepts'.

[71] Carone (2005) 73 argues that, whereas the middle dialogues tend to stress the affinity between humans and forms, the *Timaeus* stresses the affinity between humans and god.

[72] Sedley (2000) 794 notes that *Theaetetus* 176a5–c3 describes a divine paradeigma for mortal justice. Broadie (2001) 10–11 suggests that man's attempt to represent god is a necessary requirement for the success of the overall struggle towards the triumph of reason. This victory is shown to take place on two levels. The first is that of the Demiurge imposing order upon his material. The second is man imposing the order of reason upon his own potentially disordered soul. Carone (2005) 27 proposes that the 'mythic' status of Timaeus' account is partly motivated by the desire to present a mythical image of god to be emulated by man.

to strive to be like god and, after all, to search for something more than uncertain μῦθος.

Conclusion

I have attempted to present an interpretation of Timaeus' *proemium* that is in keeping with the positive interpretation of his use of εἰκὼς for which I argued in Chapter 3. Reading 29c3 as, in part, an allusion to Parmenides is useful in two ways. First, it indicates a way of reading the proportion as describing a relationship between two kinds of account (and the objects of those accounts). Such a reading seems to be more consistent with the context of the proportion than those which, influenced by perceived parallels with the *Republic*, seek to read ἀλήθεια and πίστις as cognitive states. Further, recognizing an allusion to Parmenides helps us to understand the significance of the proportion. My suggestion is that Timaeus is deliberately engaging with and seeking to correct Parmenides' absolute dismissal of the value of thinking about the perceptible world. Whilst Parmenides recognizes no more than a specious connection between the realm of Coming-to-be and that of Being, the cosmos that Timaeus describes is connected to the realm of Being insofar as it is created as an image of Being. Just as there is an important connection between Coming-to-be and Being, so there should be a significant relation between the accounts given of these two realms. Cosmological accounts are devoid of the stable and unqualified truths which describe Being. However, because the cosmos is a likeness of Being, it represents, in a qualified fashion, the nature of its model. Thus, in describing a likeness of Being, a cosmological account should express qualified truths which are informed by the unqualified truth that belongs to an account of Being. Cosmology, for all that it is a description of Coming-to-be, should be founded on and informed by understanding of the Forms. Plato takes the Parmenidean πίστις and applies it to the account of Coming-to-be, rather than that of Being. In so doing, he demonstrates that, insofar as the cosmos is a likeness of Being, there is real value in engaging in cosmology; it is not mere speciousness. I do not want to suggest that cosmology, which is essentially a study of a qualified representation of the Forms, is intended as an alternative to pure contemplation of the original. I do think however, that Plato presents it in the *Timaeus* as a useful and worthwhile activity. It is useful because it allows us to incorporate the perceptible world and, significantly, our place within it into our more 'intellectual' pursuits. The intelligible and the perceptible are not subject to an absolute Parmenidean divide for the latter is modelled on the former. Thus, our understanding of one realm informs our comprehension of the other.

Although I have been arguing for a positive interpretation of Timaeus' εἰκώς-claim, I have no desire to deny that his *proemium* expresses a certain degree of pessimism. On my reading, however, the limitations on the cosmological project are described not by the term εἰκώς, but by the shift from λόγος to μῦθος. On my reading, Timaeus is warning not that, being human, we are limited to likelihood, but that we are limited to unverified accounts, i.e. μῦθοι. I suggested that this limitation indicates an attitude to human epistemology markedly similar to that expressed by Xenophanes' use of ἐοικώς. Both seem to agree that humans are capable of no more than uncertain access to the truth. For Xenophanes, recognition of this limitation causes him to describe his teachings as ἐοικότα τοῖς ἐτύμοισι. For Timaeus, human nature limits us to uncertain μῦθοι. However, Timaeus goes on to offer the possibility of surpassing these limits. This potential for certainty derives, on the one hand, from the fact that, in addition to our human nature, we possess a share in the divine. On the other hand, the fact that the world is an εἰκών enables us to recognize and describe the influence of the intelligible realm on the perceptible. In fact, by engaging in cosmology and working through our εἰκὼς λόγος, i.e. describing the cosmos as a likeness of Being, we can improve ourselves and become as like god as is possible.

CONCLUSION

I have argued that there are significant and interesting differences in the way that Xenophanes, Parmenides and Plato in the *Timaeus* each employ the term ἐοικώς/εἰκώς. Each characterizes his account as such in order to describe its relation to the truth. Thus, Xenophanes describes his teachings as ἐοικότα τοῖς ἐτύμοισι because they enjoy some kind of *likeness* to the truth. It may even be that they are accurate. However, by his choice of ἐοικώς rather than ὁμοῖος, he seeks to remind us that we can never be certain of the truth of his teachings. We will, as B34 tells us, never be able to verify his account, for it can never surpass its status as a possible but potentially specious candidate for truth.

Parmenides, in labelling his cosmology ἐοικώς, admits that it possesses likelihood, i.e. plausibility. But, whilst Xenophanes admits that his account is potentially specious, Parmenides is at pains to emphasize that the *Doxa* is only apparently true. The plausibility of descriptions of the realm of Coming-to-be is merely subjective and ultimately unfounded. In describing something that has no reality and is essentially unrelated to reality, misguided mortals convince themselves that falsehoods are true. For Parmenides, deceptive cosmologies of the type he presents are, precisely because they describe something unrelated to reality, utterly untrue. To believe them is to be deceived.

Plato's *Timaeus* develops a specifically technical sense of εἰκώς explicitly related to εἰκών. His 'likelihood' is the quality possessed by a *successful account of a likeness as a likeness*. Such a likely account must acknowledge and, to some extent, explain the connection between the likeness and its model, specifically the way the model's nature influences that of the likeness. Timaeus' εἰκώς does not, of itself, imply a lack of truth or certainty. It is the fact that cosmology's subject-matter, being a likeness, is created and is therefore in the realm of Coming-to-be which dictates the relationship of a likely description of that likeness to the stable truth which describes Being. Thus, just as Coming-to-be represents Being, albeit in a qualified fashion, so the truths with which one can talk about the realm of Coming-to-be are qualified and contingent truths related to the stable and permanent truth of the intelligible realm.

In addition to highlighting these essential differences in the way that each uses ἐοικώς/εἰκώς, I have sought to demonstrate that there is an important similarity in the manner in which Xenophanes, Parmenides and the *Timaeus* situate themselves in opposition to their forerunners in epistemology and cosmology. I have argued that each account should be read as reflecting on and aiming to correct the epistemologies of its predecessors. In each case, the corrective element is indicated in part by the allusive tag ἐοικώς/εἰκώς. In the case of Xenophanes, it is vital to recognize his engagement with not only the language but also the epistemology of Homer and Hesiod. B35 alludes to the poetic claim to offer lies that are ἐτύμοισιν ὁμοῖα and, by altering the term for similarity to ἐοικώς, indicates the substance of Xenophanes' criticism. Whilst the poets traditionally claim access to divine certainty, he rejects such claims in favour of his fallibilist epistemology.

In discussing the deliberate ambiguity of Parmenides' use of ἐοικώς, I argued that it should be understood, in part, as alluding to Xenophanes' apparent optimism about the possibility of achieving truth about the perceptible cosmos. Whilst some contend that B8.60's ἐοικώς cannot mean 'plausible' because of lack of a dative along the lines of Xenophanes' τοῖς ἐτύμοισι, my proposal is that Parmenides can be understood as deliberately omitting such a dative in order to emphasize the vacuity of ἐοικώς talk about Coming-to-be. Parmenides is rejecting the possibility of offering a description of the cosmos that is a potential candidate for truth, because there is no truth to be had about Coming-to-be. Cosmology is not, for Parmenides, apparently true but potentially specious, as it is for Xenophanes; rather, it is apparently true only to those who know no better. It is inevitably specious.

The allusive nature of εἰκώς in the *Timaeus* is somewhat less specific. However, it seems to me almost inconceivable that Plato could have labelled the cosmology εἰκώς without intending it to be read as an allusion to the words of Parmenides' goddess. In fact, as I argued in Chapter 4, the relationship he sets up between ἀλήθεια and πίστις can plausibly be read as an evocation of Parmenides' denial of πίστις ἀληθής in the thought of mortals. Whilst thought about Coming-to-be possesses only apparent truth and convincingness for Parmenides, for Plato, the fact that the cosmos is an εἰκών of Being means that it can be described by accounts which are of real value. For, in the same way that the cosmos derives ontological value from being likened to Being, so talk about the Coming-to-be is of epistemological value insofar as it describes a likeness of Being. In addition, the *Timaeus*' blend of epistemological pessimism about the human capacity to achieve certainty and optimism about our divine potential to surpass such limitations can usefully be contrasted with the position of Xenophanes. For, whilst Xenophanes rejects the possibility that we can share god's knowledge, limiting us to what is ἐοικότα τοῖς ἐτύμοισι, Plato seems to allow that, since we have a share in the divine, we may have a share in divine certainty. For Xenophanes, man and god are in no way ὁμοῖος in mind. Plato, meanwhile, suggests that recognizing the status of the cosmos as an εἰκών and consequently attempting to give an εἰκώς account of it will enable us to achieve the goal of becoming 'as much like god as is possible'.[1]

To my mind, it is a particular attraction of this developmental and allusive account of the ἐοικώς/εἰκώς that it need assume no misunderstanding of their predecessors on the part of any of the authors discussed. The continuity of influence and reaction for which I have argued attributes a critical understanding of Homer and Hesiod to Xenophanes, of Xenophanes to Parmenides, and of Parmenides and (perhaps) Xenophanes to Plato. In aligning my interpretation of each author with that of their philosophical 'descendants', I have not, I trust, sought to impute anything implausible to these original thinkers. At any rate, I hope that my account is εἰκώς in at least two of the senses that I have described. It is, I hope, a potential, if necessarily uncertain, candidate for truth. In addition, it is likely in the technical sense put forward

[1] *Theaetetus* 176b1–2.

in the *Timaeus*, insofar as it describes the way that Xenophanes, Parmenides and Plato liken their accounts to those of their predecessors by employing critical allusion. I can only hope that I have managed to avoid, for the most part, the deceptive and vacuous plausibility of Parmenides' ἐοικώς cosmology.

BIBLIOGRAPHY

Albertelli, P. (1939) *Gli Eleati*, Bari.

Allen, R. E. (ed.) (1965) *Studies in Plato's Metaphysics*, London.

Annas, J. and Rowe, C. (eds.) (2002) *New Perspectives on Plato: Modern and Ancient*, Cambridge, Mass.

Archer-Hind, R. D. (1888) *The Timaeus of Plato*, London.

Ashbaugh, A. F. (1988) *Plato's Theory of Explanation*, New York.

Atherton, C. (ed.) (1998) *Form and Content in Didactic Poetry*, Bari.

Aubenque, P. (ed.) (1987) *Études sur Parménide*, vol. **2**, Paris.

Austin, S. (1986) *Parmenides: Being, Bounds, and Logic*, New Haven.

Ballew, L. (1974) 'Straight and Circular in Parmenides and the *Timaeus*' *Phronesis* **19**, 189–209.

Bambrough, R. (ed.) (1965) *New Essays on Plato and Aristotle*, London.

Barnes, J. (1982) *The Presocratic Philosophers*, London.

Barrett, J. (2004) 'Struggling with Parmenides' *Ancient Philosophy* **24**, 267–91.

Belfiore, E. (1985) '"Lies Unlike the Truth": Plato on Hesiod, *Theogony* 27' *TAPA* **115**, 47–57.

Berti, E. (1997) 'L'oggetto dell' εἰκὼς μῦθος nel *Timeo* di *Platone*' in Calvo and Brisson (eds.) *Interpreting the* Timaeus–Critias, 119–31.

Betegh, G. (2010) 'What Makes a Myth *eikôs*? Remarks Inspired by Myles Burnyeat's "EIKÔS MYTHOS" in Mohr and Sattler (eds.) *One Book, the Whole Universe*, 213–24.

Boeder, H. (1962) *Grund und Gegenwart als Frageziel der frühgriechischen Philosophie*, The Hague.

Bormann, K. (1971) *Parmenides: Untersuchungen zu den Fragmenten*, Hamburg.

Boudouris, K. J. (ed.) (1989) *Ionian Philosophy*, Athens.

Bowerstock, G. W., Burkert, W. and Putnam, M. C. J. (eds.) (1979) *Arktouros: Hellenic Studies Presented to Bernard M. W. Knox on the Occasion of his 65th Birthday*, Berlin.

Bowie, E. L. (1993) 'Lies, Fiction and Slander in Early Greek Poetry' in Gill and Wiseman (eds.) *Lies and Fiction in the Ancient World*, 1–37.

Boys-Stones, G. R. and Haubold, J. H. (2010) *Plato and Hesiod*, Cambridge.

Bradley, E. (1967) 'Hector and the Simile of the Snowy Mountain' *TAPA* **98**, 37–41.

Brisson, L. (1982) *Platon: Les Mots et les Mythes*, Paris.

(2001) *Timée Critias*, Paris.

Brisson, L. and Meyerstein, F. W. (1995) *Inventing the Universe*, New York.

Broadie, S. (1999) 'Rational Theology' in Long (ed.) *The Cambridge Companion to Early Greek Philosophy*, 205–24.

(2001) 'Theodicy and Pseudo-History in the *Timaeus*' *OSAP* **21**, 1–28.

Bugno, M. (ed.) (2005) *Senofane ed Elea tra Ionia e Magna Grecia*, Naples.

Burnet, J. (1905) *Platonis Opera*, vol. **4**, Oxford.

(1930) *Early Greek Philosophy*, London.

Burnyeat, M. (2005) 'Εἰκὼς Μῦθος' *Rhizai* **II**.2, 7–29; reprinted in Partenie (ed.) *Plato's Myths*, 167–86.

Bury, R. (1929) *Plato with an English Translation*, vol. **7**: *Timaeus* etc., Cambridge, Mass.

Buxton, R. (ed.) (1999) *From Myth to Reason?*, Oxford.

(2004) 'Similes and other Likenesses' in Fowler (ed.) *The Cambridge Companion to Homer*, 139–55.

Calvo, T. and Brisson, L. (eds.) (1997) *Interpreting the* Timaeus–Critias, Sankt Augustin.

Capelle, W. (1963) *Die Vorsokratiker*, Stuttgart.

Capra, A. (2010) 'Plato's Hesiod and the Will of Zeus: Philosophical Rhapsody in the *Timaeus* and *Critias*' in Boys-Stones and Haubold (eds.) *Plato and Hesiod*, 200–18.

Carey, C. (1994) 'Rhetorical Means of Persuasion' in Worthington (ed.) *Persuasion: Greek Rhetoric in Action*, 26–45.

Carone, G. R. (2005) *Plato's Cosmology and its Ethical Dimensions*, Cambridge.

Chalmers, W. (1960) 'Parmenides and the Beliefs of Mortals' *Phronesis* **5**, 5–22.

Chantraine, P. (1968) *Dictionnaire Étymologique de la Langue Grecque*, Paris.

Cherniss, H. (1951) 'The Characteristics and Effects of Presocratic Philosophy' in Furley and Allen (eds.) *Studies in Presocratic Philosophy*, vol. **1**, 1–28.

(1965) 'The Relation of the *Timaeus* to Plato's Later Dialogues' in Allen (ed.) *Studies in Plato's Metaphysics*, 339–78.

Cherubin, R. (2005) 'Light, Night, and the Opinions of Mortals' *Ancient Philosophy* **25**, 1–24.

Classen, C. J. (1989) 'Xenophanes and the Tradition of Epic Poetry' in Boudouris (ed.) *Ionian Philosophy*, 91–103.

Cole, T. (1983) 'Archaic Truth' *Quaderni Urbinati di Cultura Classica*, n.s. **13**, 7–28.

Cook Wilson, J. (1889) *On the Interpretation of Plato's* Timaeus, London.

Cornford, F. M. (1933) 'Parmenides' Two Ways' *CQ* **27**, 97–11.

(1935) *Plato's Theory of Knowledge*, London.

(1937) *Plato's Cosmology*, London.

(1939) *Plato and Parmenides*, London.

Coxon, A. (2009) *The Fragments of Parmenides*, Las Vegas.

Curd, P. (1998) *The Legacy of Parmenides*, Princeton.

Curd, P. and Graham, D. (eds.) (2008) *The Oxford Handbook of Presocratic Philosophy*, New York.

Dalfen, J. (1994) 'Parmenides, der Vorsokratiker oder: nicht der Philosoph schafft die Probleme sondern seine Interpreten' *Philologus* **138**, 194–214.

Deichgräber, K. (1938) 'Xenophanes περὶ φύσεως' *Rheinisches Museum für Philologie*, 1–31.

Denniston, J. D. (1954) *The Greek Particles*, Oxford.

Diels, H. (1897) *Parmenides Lehrgedicht*, Berlin.

(1929) *Doxographi Graeci*, Berlin.

Diels, H. and Kranz, W. (1951–2) *Die Fragmente der Vorsokratiker*, vols. **1–3**, Berlin.

Dillon, J. (1977) *The Middle Platonists*, Rome.

Donini, P. (1988) 'Il *Timeo*: unità del dialogo, verosimiglianza del discorso' *Elenchos* **9**, 5–52.

Ebert, T. (1983) 'Aristotle on What Is Done in Perceiving' *ZPF* **37**, 181–98.

Edwards, M. (1991) The Iliad: *A Commentary*, vol. **5**: Books 17–20, Cambridge.

Everson, S. (ed.) (1990) *Epistemology*, Cambridge.

Fairbanks, A. (1897) 'On Plutarch's Quotations from the Early Greek Philosophers' *TAPA* **28**, 75–87.

Fine, G. (ed.) (2000) *Plato*, Oxford.

Finkelberg, A. (1990) 'Studies in Xenophanes' *Harvard Studies in Classical Philology* **93**, 104–67.

Fowler, R. (ed.) (2004) *The Cambridge Companion to Homer*, Cambridge.

Fränkel, H. (1921) *Die homerischen Gleichnisse*, Göttingen.

(1974) 'Xenophanes' Empiricism and his Critique of Knowledge (B34)' in Mourelatos (ed.) *The Pre-Socratics*, 118–31.

(1975) *Early Greek Poetry and Philosophy*, Oxford.

Frede, D. and Laks, A. (eds.) (2002) *Traditions of Theology*, Leiden.

Frère, J. (1987) 'Parménide et l'Ordre du Monde' in Aubenque (ed.) *Études sur Parménide*, 193–212.

Furley, D. and Allen, R. (eds.) (1970–5) *Studies in Presocratic Philosophy*, vols. **1** and **2**, London.

Gadamer, H. (ed.) (1968) *Um die Begriffswelt der Vorsokratiker*, Darmstadt.

Gagarin, M. (1994) 'Probability and Persuasion' in Worthington (ed.) *Persuasion: Greek Rhetoric in Action*, 46–68.

Gallop, D. (1984) *Parmenides of Elea*, Toronto.

Garvie, A. (1969) *Aeschylus'* Supplices: *Play and Trilogy*, Cambridge.

Gentili, B. and Prato, C. (1979) *Poetae Elegiaci: Testimonia et Fragmenta*, Leipzig.

Geuss, R. (2005) *Outside Ethics*, Princeton.

Gigon, O. (1945) *Der Ursprung der Griechischen Philosophie*, Basel.

Gildersleeve, B. (1890) *The Olympian and Pythian Odes*, London.

Gill, C. (1993) 'Plato on Falsehood – not Fiction' in Gill and Wiseman (eds.) *Lies and Fiction in the Ancient World*, 38–87.

Gill, C. and McCabe, M. M. (eds.) (1996) *Form and Argument in Late Plato*, Oxford.

Gill, C. and Wiseman, T. P. (eds) (1993) *Lies and Fiction in the Ancient World*, Exeter.

Gomperz, H. (1924) *Psychologische Beobachtungen an griechischen Philosophen*, Vienna.

Goodwin, W. W. (1946) *A Greek Grammar*, London.

Görgemanns, H. (1976) 'Rhetorik und Poetik im homerischen Hermes-hymns' in Görgemanns and Schmidt (eds.) *Studien zum antiken Epos*, 113–28.

Görgemanns, H. and Schmidt, E. A. (eds.) (1976) *Studien zum antiken Epos*, Hain.

Graham, D. W. (2006) *Explaining the Cosmos*, Princeton.

Gregory, A. (2000) *Plato's Philosophy of Science*, London.

Guthrie, W. K. C. (1962–5) *A History of Greek Philosophy*, vols. **1** and **2**, Cambridge.

Halliwell, S. (2002) *The Aesthetics of Mimesis*, Princeton.

Hankinson, R. J. (1998) *Cause and Explanation in Ancient Greek Thought*, Oxford.

Havelock, E. A. (1958) 'Parmenides and Odysseus' *HSCP* **63**, 133–43.

(1978) *The Greek Concept of Justice*, London.

(1983) 'The Linguistic Task of the Presocratics' in Robb (ed.) *Language and Thought in Early Greek Philosophy*, 7–81.

Hayman, H. (1866–82) *The* Odyssey *of Homer*, vols. **1–3**, London.

Heidel, W. A. (1912–13) 'On Certain Fragments of the Pre-Socratics: Critical Notes and Elucidations' *Proceedings of the American Academy of Arts and Sciences* **48**, 679–734.

(1943) 'Hecataeus and Xenophanes' *AJPh* **64**, 257–77.

Heitsch, E. (1974) 'Evidenz und Wahrscheinlichkeitsaussagen bei Parmenides' *Hermes* **102**, 411–19.

(1966) 'Das Wissen des Xenophanes' *RhM* **109**, 193–235.

(1983) *Xenophanes*, Munich.

Hermann, A. (2004) *To Think like God: Pythagoras and Parmenides – The Origins of Philosophy*, Las Vegas.

Hershbell, J. P. (1974) 'Empedoclean Influences on the *Timaeus*', *Phoenix* **28**, 145–66.

(1983) 'The Oral–Poetic Religion of Xenophanes' in Robb (ed.) *Language and Thought in Early Greek Philosophy*, 125–33.

Heubeck, A. and West, S. (1981) *Omero* Odissea, vol. **1**, Milan.

Hinds, S. (1998) *Allusion and Intertext: Dynamics of Appropriation in Roman Poetry*, Cambridge.

Hinks, D. (1940) 'Tisias and Corax and the Invention of Rhetoric' *CQ* **34**, 61–9.

Howald, E. (1922) 'Εἰκὼς Μῦθος', *Hermes* **57**, 63–79.

Hussey, E. (1972) *The Presocratics*, London.

(1990) 'The Beginnings of Epistemology: From Homer to Philolaus' in Everson (ed.) *Epistemology*, 11–38.

Inwood, B. (2001) *The Poem of Empedocles*, Toronto.

Ioli, R. (2003) 'Senofane B34DK e il conoscere' *Giornale Italiano di Filologia* **55**, 199–219.
Jacoby, F. (1923) *Die Fragmente der griechischen Historiker*, vol. **1**, Berlin.
Jaeger, W. (1947) *Theology of the Early Greek Philosophers*, Oxford.
Jameson, G. (1958) '"Well-Rounded Truth" and Circular Thought in Parmenides' *Phronesis* **3**, 15–30
Janko, R. (1982) *Homer, Hesiod and the Hymns*, Cambridge.
Johansen, H. and Whittle, E. (1980) *Aeschylus* The Suppliants, vol. **2**, Copenhagen.
Johansen, T. K. (2004) *Plato's Natural Philosophy: A Study of the* Timaeus–Critias, Cambridge.
Jones, C. P. (1961) 'The Teacher of Plutarch' *HSCP* **71**, 205–13.
Kahn, C. (1979) *The Art and Thought of Heraclitus*, Cambridge.
Karsten, S. (1830) *Philosophorum Graecorum Veterum: praesertim qui ante Platonem floruerunt, operum reliquiae*, vol. **1**, Brussels.
Kennedy, A. (1963) *The Art of Rhetoric in Greece*, London.
Kerferd, G. (1981) *The Sophistic Movement*, Cambridge.
Kirk, G., Raven, J. and Schofield, M. (1983) *The Presocratic Philosophers*, Cambridge.
Kirkwood, G. (1982) *Selections from Pindar*, Chicago.
Krischer, T. (1965) 'ἔτυμος und ἀληθής' *Philologus* **109**, 161–74.
Ledbetter, G. (2003) *Poetics before Plato*, Princeton.
Lee, D. (1964) *The Similes of the Iliad and the Odyssey Compared*, Melbourne.
Lesher, J. (1984) 'Parmenides' Critique of Thinking: The *Poludêris Elenchos* of Fragment 7' *OSAP* **8**, 1–18.
(1992) *Xenophanes of Colophon*, Toronto.
(1999) 'Early Interest in Knowledge' in Long (ed.) *The Cambridge Companion to Early Greek Philosophy*, 225–49.
(2008) 'The Humanizing of Knowledge in Presocratic Thought' in Curd and Graham (eds.) (2008) *The Oxford Handbook of Presocratic Philosophy*, 458–84.
Liddell, H. G., Scott, R. and Jones, H. S. (1940) *A Greek–English Lexicon*, Oxford.
Lloyd, G. E. R. (1966) *Polarity and Analogy*, Cambridge.
(1991a) 'Plato on Mathematics and Nature, Myth and Science' in Lloyd *Methods and Problems in Greek Science*, 333–51.
(1991b) *Methods and Problems in Greek Science*, Cambridge.
Long, A. A. (1963) 'The Principles of Parmenides' Cosmogony' *Phronesis* **8**, 90–107.
(1996) *Adversaries and Authorities*, Cambridge.
(1999a) 'The Scope of Early Greek Philosophy' in Long (ed.) *The Cambridge Companion to Early Greek Philosophy*, 1–21.
(ed.) (1999b) *The Cambridge Companion to Early Greek Philosophy*, Cambridge.

Longrigg, J. (1993) *Greek Rational Medicine*, London.
Mackenzie, M. M. (1982) 'Parmenides' Dilemma' *Phronesis* **27**, 1–12.
Mansfeld, J. (1964) *Die Offenbarung des Parmenides und die menschliche Welt*, Assen.
(1990a) 'Aristotle, Plato, and Preplatonic Doxography and Chronography' in Mansfeld *Studies in the Historiography of Greek Philosophy*, 22–83.
(1990b) *Studies in the Historiography of Greek Philosophy*, Assen.
Martijn, M. (2006) ' The *eikôs mythos* in Proclus' commentary on the *Timaeus*' in Tarrant and Baltzly (eds.) *Reading Plato in Antiquity*, 151–67.
McKirahan, R. D. (1994) *Philosophy before Socrates*, Indianapolis.
(2008) 'Signs and Arguments in Parmenides B8' in Curd and Graham (eds.) (2008) *The Oxford Handbook of Presocratic Philosophy*, 189–229.
Merry, W. and Riddell, J. (1886) *Homer's Odyssey*, Oxford.
Meyer-Abich, K. M. (1973) 'Eikos Logos: Platons Theorie der Naturwissenschaft' in Scheibe and Suessmann (eds.) *Einheit und Vielheit*, 20–44.
Mogyoródi, E. (2006) 'Xenophanes' Epistemology and Parmenides' Quest for Knowledge' in Sassi (ed.) *The Construction of Philosophical Discourse in the Age of the Presocratics*, 123–60.
Mohr, R. and Sattler, B. (eds.) (2010) *One Book, The Whole Universe*, Las Vegas.
Morgan, K. (2000) *Myth and Philosophy from the Presocratics to Plato*, Cambridge.
Most, G. (1999) 'The Poetics of Early Greek Philosophy' in Long (ed.) *The Cambridge Companion to Early Greek Philosophy*, 332–62.
Mourelatos, A. (1974) *The Pre-Socratics*, New York.
(2008) *The Route of Parmenides*, Las Vegas.
(2010) 'The Epistemological Section (29b–d) of the Proem in Timaeus' Speech: M. F. Burnyeat on *eikôs mythos*, and Comparison with Xenophanes B34 and B35' in Mohr and Sattler (eds.) *One Book, The Whole Universe*, 225–47.
Murray, A. T. (1919) *Homer* The Odyssey, Cambridge, Mass.
(1925) *Homer* The Iliad, vols. **1** and **2**, Cambridge, Mass.
Murray, P. (1981) 'Poetic Inspiration in Early Greece', *JHS* **101**, 87–100.
(1999) 'What Is a *Muthos* for Plato?' in Buxton (ed.) *From Myth to Reason?*, 251–62.
Naddaf, G. (1997) 'Plato and the Περὶ Φύσεως Tradition' in Calvo and Brisson (eds.) *Interpreting the* Timaeus–Critias, 27–36.
Nagy, G. (1990) *Greek Mythology and Poetics*, Ithaca.
Natali, C. and Maso, S. (eds.) (2003) *Plato Physicus: Cosmologia e Antropologia nel* Timeo, Amsterdam.
Neitzel, H. (1980) 'Hesiod und die lügenden Musen' *Hermes* **108**, 387–401.
Netz, R. (2002) 'Did Plato Have a Philosophy of Science? A Discussion of Andrew Gregory, *Plato's Philosophy of Science*', *OSAP* **23**, 247–63.
O'Brien, D. (1987) *Études sur Parménide*, vol. **1**, Paris.

Osborne, C. (1996) 'Space, Time, Shape, and Direction: Creative Discourse in the *Timaeus*', in Gill and McCabe (eds.) *Form and Argument in Late Plato*, 179–212.

(1998) 'Was Verse the Default Form for Presocratic Philosophy?' in Atherton (ed.) *Form and Content in Didactic Poetry*, 23–35.

Owen, G. E. L. (1960) 'Eleatic Questions' *CQ* **10**, 84–102.

(1965) 'The Place of the *Timaeus* in Plato's Dialogues' in Allen (ed.) *Studies in Plato's Metaphysics*, 313–38.

Palmer, J. (1998) 'Xenophanes' Ouranian God in the 4th Century' *OSAP* **16**, 1–34.

(1999) *Plato's Reception of Parmenides*, Oxford.

(2009) *Parmenides and Presocratic Philosophy*, Oxford.

Partenie, C. (ed.) (2009) *Plato's Myths*, Cambridge.

Patterson, R. (1985) *Image and Reality in Plato's Metaphysics*, Indianapolis.

Pellikaan-Engel, M. (1978) *Hesiod and Parmenides: A New View on their Cosmologies and on Parmenides' Proem*, Amsterdam.

Pender, E. E. (2010) 'Chaos Corrected: Hesiod in Plato's Creation Myth' in Boys-Stones and Haubold (eds.) *Plato and Hesiod*, 219–45.

Petersen, W. (1915) 'Greek Pronominal Adjectives of the Type τοῖος', *TAPA* **46**, 59–73.

Philippoussis, J. (1989) 'The Gnoseological and Metaphysical Particularity in Xenophanes' Thought' in Boudouris (ed.) *Ionian Philosophy*, 327–36.

Popper, K. (1998) *The World of Parmenides*, London.

Pratt, L. (1995) *Lying and Poetry from Homer to Pindar*, Ann Arbor.

Pucci, P. (1977) *Hesiod and the Language of Poetry*, Baltimore.

Race,W. (1986) *Pindar*, Boston.

Reinhardt, K. (1916) *Parmenides und die Geschichte der griechischen Philosophie*, Bonn.

Rieu, E. (1946) *Homer The Odyssey*, London.

Rivier, A. (1956) 'Remarques sur les Fragments 34 et 35 de Xénophane' *Revue de Philologie* **30**, 37–61.

Robb, K. (ed.) (1983) *Language and Thought in Early Greek Philosophy*, La Salle.

Robbiano, C. (2006) *Becoming Being: On Parmenides' Transformative Philosophy*, Sankt Augustin.

Rowe, C. (2003) 'The Status of the "Myth" in Plato's *Timaeus*', in Natali and Maso (eds.) *Plato Physicus: Cosmologia e Antropologia nel* Timeo, 21–31.

(2007) *Plato and the Art of Philosophical Writing*, Cambridge.

Runia, D. (1989) 'Plato, *Timaeus* 30b6–c1', *Elenchos* **10**, 435–43.

(1997) 'The Literary and Philosophical Status of Timaeus' Prooemium' in Calvo and Brisson (eds.) *Interpreting the* Timaeus–Critias, 101–18.

Santa Cruz, M. I.(1997) 'Le Discours de la Physique: *eikos logos*' in Calvo and Brisson (eds.) *Interpreting the* Timaeus–Critias, 133–40.

Sassi, M. M. (2005) 'De Senofane al *Timeo*: il problema del discorso "verosimile" in Bugno (ed.) *Senofane ed Elea tra Ionia e Magna Grecia*, 141–6.
(ed.) (2006) *The Construction of Philosophical Discourse in the Age of the Presocratics*, Pisa.
Schäfer, C. (1996) *Xenophanes von Kolophon*, Stuttgart.
Scheibe, E. and Suessmann, G. (eds.) (1973) *Einheit und Vielheit*, Göttingen.
Schofield, M. (1987) 'Coxon's Parmenides' *Phronesis* **32**, 349–59.
(1997) 'The Ionians' in Taylor (ed.) *Routledge History of Philosophy*, 47–87.
(2003) 'The Presocratics' in Sedley (ed.) *The Cambridge Companion to Greek and Roman Philosophy*, 42–72.
Schwabl, H. (1968) 'Sein und Doxa bei Parmenides' in Gadamer (ed.) *Um die Begriffswelt der Vorsokratiker*, 391–422.
Sedley, D. (1989) 'Teleology and Myth in the *Phaedo*' *Proceedings of the Boston Colloquium in Ancient Philosophy* **5**, 359–83.
(1999) 'Parmenides and Melissus' in Long (ed.) The Cambridge Companion to Early Greek Philosophy, 113–33.
(2000) 'The Ideal of Godlikeness' in Fine (ed.) *Plato*, 791–810.
(2002a) 'The Origins of Stoic God' in Frede and Laks (eds.) *Traditions of Theology*, 41–83.
(2002b) 'Socratic Irony in the Platonist Commentators' in Annas and Rowe (eds.) *New Perspectives on Plato: Modern and Ancient*, 37–57.
(ed.) (2003) *The Cambridge Companion to Greek and Roman Philosophy*, Cambridge.
(2006) 'Form-Particular Resemblance in Plato's *Phaedo*' *Proceedings of the Aristotelian Society* **106**, 311–27.
(2007) *Creationism and its Critics in Antiquity*, Berkeley.
(2010) 'Hesiod's *Theogony* and Plato's *Timaeus*' in Boys-Stones and Haubold (eds.) *Plato and Hesiod*, 246–58.
Shorey, P. (1938) *Platonism, Ancient and Modern*, Berkeley.
Snell, B. (1982) *The Discovery of Mind*, New York.
Sommerstein, A. (1989) *Aeschylus Eumenides*, Cambridge.
Stallbaum, G. (1888) *Platonis Timaeus et Critias*, London.
Stanford, W. B. (1959) *The Odyssey of Homer*, vol. **I**, New York.
(1972) *Ambiguity in Greek Literature*, New York.
Stroh, W. (1976) 'Hesiods lügenden Musen' in Görgemanns and Schmidt (eds.) *Studien zum antiken Epos*, 85–112.
Szaif, J. (1996) *Platons Begriff der Wahrheit*, Freiburg.
Tarán, L. (1965) *Parmenides*, Princeton.
Tarrant, H. and Baltzly, D. (eds.) (2006) *Reading Plato in Antiquity*, London.
Taylor, A. E. (1928) *A Commentary on Plato's Timaeus*, Oxford.
Taylor, C. C. W. (1976) *Plato's Protagoras*, Oxford.
(ed.) (1997) *Routledge History of Philosophy*, vol. **I**, *From the Beginning to Plato*, London.

Teodorsson, S. (1996) *A Commentary on Plutarch's Table Talks*, vol. **3**, Gothenburg.
Tucker, T. G. (1889) *The Supplices of Aeschylus*, London.
Turnbull, R. G. (1998) The *Parmenides and Plato's Late Philosophy*, Toronto.
Verdenius, W. J. (1964) *Parmenides*, Amsterdam.
(1972) 'Notes on the Proem of Hesiod's *Theogony*' *Mnemosyne* **25**, 225–60.
Vlastos, G. (1965a) 'The Disorderly Motion in the *Timaeus*' in Allen (ed.) *Studies in Plato's Metaphysics*, 379–99.
(1965b) 'Degrees of Reality in Plato' in Bambrough (ed.) *New Essays on Plato and Aristotle*, 1–19.
(1975) *Plato's Universe*, Oxford.
Warren, J. (2007) *Presocratics*, Stocksfield.
West, M. L. (1966) *Hesiod's Theogony*, Oxford.
Wilamowitz, U. von (1899) 'Lesefrüchte' *Hermes* **34**, 203–6.
Wilson, J. R. (1970) 'Parmenides, B8.4', *CQ* **20**, 32–4.
Woodbury, L. (1966) 'Equinox at Acragas: Pindar Ol. 2.61–62' *TAPA* **97**, 597–616.
Worthington, I. (ed.) (1994) *Persuasion: Greek Rhetoric in Action*, London.
Wright, M. R. (1979) 'How Credible Are Plato's Myths?' in Bowerstock, Burkert and Putnam (eds.) *Arktouros*, 364–71.
(2000a) 'Myth, Science and Reason in the *Timaeus*' in Wright (ed.) *Reason and Necessity*, 1–22.
(ed.) (2000b) *Reason and Necessity*, London.
Zeller, E. and Nestle, W. (1919–20) *Die Philosophie der Griechen in ihrer geschichtlichen Entwicklung*, Leipzig.
Zeyl, D. J. (2000) *Plato Timaeus*, Indianapolis.

INDEX LOCORUM

Lightning Source UK Ltd.
Milton Keynes UK
UKHW051129300620
365693UK00009B/25

9 780521 762946